SWIMMING IN CIRCLES

SWIMMING IN CIRCLES

PAUL MOLYNEAUX

AQUACULTURE AND THE END OF WILD OCEANS

Thunder's Mouth Press
New York

SWIMMING IN CIRCLES:
Aquaculture and the End of Wild Oceans

Copyright © 2007 Paul Molyneaux

Thunder's Mouth Press
An imprint of Avalon Publishing Group, Inc.
245 West 17th St., 11th floor
New York, NY 10011
www.thundersmouth.com

AVALON
publishing group incorporated

First printing, 2007

Library of Congress Cataloging-in-Publication data is available.

ISBN-10: 1-56025-756-3
ISBN-13: 978-1-56025-756-1

10 9 8 7 6 5 4 3 2 1

Interior design by *Ivelisse Robles Marrero*

Printed in the United States of America
Distributed by Publishers Group West

To Bill Crowe

CONTENTS

Part IV

The End of the Wild

The trilobites tell us, and it's an old lesson, "Trust nothing, even the ocean can desert you."

And it will. The laws of thermodynamics say that the matter and energy of the sea and everything else, including us, will eventually dissipate. Entropy will claim all, but how fast? In my brief lifetime working on the water, a mere thirty years, the earth's oceans have been degraded to the point that they can no longer supply the global demand for seafood. In 1969 many government scientists claimed that the ocean could produce upwards of five hundred million tons of seafood a year, primarily from wild-harvest fisheries. Today, no one of stature would support an annual production estimate higher than one hundred million tons, and many call that optimistic.

Pollution, overfishing, and other human impositions have lead to largely invisible changes in ocean ecology, such as the composition and abundance of phytoplankton communities, the primary production of the marine food chain. Almost half the United States' nearshore and estuarine waters—where 70 percent of commercially important species spend some portion of their life cycles—are "impaired," as the National Oceanic and Atmospheric Administration says, creating bottlenecks in the marine ecosystem.

By taking more than the sea can offer in terms of resources and waste absorption capacity, humankind has overdrawn its account with Mother Nature. Rather than living off the interest of natural capital, we have taken a large portion of the principal. Many economists, scientists and activists believe that principal needs to be paid back—but that would require actually shrinking the economy. Instead, the eminent political and business

INTRODUCTION

The train rolls east across America's West, en route from the Sea of Cortez to the Atlantic, and I look out the window as we pass over a now-dry ocean floor. The layered mesas, washed clear of soft earth, tell a submarine history. Within the arid rocks lie signs of the old ocean: fossils of shells and trilobites from millions of years ago present uncluttered historical evidence. Paleontologists do not find Coke bottles among the trilobites.

In the high-speed media age, contradictory information confronts the investigator on a daily basis. Spin has become the dominant postmodern art form, distorting realities past, present, and future. One week an ad in the *New York Times* touts the benefits of eating farmed salmon, the next week an op-ed points out the dangers. When people are unable or unwilling to make up their minds, their ability to reason undermined by an information landscape crowded with dubious material, the leaders of business and government step in and say, "Trust us."

leaders of the world advocate replacing natural capital with human ingenuity. They contend that aquaculture offers a way to bypass environmental bottlenecks and maintain economic growth on the high seas. A salmon or a shrimp hatched and reared in a laboratory, and coddled through its most vulnerable life stages, can then survive, capitalizing on what remains of a compromised ecosystem. Industrial-scale farming of relatively high-priced shrimp and salmon promises big returns, and the industry has become the darling of politicians everywhere. The United States aims to increase the value of its aquaculture industry fivefold by 2025, and Mexico hopes to double its farmed shrimp production. In a way, aquaculture enables humanity to continue to draw down natural capital and count it as growth. Sort of like paying off one's mortgage with a credit card: it simply raises the interest rate and puts off the day of reckoning.

"We have to have growth," said economist Mark Weisbrot, director of the Center for Economic Policy Research. "Let's face it, you're not going to take anything away from the rich without violence."

This is essentially a travel book through the communities of marine organisms, fishing people, seafood farmers, and the offices of those who run aquaculture industries on one level or another. The journey moves through Maine and Mexico, looking at aquaculture from four basic perspectives: first, that of an expanding universe, where those on the cutting edge of biotechnology and aquaculture experience the thrill of opening a new frontier. One aquaculture advocate invoked manifest destiny as a rationale for the fish farming expansion into offshore waters. These techno-optimists believe that human ingenuity will overcome all limitations to an infinitely growing economy; they believe they can develop sustainable aquaculture systems that will feed the world. "We're on page one," as Bob Rosenberry, editor of *World Shrimp News*, likes to tell people.

Next, we see aquaculture from the world of ecological economics, which recognizes limits to growth and advocates strong sustainability and a new approach to using the earth's resources. Ecological economists operate in an economy of calories; they count carbon along with natural and social capital and other forms of wealth ignored by the neoclassical economic model. Eco-economics provides the impetus for a new paradigm, one geared to a world with limits, where equitable distribution of wealth within and among generations—an idea panned by Weisbrot—would become the norm.

Then comes the view from the shrinking universe, the one seen by people who lack the resources—the technology and capital—to participate in fisheries and aquaculture geared for the global economy. People such as the artisanal fishermen of coastal Sonora, Mexico, and Lubec, Maine, whose world began collapsing with depleted fish stocks long before the arrival of modern aquaculture are now divided between fighting and supporting shrimp and salmon farms.

Last, I try to speak for the wild fish and shrimp, the poorest of the poor. They have no voice in their own future, no title to their franchise, and while they still supply 85 percent of most nations' seafood, they bear the heaviest burden in terms of compromised welfare.

In creation stories from evolution to Genesis, the sea comes first, the source of life. Aquaculture offers an opportunity to either turn the sea into a larger food source than it has ever been, or destroy what remains of its productivity. Considering the high degree of uncertainty involved, aquaculture looks like a gamble, with different payoffs and consequences for different groups. Venture capitalists can score big and then move on if disease or pollution wipe out their enterprises. For coastal residents without mobility, aquaculture development becomes a desperate attempt to continue to profit from the ecosystems they have often relied on for generations. In what remains of the wild, creatures simply encounter an environment that no longer sustains them.

For a professional journalist in a world of cloudy and subjective perceptions, finding truth has become almost impossible. The polestar has shifted, and all compasses point in the varied directions of self-interest.

"But that's human nature," said Rosenberry, and though I've seen a lot that would support that argument, I still wonder if it's true—that we're all looking out for ourselves—and if so, where it will lead. This journey through a slice of the world of shrimp and ocean-fish farming gives a look at the course we are on in search of profit, sustainable seafood, and ultimately, survival.

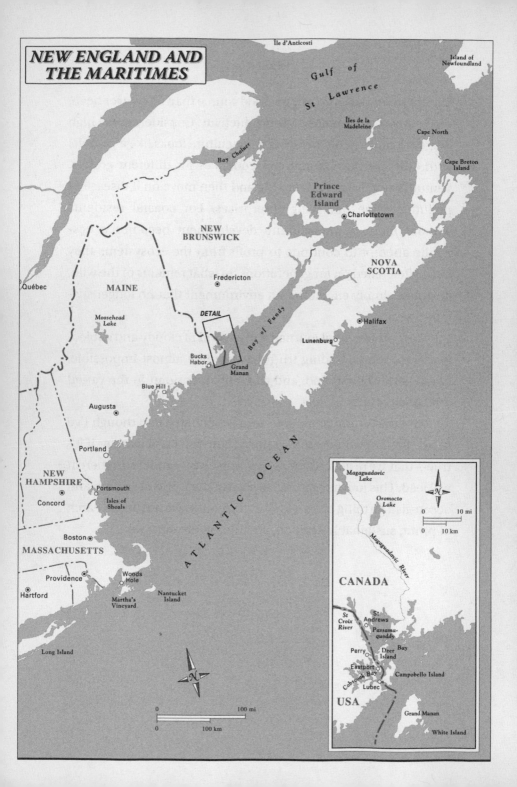

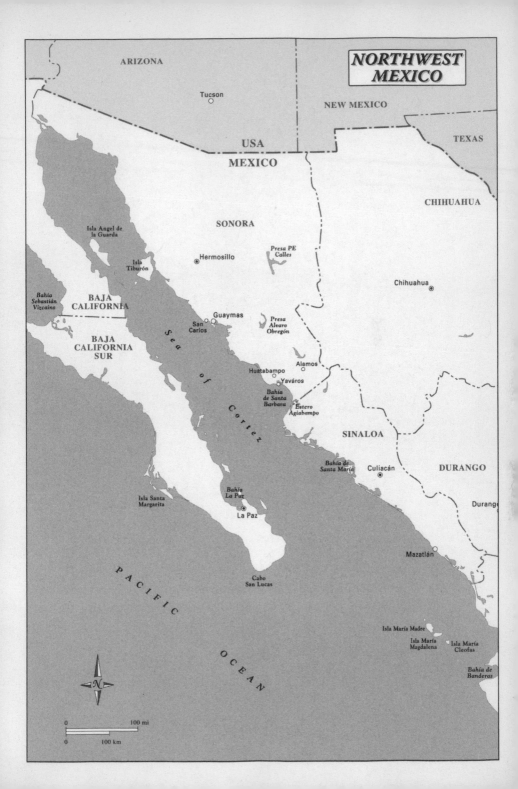

PART I

THE EXPANDING UNIVERSE

A Beautiful Fish

Cobscook Bay, Maine, 1987

A chill breeze blew across Cobscook Bay on a late summer day, raising a few white caps. Charlie Leppin, foreman for the Passamaquoddy Towing Company, watched them from the calm waters of Johnson's Bay—a broad cove off the larger bay. He stood on a barge loaded with granite blocks five feet square, piles of thick steel chain and big steel mooring balls painted bright yellow. Leppin raised his hand, pointing one finger up in a spiraling motion, signaling Dana Gardner on the crane to lift a mooring rock and swing it out over the side. Two solid tons of granite trailing a heavy chain, each rusty link a foot long and weighing twenty pounds, dangled over the deep green water, ready to drop.

When it went, it would drag over one hundred feet of chain and mooring ball. I stood by with an ax, ready to cut the ropes holding the rock, trading looks of anticipation with Dana in the crane.

While a tugboat maneuvered the barge into position, a small boat run by Frank Rier circled nearby. Rier, an intense man with wiry red hair, held a portable GPS unit that gave him his position within thirty feet. He had grown up on the shores of the bay, and picked this protected site for his salmon farm. He glanced between the GPS machine and the speckled granite block swaying from the crane. He waved his hand, Charlie waved to me, and I swung the ax at the tight hawser: it parted with a single stroke; the rock dropped and the chain followed.

I turned at a shout and saw Charlie standing between the edge of the barge and the chain sweeping toward him. He jumped just as the chain passed under him, and fell to the deck as the mooring ball whipped off the barge, leaving only a ringing sound and a cloud of rusty dust. Charlie stood up, looked at us, brushed himself off, and directed us to hook up the next rock.

The first mooring for what Rier called "the first privately owned salmon farm in Cobscook Bay" almost took a life to the bottom with it. But it didn't happen. With a bit more attention to detail, Charlie directed the setting of three more rocks, each marked on the surface by a yellow buoy.

Frank Rier looked from the moorings to the Lubec shore, where six square steel frames sat on the beach below his father's house. Later in the fall, he and his brothers and a few helpers floated the frames, towed them out, and hooked them to the moorings.

The tides ranged twenty-seven feet from high to low and controlled to a large degree what went on in the bay—sometimes acting as a limiting factor, but also making it a perfect place to grow salmon. The massive volumes of water surging in and out of the bay—over one cubic kilometer a day, equal to the flow of the Mississippi river for the same period—carried oxygen-rich water in from the Gulf of Maine, and essentially flushed the toilet for the farms, dispersing tons of feces and other waste over a wide area.

Relatively clean water is the most valuable input for successful fish farming, and while truly wild salmon had long been extirpated from their spawning rivers in the Cobscook Bay watershed, the waters of the bay itself remained pristine enough to host the well-fed smolts that would soon fill Rier's net pens. In 1987, he was one of the first to capitalize on this abundant source of clean water, free for the taking. Others followed, and in thirteen years, over half the salmon grown in the United States would come from Cobscook Bay. But on that bright autumnal day, Rier had it almost all to himself.

The week after we set the moorings, with the frames in place, Frank's crew installed the first nets; some of the men held armfuls of the fine-mesh nylon twine hanging in the water, while others lashed the upper edge tight to the frame. Secured, the net created a porous bag forty feet square and thirty feet deep. Below, a scuba diver worked on the moorings, mindful of a massive black cloud shifting above him. He checked their weight belts. A diver working beneath one of the earliest pens had lost his weight belt and risen uncontrollably into the net above him. Unable to get free, he ran out of air and drowned.

"That had only happened once," said former diver Greg Biss of nearby Eastport. "But we all remember it."

＊

In 1987, Atlantic salmon still qualified as a luxury food, the distinctive orange meat of a fillet looked beautiful served on white China plates in fine restaurants. A market-size fish, two feet long and weighing ten pounds or so, sold for eight dollars a pound. For most consumers, eating a salmon represented a rare treat. The experience created a connection between the diner and the image of a silversided fish leaping over the falls of a clear-running northern river, determined to reach its native spawning grounds.

Whenever a related subject came up, my uncle Donald waxed eloquent about the salmon he once ate in Ireland. Hitchhiking around the Emerald Isle in the late 1960s, he had found himself pretty lean. "I walked into this little restaurant, it was like a little house, and this fisherman walks in behind me with a big salmon and lays it on the kitchen table. He said he just caught it. I looked at that thing laying there and said to the waitress, 'I'll have that.' Man, they brought that out and put it in front of me. I'm tellin' you, no shit, that was the best fish I have ever eaten in my life."

The fisherman's timing may have been Irish hijinks, but the event never faded for my uncle and decades later he still told the story with enthusiasm. Atlantic salmon have that impact on people, particularly in Ireland, where eating the iconic fish holds a mythical significance.

The story goes that Finn McCool, a legendary hero of Ireland's common people, got his start by tasting the salmon of wisdom. As a young man, Finn served an ambitious master who caught the sacred fish in the depths of the River Boyne and proceeded to cook it. It was believed that whoever ate first from the fish would receive all its wisdom. "Wake me when it's ready," Finn's master said to him, and dozed off.

After a while the fish fell into the coals and started to burn. When Finn reached in to save it, a bit of the fish's skin stuck to his thumb, burning him. Reflexively he put his thumb in his mouth, and in that instant he absorbed all the wisdom from the fish. When the master woke he looked at Finn and saw immediately what had happened. "So it's you, then," he said, and walked away. In later years, as Finn charged around Ireland, leading his warriors in their defense of the poor, he was known to suck his thumb when confronted with perplexing problems.

My first salmon experience involved no actual fish, yet it stuck indelibly in my mind. One May evening in 1985 as the day cooled and the late sun lit everything a bit gold, I stopped to watch a man fly-fishing in Maine's East Machias River, about a mile above the falls that flow through the picturesque town of East Machias and into the saltwater estuary below. He stood on a small dome of rock in his hip waders, waving the long rod gracefully through the air, laying the line out and settling his fly in the rippling current. It looked so idyllic, I told a friend about it.

"What was he fishing for?" I asked.

"Probably salmon."

"There's salmon in that river?"

"Oh yeah, that's one of the best."

He should have said, one of the last.

The Atlantic salmon runs once extended as far as the Connecticut River, but by the late 1980s the last salmon runs in the United States hung on tentatively in a dozen Maine rivers. The Penobscot River hosted the strongest run, augmented by hatchery releases. Wild fish still managed to make their journeys up fish ladders and into other rivers such as the Pleasant, Narraguagus, Machias, and Dennys, all in Washington County, the easternmost corner of the state.

"They ain't what you could call a wild Atlantic salmon," said Jimmy Robinson, whose family has run a fishing lodge on the Dennys since 1920. "For all intents and purposes the wild Atlantic salmon is extinct. The fish in these rivers have been stocked for over a hundred years. I know because my great grandfather brought the first hatchery eggs up here by stagecoach."

The real wild salmon coexisted thousands of years with the Passamaquoddy, the Native American tribe of the region. But with European settlers they did not last a century.

Mature salmon fight their way from the ocean up into the boreal rivers to spawn. In late autumn they lay their eggs, burying them in gravel nests called redds. By late spring they hatch below the gravel as alevin and begin their complex development. The alevin absorb their yolk sacs and emerge from the gravel as fry, which quickly develop into parr, identifiable by their horizontal stripes. The parr live in their natal rivers for two years before swimming to sea as smolt.

The salmon have other names that tell their status in life and in the river. "A grilse is a one year return, a fish less than twenty-five inches that comes back but is too young to spawn," said Robinson. "We never had any in the Dennys. A kelt is an adult fish that has spent the winter in the river, you catch 'em in the spring. Some call 'em blacks cause they're blacker than a boot, and stink!"

The history of the Dennys River is fairly typical of salmon streams. A dam constructed in 1846 cut the river off only a mile up from the estuary, blocking the salmons' passage for nine years. Another dam at that site blocked the salmons' upstream migration from 1869 to 1874.

In addition, the Dennys emptied into Cobscook Bay, and wild fish returning to spawn sometimes had to share the river with escaped salmon from the farms, but Robinson did not see any problem with that. An escaped farmed salmon seemed better than nothing, and he considered them little different than hatchery fish. "A salmon is a salmon as far as our customers care. They just want to catch a fish." In spite of almost four million fish stocked in the river over a period of 130 years, returns number in the dozens. Robinson blamed the commercial fisheries for the poor returns. "The U.S. Navy found their winter grounds off Greenland in the 1960s," Robinson said. "A submarine ran right into huge schools of salmon. After that, folks up there got the fishery going that wiped them out."

Beginning in 1963, commercial salmon fisheries in the remote waters off Greenland took an estimated five million fish a year from the combined stocks of many North Atlantic–rim countries, depleting river returns from Maine to Norway. The intense fishery ended in 1998, but, coupled with habitat degradation in spawning rivers, it left wild salmon sorely depleted. Markets remained strong, however, and Rier set out to grow a fish not unlike its wild cousin. He focused on producing a quality product worthy of its price.

"We stocked at low density," he recalled, "looking for a harvest of around eighteen kilos per cubic meter of pen space. But the most important thing was the feed. We maintained health by feeding high-quality food. And by not feeding if the fish looked stressed."

Not long after Rier started, however, Maine set the lower limit for lease holdings at two hundred acres per company. He realized the game was being set up for much larger enterprises than he intended to create, and sold his operation to Stolt Sea Farms before his first harvest. He stayed in the game, however, forming several partnerships with his brothers and overseas investors.

Bobby Peacock, another Lubecker with a long family history in the seafood business, inherited a processing plant that began operation in the glory days of the canned sardine: the late nineteenth and early twentieth centuries, when the sardine canning industry supported a bustling coastal economy. Lubec and neighboring Eastport had been the centers of activity. In 1917,

Lubec boasted twenty factories that canned close to five million dollars' worth of herring a year. Old-timers often recalled the days when the bay brimmed with herring and haddock every summer. "You could walk across the bay on the backs of the haddock," Peacock's foreman, Albert Gardner, once told me. By 1988, only two canneries remained in Lubec, both showing signs of dereliction.

The wooden floors and antique machinery of Peacock's had seen better days, health inspectors viewed it with a jaundiced eye, but the sardine business did not warrant the investment needed to upgrade the facility. Prices remained flat and the market had shrunk. In addition, fleets of high-tech trawlers had decimated the stocks that once filled the bay. Most of the fish Peacock's packed arrived in Lubec aboard trucks, some from Rhode Island, five hundred miles away.

Like Frank Rier, Bobby Peacock joined the salmon business early on. He converted an unused portion of the plant into a salmon processing room, and hung out his shingle for contract processing. For his business, salmon looked like the ticket to survival.

~

By the spring of 1989, most of the major fishing families in downeast Maine—the Harrises of Eastport, the Preniers of Pembroke, and the Cates of Cutler—had all taken out leases for salmon farms. Periodically I helped friends feed fish, tossing scoopfuls of pellets out into the middle of the net pen and watching the fish rise to the surface and gobble them up. The large, densely packed fish swam around the edge of the cage. In most of my fishing career I only saw fish spilling out of a net, or rising to the surface on the end of a hook. At a salmon pen I watched the salmon in the water, somewhat hypnotized as they circled relentlessly, struggling to go nowhere.

Eventually I tried to sign on with one of the salmon farms. Having run boats and processing plants, I expected a reasonably well-paying job, overseeing a processing line or a cage site.

But Stolt Sea Farms, a Norway-based firm with salmon farming operations there as well as in Canada, Chile, and Lubec, turned me down. The local manager hired an inexperienced friend of a friend.

Maine Pride, a U.S. company, offered me seven dollars an hour to feed fish. "That's good money for downeast Maine," said their financial advisor, Mike Faunce. I didn't think so. I told him I was an experienced twine man; I could build the nets and keep them together. "We get all that done in Canada," said Faunce.

The high arc of the international bridge spanned the Lubec Narrows, one of two gateways for the water coming in and out of the bay. The sea ran back and forth in a virtual millrace between Campobello Island, in New Brunswick, Canada, and Lubec, or L.A., as the locals liked to say—Lubec, America. Below the bridge on the U.S. side, the lights at Peacock's burned brightly in a darkening December evening, and I backed an empty truck up to the processing room as workers prepared to send their first load of fish to market. The fish had come out of the pens Stolt had bought from Rier: the ones I had helped set a year and a half earlier, and I landed a truck-driving job in time to take them to market.

Under neon lights, amid gray plastic boxes full of ice, fish, and blood, a line of people worked in animated confusion, clear on the mission if not the means. Clad in waterproof gear, slickers and oil pants, hands gloved, the workers passed the glistening salmon from the boxes onto stainless-steel tables, gutted them, washed them, weighed them, and slid them into plastic bags, which others laid gently in Styrofoam-lined cardboard boxes. When the workers filled a box, the foreman wrote down the weight, and scribbled a shipping number on the box.

"Four Gel Paks," plant manager Gene Greenlaw told a worker about to close a box without having put in the blue frozen Gel Paks that would keep the fish cool on their journey.

The worker put four bags of frozen chemical into the box to keep it cool. Another stapled the bag shut and slid the box down a roller ramp. It landed on a table where another worker taped it shut and tossed it onto a waiting truck. It slammed heavily on the bed.

"Easy now," said Greenlaw. "That ain't a case a sardines."

A young assistant manager for the Stolt's ran around in the back of the truck trying to put the correct shipping labels on the boxes. It shouldn't have been too hard. The shipping labels corresponded with the number Greenlaw had written on the box. But the novice made a mistake, and that threw everything else off, until in a panic he screamed. "Stop. Stop!"

Twenty people working at full blast came to a screeching halt and looked at him in wonder.

"What's a matter?" I asked.

"Something's wrong. These are the wrong boxes."

I had shipped a few fish over the years; I found the glitch, and took over labeling the boxes while the assistant manager did the stacking.

❧

At 10:00 A.M. Greenlaw signed the manifest and waved good-bye. "Be careful now," he said. "You're overweight by about half." I slipped in a cassette of Howlin' Wolf and headed for Boston, a long way off on a snowy night. At midnight I crossed the hills on the Blacks Woods Road. Coming down a steep incline I sucked in my breath at the sight of ice glaring on the road ahead of me, and the guardrail sweeping out of sight to the left. Tapping the braks a bit until I entered the turn and could no longer safely touch them, I held the wheel gently, sensitive to how much traction the truck had: eight thousand pounds of salmon managed to hold the Volvo on the asphalt. I let out my breath as the road straightened out and I was still on it.

At 4:00 A.M. I pulled into the last service stop on the Maine turnpike. Amid the smell of diesel engines that never stopped, I ate a bad breakfast, got my receipt. Back in the truck, I filled in my logbook, unrolled my sleeping bag across the seat and slept to the drum and roar of the highway. I woke up two hours later and twisted back into the driver's seat, shoving the warm sleeping bag out of the way.

I chased scattered red taillights down the highway until they resolved into cars and trucks at dawn. An hour later I confronted the first wave of rush-hour traffic inbound to Boston. As the sun rose I put on my shades, slipped Howlin' Wolf back into the cassette player and like a fighter pilot entering the fray, swooped smoothly from I-95 onto Route 1 entering the traffic without slowing down. Through Saugus and Lynn I raced with the pack at eighty miles per hour, four tons of fish on my back, commuter cars cutting in front of me with inches to spare. The truck barrelled along with the blues turned up loud; the surge and play of traffic seemed to coincide with the ups and downs of the music's tempo, and I found the groove.

At the Logan Airport freight terminal, I found an empty bay and backed in. I got out as a plane roared low overhead, and found my way inside. A stevedore looked at my manifest and I pointed to my bay.

"Is it on pallets?" he asked.

"No."

"I'll get someone right over there to unload you."

"Mind if I just stack it on pallets?"

He shook his head. "Can't let you do that."

I unlocked the bay door, and pushed a green button next to it. The broad steel door rose up along a pair of tracks, and there sat the truck, filthy with highway grunge. Big cakes of frozen slush from Maine fell from the wheel wells as the day warmed up.

I opened the back and looked around for the promised help. While waiting, I watched a tractor-trailer that had come in after me get unloaded. Maybe the drivers were union, too, or they bribed the stevedores. At $120 for fourteen hours of driving, I didn't have any bribe money, so I walked across the cavernous warehouse, stacked a hand-operated forklift with pallets, and brought it back to my truck. Nobody seemed to notice. As I set each box on the pallet I read the labels again. They bore the names of restaurants, retailers, and wholesalers scattered all over the northeast: Alexandria, Virginia; Wilmington, Delaware; and Philadelphia, with one consignment headed for Chicago.

An hour later I handed my manifest to the stevedore. "Hey thanks, I'm all unloaded. Can you sign this?"

He walked over to the pallets, counted the boxes and signed.

Like a lot of folks around Lubec and Eastport, I expected the industry to grow. I assumed a good job would eventually open up and enable me to ride what many of us believed was the wave of the future.

2

ENDLESS NAKED SHRIMP

In late May, a mature female blue shrimp crawls through the moonlit shallows of the Gulf of California near the mouth of Agiabampo Estuary in southern Sonora, Mexico. Thousands and thousands of her kind join her in a determined ritual. Her eight-inch-long translucent form becomes part of a larger organism, a soft, glowing mass of gravid shrimp, and males eager to fertilize them. The shrimp's antennae, longer than her body, search and touch the forms around her. Her eyes function not so much to see as to register light; the moon above is full, and it reflects thin traces of the sun's rays into the depths. A few hours before, at dusk, females and males had separated into pairs, the males chasing the females for several yards before briefly diving beneath them to deposit a packet of sperm. Now, near midnight, almost on cue, she and the others begin expelling millions upon millions of microscopic eggs into the silver black sea.

Zooplankton, the larval young of squid, snapper, jellyfish, and other marine organisms, feed on the new eggs. After eight hours the surviving eggs hatch. The naupliae emerge, looking more like creatures from outer space than anything that would grace the plate of a diner at a fancy restaurant.

While floating among the plankton, and grazing on micro-algae, the naupliae transform rapidly through eleven life stages, the first five in thirty-six hours, sometimes morphing into new shapes over the course of a few hours. After eight to ten days, the tiny shrimp settle to the bottom and begin their migration back to the nutrient-rich estuaries where they will feed on bacteria and detritus among the mangroves.

The post-larval shrimp surf the tides, as the current shifts toward the coast they rise in the water column, riding the flow and settling to bottom again before the tide turns and sweeps them back offshore. The strongest currents run into the estuaries, and from May through July millions of post-larvae (PLs) passed through the entrance of Agiabampo. As each tide rises, the small shrimp rise with it as the ocean water surges into the wide bay. Predators await, huge schools of mullet guard the gateway the shrimp must pass; they take their toll. Of the millions of eggs laid offshore, a tiny percentage will grow to maturity, most provide food for one species or another, supporting a food chain that ends with the top predators such as dolphins and local fishermen. None of these species exist in the numbers they once did, not even the fishermen. The inshore waters have suffered many insults over the years: siltation, agricultural runoff, and sewage, to name a few. To an observer ignorant of history, life in the relatively pristine Agiabampo Estuary looks abundant, but the fishermen who once earned a good living on the extensive bay see the steady degradation.

～

On a Thursday morning in late November 2000, Victor Alcantar cast his *ataraya* into the shallow slough north of Navopatia, a very small part of the extensive Agiabampo estuary system that spanned the border between the Mexican states of Sonora and Sinaloa. The shrimp season opened in September and the best days had passed. Several pangas, the open boats of Mexico's nearshore fishermen, lay broken and abandoned along the shore, attesting that the best years were also in the past, but still Alcantar tried. His wife waited on the shore with a bucket as Alcantar walked deeper into the slough, the water over his knees.

He wrapped the line from the center of the twelve-foot-diameter net around his hand, and gathered the folds of fine mesh together and held them draped over his shoulder; the lead weights edging the net hung heavily behind him. With a grunt, he twisted like a shotputter and whipped the net out in front of him; it spread in a ragged circle, landed flat on the water with a splash, and sank quickly to bottom. Alcantar hauled in on the line, the net came toward him like a collapsed parachute, bits of life caught in the meshes.

His wife watched intently as he lifted the net and shook an immature snapper and two shrimp into his bucket. Nothing that came up in the net went back except some mud and bits of grass. He left the four-inch fish in with the shrimp, and prepared to cast again.

He fished illegally; he did not belong to the Agiabampo *ejido*—a community of families that owned in common most of the land around the estuary—or any fishing cooperative. They all called fishermen like him *independentes* and spit the word out.

~

From the other side of the mangroves he heard noises: idling engines, and the ringing of steel. Suddenly, the roar of powerful engines drowned out the songs of nearby birds. Alcantar kept casting his net, he had to; it would take all day to gather a kilo or two of shrimp that his wife could sell for fifty to ninety pesos a kilo, depending on the size of the shrimp. But most of the shrimp had left the shallows. They migrated out to sea, the *alta imar,* where the big boats trawled for shrimp all winter. Harvesting the large shrimp for buyers like Ocean Garden Products, Mexico's government-owned company that handled over 60 percent of the country's shrimp exports.

As Alcantar drove down the rutted road back to Las Aquilas, a waterless ejido surrounded by barren fields, tall cactus, and desert shrubs, he noticed the wide tracks of tractor-trailers in the soft sand and saw where they turned of the main track, heading north toward where all the noise came from. He would find out soon enough what was happening.

That evening when the *pangeros*, the panga fishermen, returned, they told of four huge bulldozers dragging heavy chains between them and plowing through the matoral, clearing away the virgin cactus forest and scrubby growth. A *desmonte*, they called it, literally translated: a dismounting of the fauna from the land.

Soon word spread along the grapevine that a powerful patron had leased the land from Agiabampo ejido, which owned the entire shore along much of the greater Agiabampo Estuary, and planned to build a two hundred hectare shrimp farm. Alcantar wondered if he could get a job there.

≈

One hundred miles to the north, in the classic Spanish colonial town of Alamos, Dave McKay, an eco-tour guide who sometimes took birding groups to Agiabampo estuary, got a call from a friend who told him about the bulldozers on the shore. A year later sitting in a leather chair under the arches of the hacienda that he and his wife Jen ran as a bed & breakfast, McKay gave me the basic story, and a file.

"We managed to stop them," he said. "They didn't have the Mexican equivalent of an environmental impact statement. But a couple of days after we filed the petition they had all their paperwork in order and the bulldozers started up again."

McKay and his wife, both sun-burnished blonds from California, tried to get the board of directors of Agiabampo ejido to stop the project, but towering above their hosts at their first meeting, they came off as a couple of foreigners who had been making money on ejido property and then wanted to stop the *ejidatarios* from cashing in on what promised to be a gold mine. The McKays got nowhere—the new shrimp farm, Acuiacola Clej, was going in.

≈

McKay and others worked for about a year to try and create a sanctuary in Agiabampo, to no avail. A year later a group gathered together at the McKays' to talk about ways to preserve migrating bird habitat. A representative of the Mexican environmental group PRONATURA presented a list of estuaries the group felt it had a good chance of protecting.

The session ended, the PRONATURA list sat on a heavy wooden table under the vaulted ceiling of the McKay's hacienda. I picked it up and searched fruitlessly for the name of Agiabampo. I asked why they didn't have it on there. "We didn't put it on there because from what we understand Agiabampo is slated for shrimp farm development," said a PRONATURA representative.

Some of the conference participants had heard stories about environmental impacts and mangrove destruction. PRONATURA's Meredith de la Garza had conducted surveys of communities near shrimp farm developments and her documentation of social decay shocked a few people. But Mexico appeared to be an exemplary shrimp farm developer, the country was among the first to institute laws protecting mangroves, and Mexican scientists acknowledged problems with effluent and began working on solutions.

Because Mexico had held private capital out of shrimp farming until 1992, the country got a late start in developing the industry. "That has proved to be a benefit," observed Professor Billie DeWalt, of the University of Pittsburgh, a specialist in the area, that enables them "to avoid many of the mistakes made by earlier development."

To its credit, Mexico had people from the University of Rhode Island working on the best management practices to reduce environmental impacts. In an effort to control the international spread of shrimp disease, the country had implemented strict importation laws on shrimp products and advocated a reduction in the use of shrimp antibiotics. In addition, the state of Sonora was working with the Natural Resources Defense Council (NRDC) to reduce the impacts of shrimp trawling in the northern Gulf of California and to protect the rare vaquita dolphin.

At a party after the conference, the guests sat at a long table under the palms in the McKay's inner courtyard, feasting on farm-raised shrimp and other delights. The McKays charged a flat rate for hosting the conference and providing the banquet; the low price of shrimp did not hurt business. Like everyone else there, they understood that the demand for shrimp was sky-rocketing and that nothing could stop Mexico, with its proximity to the United States, from making a healthy profit.

BOSTON, MASSACHUSETTS, 2003

In 2003, Ocean Garden Products and several prominent shrimp farmers formed the *Consejo de Cameron Mexicano*, the Mexican Shrimp Council, and launched a publicity campaign. Their glossy publication, *The Naked Truth About Shrimp*, left even the most critical reader feeling optimistic about aquaculture as an environmentally sound way to produce seafood.

Public relations consultant Melissa Dennis recalled the narrow entrance that led from the cold streets of Boston into the city's Institute for Contemporary Art, a small, intimate museum with a main gallery and many smaller rooms on three floors. "It was more like a townhouse than a museum," said Dennis. "People came through this, like, passage, that opened out then into the main gallery. The weather was what you would expect for late winter, cold and cloudy, but the museum had a Mexican art exhibit and we'd set up tables of these amazing shrimp dishes and the colors and smell created this very warm, intimate, almost tropical feeling."

Attendees wrapping up a day at the Boston International Seafood Show found their way via invitation or word of mouth to the "Naked Cocktail Party," an event intended to show off the culinary appeal of unbreaded—*naked*—shrimp, and make Mexico as synonymous with high-quality shrimp as Maine was with lobster, and Russia with caviar.

The men and women Dennis called "the influential leaders of the seafood industry" loosened their ties, kicked off their high heels and, amid the bright colors of Mexican art, proceeded to devour offerings such as grilled shrimp glistening with a cilantro marinade on sugar cane skewer; shrimp tacos with tomatilla salsa and chili sour cream; tequila-laced melon gazpacho cocktail with grilled shrimp; among other delights.

"And they emptied the bar," said Dennis. "They drank every drop of tequila and every Corona we had."

Though Dennis knew the "naked" angle was a marketing gimmick, the party still had an edgy feel, and organizers fed the resulting anticipation with more "naked" publicity: a brochure called "The Naked Truth About Shrimp," and T-shirts that read, It's Better Naked.

"The whole presentation was really well done," said Dennis. "You had these white T-shirts rolled up with a red band around them and the word *naked* just peeking out. It really got people's attention in a memorable way."

Her clients at the Mexican Shrimp Council got exactly what they wanted. Formed by Ocean Garden Products, the Mexican Shrimp Council had launched the three-million-dollar campaign to do what all advertising does, increase market share without lowering prices. In the competitive shrimp market, the Mexicans wanted to carve out a niche for their "affordable luxury," as Dennis called it.

Not far from the museum, a Red Lobster offered "endless shrimp" specials: all the frozen and breaded product from Asia and South America you could eat, for twenty bucks. In 2003, the United States imported over a billion pounds of shrimp, most of it coming from Thailand, India, and other Asian countries where production costs float around eighty cents a pound compared to two dollars a pound in Mexico. The "Naked Shrimp" marketing ploy strove to give Mexican shrimp an identity of their own, rather than compete in a market for generic shrimp,

"We flew in some producers from Mexico," said Dennis. "Including Daniel Gutierrez [owner of one of the most successful shrimp farms in the northwest Mexican state of Sonora] and the president of the Mexican Shrimp Council so that people could meet them face to face."

Dennis called the event a major success, and wrote several flattering articles for *Seafood Business*—and other trade publications. She praised the marketing strategy for raising the profile of Mexican shrimp "whether caught on the high seas or farm raised."

Flying from Huatabampo south to the Agiabampo estuary in 2003, shrimp farms dotted the coastline. Some looked operational, others abandoned, having failed due to disease, mismanagement, or lack of capital. Diseases, particularly the fast mutating Taura syndrome virus, and the incurable white spot syndrome virus, cut production by an estimated 20 percent in 2005, but in the risky business of shrimp production, the government and investors continued to put their chips on the aquaculture number. Small-boat fishermen in places like Navopatia realized that shrimp farming radically changed the landscape they operate in, both literally and in the markets, but they shrugged and went about the business of trying to harvest a few kilos of wild shrimp every night.

Consumers in Boston and other affluent areas of the world saw only the constant flow of shrimp into seafood cases and restaurant menus. The complex questions about how that can continue on a sustainable level remained imbedded within a matrix of issues, such as the rights of traditional fishermen versus adventurous entrepreneurs, and the fate of wild shrimp. The answers—less than empirical—often boiled down to elements of philosophy, taste, and faith.

3

THE AQUABOOM

MAZATLÁN, MEXICO, 2003

Rohana Subasinghe stood in shirtsleeves under the cathedral ceiling of the El Cid Hotel, one of the several four-star establishments in Mazatlán's "Golden Zone." Not too tall, but alert and focused, the Sri Lankan native stood out even among the hotel's cosmopolitan clientele.

Subasinghe, the senior fisheries officer for the United Nation's Food and Agriculture Organization (FAO), had come to Mexico for a conference on the major diseases—the white spot and Taura viruses in particular—affecting shrimp farms all over the world. Although I knew he had spent a hot day in a series of meetings, he looked a bit more rumpled than I expected.

"The airline lost my luggage," he said, smiling, as he glanced down at his wrinkled shirt.

"What are you going to do?" I asked with a laugh.

He shrugged nonchalantly. "This happens to me all the time. It'll turn up."

We walked out of the bright lobby and into the sultry heat of Mazatlán. We talked about our families as we ambled down the street. "What do you think of that place?" asked Subasinghe, pointing to an open air beachfront restaurant.

"Looks good to me."

A few moments after the maitre d' seated us and we'd begun to talk shrimp, a band started playing. We looked up from our menus to see men in sequined sombreros blowing the opening notes of a lively tune on trumpets: mariachis. The tuba player joined in, accompanied by two others strumming hard on giant guitars. Subasinghe and I looked at each other, realizing that what had promised to be a relaxing interview was about to turn into work. Life's that way, and aquaculture is no different, full of unexpected events like shrimp viruses that spread around the world through international trade.

Striving to overcome the noise, Subasinghe and I launched into a shouted conversation about shrimp and salmon farming and its risks. In spite of irremediable viruses and the other problems it faced, Subasinghe insisted that the industry had to go forward. He took my notepad and pen, and drew a line angling upward across the page. "This is population growth," he said. "Expected to reach over eight billion by 2025." Then he drew another line straight across the page. "And this is fisheries' production, steady at a little under one hundred million tons per year. If we're lucky, we can raise that by another ten million through better management. But it's still going to leave a significant gap," he said, pointing to the widening disparity between population growth and natural production of seafood. "We need aquaculture to fill that gap."

Of course, aquaculture—aquatic organisms being grown under controlled conditions—began filling the gap thousands of years ago. The new versions of shrimp and fish farming that Subasinghe promoted had their origins in some of the oldest civilizations on earth. Archeologists probing a three-thousand-year-old Egyptian tomb found images of men removing tilapia from fish ponds. As early as the sixth century, Romans kept sea bass, mullet, oysters, and other marine organisms alive in pens off the coast of what is now Italy. But these systems did not endure.

The real aquaculture boom began in China, where farmers have continually grown carp and other vegetarian fish in flooded fields at least since 1100 B.C. The Chinese have long been the world leaders in aquaculture development, and in the 1950s, they married twentieth-century technology with fish farming in an attempt to provide protein to a growing population.

Traditional fish farming promised to relieve the problem of declining food availability per capita, but it relied on collecting wild juveniles from the Yangtze and other rivers, and transferring them to ponds—a system limited by the availability of the wild fish. In the 1950s, the Chinese government mobilized their scientists in a major effort to overcome those constraints.

In 1958, on the eve of the largest famine in Chinese history, researchers succeeded for the first time in spawning several species of carp in captivity. From 1959 to 1960, an estimated thirty million people died of hunger in China. Chroniclers of the famine blamed it on government policies that forced peasants to make steel rather than grow grain. But while the millions starved, scientists made several other breakthroughs in spawning fish in captivity and the government published a 612-page book on the new system. China's freshwater fish farming industry took off, and in 1962, growers spawned three billion carp in captivity.

A push to develop marine aquaculture followed and soon made China the biggest exporter of farmed seaweed in the world. According to the FAO, seaweed accounted for 60 percent of China's marine aquaculture production in the 1970s. Mollusks, fish, and shrimp made up the rest.

❧

In its early stages, the modernized seafood farming industry proved it could substantially augment wild production. Subasinghe was still in University studying public policy when the FAO took a lead role in developing aquaculture on a global level. On June 2, 1976, eminent scientists and policy makers from around the world gathered in Kyoto, Japan for the FAO Technical Conference on Aquaculture.

Panels at the conference discussed various types of aquaculture, from seaweed farming to raising shrimp and salmon. They predicted problems such as securing adequate levels of clean water and feed, and issued warnings—among them that "the hazards of spreading communicable diseases through introduction and transplantation of aquatic organisms are becoming increasingly serious with the expansion of aquaculture." The conference recommended that the FAO, the Office International de Èpizootics (OIE), and other organizations form an international convention for the control of selected communicable diseases "as soon as possible."

❦

None of the concerns raised ever threatened to slow development. Most of the conference participants believed that real and potential obstacles to expanding aquaculture could all be surmounted through better management and advanced technology. To that end, the conference report recommended that nations move to increase aquaculture production fivefold between 1976 and 2006. Participants called on the World Bank and other international finance agencies to "recognize aquaculture as a priority sector for investment and provide adequate financial support for aquaculture in developing countries, taking into full account the social values of rural aquaculture."

Not long after the conference, development banks began pouring money into the aquaculture industry, particularly marine and brackish water aquaculture. According to a report by Public Citizen, between 1977 and 1997 the World Bank claims to have loaned almost a billion dollars for shrimp farm development in Africa, Asia, and Latin America: 10 percent of the estimated nine billion dollars the industry received from public lenders. Public Citizen estimated that when infrastructure supports for shrimp farm development, such as roads and power were included, the World Bank, along with USAID, the IMF and other finance institutions, put almost two billion dollars into South America, primarily Ecuador, during those same two decades. However, while advocating technically advanced aquaculture as a boon for the poor, the conference report noted that "the adoption of intensive culture techniques has resulted in increased yields, but this also involves increased production costs. This situation has led to a trend toward the culture of high-valued species for export even in countries that need to produce cheap fish to feed the local people."

❤

The report made a fair prediction. An acre of pond stocked with shrimp proved far more valuable than one stocked with carp, and with capital available, the shrimp farming industry exploded in Asia and South America in the 1980s, when countries like Thailand, Ecuador, India, and Vietnam, saw double-digit growth in shrimp production and surpassed the Untied States as aquaculture producers. By 2005, Thailand alone produced four hundred thousand tons of farmed shrimp that accounted for 25 percent of the country's agricultural exports. For many nations in Asia, aquaculture played a key role in their economic expansion.

"In the early days," said Subasinghe, "anybody could make money growing shrimp. But now you have to know what you are doing."

❤

As with China's freshwater fish farms, modern shrimp farming built on an existing system called extensive shrimp farming. In Southeast Asia and South America, coastal residents had often trapped wild shrimp post-larvae in natural lagoons or man-made ponds and, with little input, reaped a small harvest after a few months. A variation of this low-tech system became the backbone of the global shrimp farming network.

With backing from the banks and help from development agencies, shrimp farmers bulldozed shallow ponds near lagoons and other sources of reasonably clean water. After filling the ponds, they stocked them with post-larval shrimp harvested from the wild, but at higher densities than with the extensive method. They pushed densities up above twenty PLs per square meter, fed them enough prepared feeds to ensure steady growth, and circulated water from nearby sources through their ponds in order to provide oxygen and flush wastes. In the early days of global expansion, this method, known as semi-intensive, offered the highest returns on investment, and became the most popular for both poor farmers and larger companies.

Mexico, too, hoped to cash in, but the country had to find a place for aquaculture. In Mexico, shrimp aquaculture was reserved for the ejidos and fishing cooperatives established by the Mexican Constitution of 1917. Under the banner of "Land and Liberty," a million people died in the Mexican Revolution between 1910 and 1920. That ten-year struggle sought to free the general population from the heavy hands of foreign capital and the Catholic Church, but according to many, it failed as much as it succeeded. The land reform promised by Article 27 of the 1917 Constitution came slowly, and in the form of ejidos, communally owned properties that could not be sold to nonmembers or used as collateral for loans. Fishing cooperatives gave established communities clear rights to inshore and offshore fishing areas, but often required fishermen to sell to state-owned companies such as Ocean Garden Products. Nonetheless, what little the Mexican campesinos and fishermen gained from the revolution, they clung to.

At the dawn of modern shrimp aquaculture, the conservative fishing and farming communities of Sonora and Sinaloa—many of them rooted in ancient Mayo, Yaqui, and Seri Indian villages—held exclusive rights to the Sonoran coast, and they did not join the rush to aquaculture. By the early 1990s, there were no shrimp farms in Sonora.

But in 1992, with the aim of fostering economic growth on the coast and elsewhere, as well as integrating the country into the global economy, Mexican president Carlos Salinas de Gortari succeeded in amending the Constitution. Suddenly, ejidatarios received clear titles to their lands, and they could sell or lease them to entities outside the ejido; the market would determine the disposition of the land, as it had before the revolution.

❧

While humanitarian concerns such as creating jobs and feeding the hungry got top billing as the reason for these investments, money was to be made, and shrimp farms sprouted up from Puerto Peñasco in northern Sonora to the southern end of Sinaloa. From 1994 to 2001, the number of shrimp farms in Sonora jumped from 0 to an estimated 210. By 2005, the entire country had forty thousand hectares of shrimp farms, a quarter of Mexico's total capacity as estimated by the World Bank. Many of the earliest farms were established as joint ventures with ejidos, and aquaculture promoters called the development of high value exports a win-win situation: a boon for consumers and producers in depressed coastal areas.

"Aquaculture is good for poor people," said Subasinghe. He said it emphatically, his voice rising above the blaring mariachis, and pointed out that "over half the shrimp farms in Thailand are less than half an acre." He also espoused the popular belief that shrimp exports would enable poor countries to enjoy some of the benefits of trade liberalization. "They can sell their shrimp for a high price and buy more food than the land could have produced. This is the law of comparative advantage working in their favor." According to Subasinghe, the shrimp industry would ultimately feed more people than local fishing could, and that would lead to increased food security—an important part of the FAO mission. For Subasinghe and many people in coastal regions, the risks of not developing aquaculture seemed more threatening than the alternative.

Fishing communities in eastern Maine, northwest Mexico, and elsewhere willingly accepted the new vision of aquaculture development. As they strove to keep their resource-based economies intact, more and more fishermen realized that practicing the dogma of economic growth on the backs of limited fish and shellfish stocks has its limits. The resulting decline of wild harvest fisheries left fishing communities around the world looking for something to bail them out: aquaculture looked like a solution.

"There may be a limit," said Subasinghe in regard to the ocean's capacity to grow shrimp. "But if there is, we are so far from it, it is not really a concern."

SANTA BARBARA, SONORA, 2006

A narrow road passed a forlorn cemetery set amid the desolation of a cracked and salt-crusted landscape, a good place to be dead. A garden of white angels, crosses, and benevolent Jesus statues sprouted amid the sparse cactus that dotted the floodplain. My ride stopped where a shrine stood at the head of the dirt road leading to Santa Barbara, little more than a name on the coast of Sonora.

I planned to walk the road and see what changes had occurred since my first visit in 2003, but as I got out of the car a red Ford truck pulled in behind us. The driver, a Mexican rolled down his window. "Are you lost?" he asked in very good English.

"Not yet."

He and I looked at each other a second. "Do you work down here?" I asked.

"I own an oyster farm at the end of the road," he said.

"Can you give me a ride in?" I looked and saw a boy sitting in the passenger seat.

"Sure," he said, and turned to the boy. "Get in the back, son." His son jumped in the back and made room for me in the passenger seat. "My name is Alejo," said the man. "You can call me Alex if that is easier." Not far down the dirt road, we passed a cluster of white buildings, a shrimp hatchery. "That's Camaron Dorado," said Alejo.

"I know. I was there three years ago."

⌁

In 2003, I had traveled down the same road to Santa Barbara. In even worse shape then, it had deep ruts from tractor-trailer traffic during the rainy season, I straddled them perilously as I drove out to a complex of low white buildings among the dunes: Camaron Dorado, a shrimp hatchery gearing up for the year's production.

In 1999, the Mexican government passed a law requiring all shrimp farms be stocked with hatchery raised post-larvae. Hatchery PLs would be less likely to spread the diseases afflicting shrimp farms and would reduce pressure on wild stocks by eliminating the harvest of PLs from the region's estuaries.

A barbed wire-topped cyclone fence surrounded the compound. A guard in a small hut questioned me at the gate. I told him, more or less, that I had an appointment to meet José Reyna, a technical consultant for the hatchery. Reyna, a man in his late thirties, has worked in Mexico's shrimp aquaculture industry for almost twenty years. "I've been with this company for three years," he told me. "They started in 1992 and produced twenty-four million post-larvae. Now we produce 140 million post-larvae a year."

Shrimp farms are generally stocked with fourteen-day-old post-larval shrimp, either spawned in hatcheries or harvested from the wild. In Mexico, a ban on wild larvae harvest led to an increase of hatcheries, such as Camaron Dorado, but production has idled.

"Growth has been slow for the last couple years because of disease problems," says Reyna. In the early 1990s, two virulent viral diseases, white spot and Taura, emerged on shrimp farms in Taiwan and Ecuador, respectively. The global trade in aquaculture products has spread the pathogens to shrimp farms around the world and sometimes led to the contamination of wild stocks.

Reyna had no English, so we talked in a mix of rudimentary Spanish and mime, reiterating the questions and answers from different angles to make sure we understood each other. A secretary brought us coffee.

Among other things, I asked about the future of fisheries and aquaculture, a favorite question of mine since I read a speech by Canada's aquaculture czar, Yves Bastien, in which he called fisheries "an impediment to the development of aquaculture." Bastien predicted that future generations would see the beginning of the twenty-first century as the time when humankind switched from fishing to aquaculture as a means of producing seafood. Bastien did allow that fisheries would be an asset, in that they would provide aquaculture with a ready infrastructure of dockside facilities, processing plants, markets, and a trained seafood-processing workforce.

Reyna agreed with Bastien. "Farmed shrimp will totally replace the wild-caught shrimp in the next twenty years," he said. He repeated the answer to make sure it was clear, but made no provision for the fishermen. "They don't have the right mentality for aquaculture," he said.

After our coffee, Reyna invited me to tour the hatchery. We started at the circular tanks where the broodstock swam in circles around the edges. Most had only one eyestalk. In the complex morphology of shrimp, hormones that inhibit reproduction are located on the eyestalk. By a process called ablation, scientists remove one of the eyestalks, blinding the shrimp in one eye, but stimulating reproduction.

After ripe females spawn, Reyna's technicians pour the microscopic fertilized eggs into separate tanks laced with iodine to sterilize the rapidly growing eggs before they hatch into naupliae in eight hours. Over the course of the next ten days, the naupliae morph continuously, going through larval stages as they do in the wild.

Reyna prepared several slides and invited me to look at the larval shrimp. In the busy lab I took off my glasses and peered into a microscope. Against the white background several transparent creatures paddled around with a pair of small cilia; they looked nothing like shrimp, and would remain unrecognizable as such until they passed beyond the larval stage and dropped to the bottom.

After ten days, Reyna says, the shrimp are ready to market as PL-10s (post-larvae, ten days old) but most go at PL-14. Outside the lab, long concrete tanks hold thousands of PLs of various ages, and thousands of such hatcheries spread along the coast produce PLs for Mexico's shrimp farms. The earliest farms in Mexico and elsewhere in the world initially relied on collecting wild post-larvae.

Fishermen using fine meshed nets sieved PLs, but in addition to the shrimp post-larvae, they harvested larvae of other species, including many commercially valuable species. In addition to the wild stocks becoming identified as sources of disease, and the wild fish larvae often preying on shrimp in the ponds, commercial fishermen complained that the larvae harvest was depleting the wild fishery. To appease fishermen protesting about the loss of wild shrimp and secure the health of its shrimp farms by limiting the spread of disease, the Mexican regulatory agency SEMARNAP (Secretaría de Medio Ambiente y Recursos Naturales) required that all ponds be stocked with certified "Specific Pathogen Free" (SPF) post-larvae from hatcheries.

With a reliable source of larvae, and secure rights to coastal property, Mexico's shrimp farming industry quickly spread from Sinaloa to Sonora, where farmers have realized record harvests. Farms expanded south into the west coast states of Nayarit and Jalisco. On the east coast, competition with a thriving tourist trade slowed, but did not stop the spread of shrimp farms: Tamaulipas, Veracruz, and Tabasco all showed continuing growth. By 2004, the geographic expansion increased farm shrimp production to the point where it topped the wild harvest for the first time in history.

～

Three years later I drove down the same rutted dirt track with Alejo Aguilera. We passed a dry shrimp farm, and Alejo pointed a finger at the crumbling dikes sprouting thorny shrubs and cactus. "They should be how do you say it, seeding?"

"Stocking."

"Stocking the tanks now, but they went broke."

"Disease?"

"No. This is an ejido farm and the owners drank all the money in the cantinas." In spite of some success stories, ejido shrimp farms had bad reputations for going broke. But the number of decaying farms in Sonora and Sinaloa, abandoned for a variety of reasons, attested to the fact that shrimp farming was fraught with uncertainty.

Alejo turned up a sandy track and after a couple of hundred yards found the road blocked by a small brown pickup truck spinning its wheels. He got out, and pulled a rope out of the back. "I'm always helping people out here," he said. His twelve-year-old son Alejito and I stood on a small, windswept knoll and looked around as his father towed the two-wheel-drive vehicle almost back to the dirt road. To the southwest, half a dozen large shrimp trawlers lay at anchor outside a shallow lagoon. Further down the beach, a glut of pangas lay grounded on the sand, and a crowd of fishermen seemed to playing volleyball. To the west, near the shore, a few old buildings stood scattered around the edge of some low mangroves. When Alejo got back I noticed that his truck had very fat, knobby tires, a necessity out among the dunes.

"That guy was lost," he said.

❧

All around Alejo, the people with capital and resources had invested in shrimp farms, but Alejo was broke when he entered the aquaculture business and his primary resources were tenacity and ingenuity.

"When the Mexican peso crashed in 1994, I lost everything," said Alejo. "I had just one account with $2,500 in it in the United States. I knew nothing about aquaculture but I decided to try and grow oysters."

Alejo got out of the truck and walked in among half a dozen masked workers. One wore a black ski mask, others had bandanas wrapped over their faces. They barely looked up from their sorting. Oysters grow at different rates and the bags must periodically be emptied and resorted for size.

"They cover their faces because of the sun and wind," said Alejo, as he guided me out beyond the workers to show me his site. We topped a dune and saw what looked like some sort of gypsy picnic or modern art: plastic bottles of various colors and sizes buoyed up dirty white bags, tied to long lines. Crooked black poles, which held the lines, poked out of the blue water bounded by the cactus-covered dunes.

"I didn't buy anything new," said Alejo. "I went to an oyster processing plant and took the empty bags. I needed something to float the bags. You see, the bottom is very sandy here and if the oysters touch bottom they get buried. Then I had an idea to use the bottles people throw away. I put them in the bags and they hold the oysters off bottom."

The colors, sharp angles and contrast promised a beautiful photo in the right light at dawn or dusk. "This would make a great shot for the Beauty of Aquaculture photo contest the Global Aquaculture Alliance is holding," I said.

"Sure, take lots of pictures, come whenever you want," said Alejo.

🐟

It took Alejo a couple of years to get organized. In 1998, he bought four hundred dollars' worth of seeds from Coast Sea Foods, in Washington State, and stocked his farm. "I told the ejidatarios here that I was working on a experiment for the government. If they knew it was a business they would never have let me do it."

He built up the business to twenty-seven lines with anywhere from seven hundred to one thousand bags per line and around two hundred oysters per bag. "You know the way this business is, I could have two million oysters today, two hundred thousand tomorrow."

I snapped some more photos, wishing I had better light and a better camera, but the contest deadline was only three days away, and I would never make it if I waited to come back.

"This is the entrance canal to Camaron Dorado's shrimp farm," said Alejo. "They were the last to get *Mancha Blanca*," he added, referring to the white spot virus that wiped out most farms in the area in 2005. "Maybe because the oysters were cleaning the water. Now other shrimp farmers want to put oysters in their canals."

We walked back through the workers and bent low to thread our way along a path overhung with mangroves. We emerged near a collapsing house. "I want to make here a restaurant where people come and eat oysters," said Alejo. "Then I want my own hatchery. I had larvae and settled them here last year. For a thousand dollars and without electricity I did what the expensive labs do, I had no ultraviolet light, none of that, just water from the bay and upwells." He described the special cages he used to get his oyster larvae to settle, made from cast-off materials. "I build everything out here out of what other people throw away."

Back under the awning with his workers, he showed me some market-size oysters. "I sell by the unit, by the oyster. I can sell to Mazatlán sometimes three thousand a week, I sell to Obregón maybe four thousand a week, to Hermosillo seven thousand. One year on *Semana Santa* I sold one hundred thousand units."

He gave me four oysters and told me to try them. On the way back out to the road he pointed to a fence separating some short mangroves from a sparse patch of mangrove stumps.

"I put this fence up and people got angry with me. They said why did you put up a fence? But look at the difference. It saves the mangroves."

"What happened to the others?"

"People take them to smoke *lisa* [mullet]."

In many ways, his oyster farm accomplished what the FAO wanted aquaculture to accomplish: it created jobs for struggling fishermen, food for local markets, and it had a positive effect on the environment by absorbing waste in more ways than one.

In spite of his success however, Alejo lacked the permit to be on ejido land, and it cost him every time the inspectors came to his farm. "I tell them I have my federal permit, but the ejido won't give me one for the land, and what can I do? I am running a profitable business and providing jobs to people. So I give them some oysters and they tell me it's okay. It's corruption, but that's Mexico."

By the late 1980s, every form of government associated with the coasts, down to the village elders, was partially focused on aquaculture. Other conferences outlining the path aquaculture should take followed the FAO's 1976 Kyoto meeting. To most it was clear: aquaculture was the food-producing system of the future. Nongovernment organizations such as Greenpeace, the Environmental Defense Fund, and the World Wildlife Fund, to name a few, initially saw aquaculture in a positive light: a source of jobs and food for a hungry world.

In economically depressed areas of the developed world— the less prosperous regions of otherwise well-off countries—

marine aquaculture development focused on another high value export product: Atlantic salmon.

Unlike the shrimp and oyster farms of the developing world, the more technologically sophisticated salmon farming industry grew out of long-running programs in the United States, Canada, and Europe that released hatchery-reared fish into the wild in an effort to supplement existing stocks. People like Jimmy Robinson's great-grandfather had long experience with augmenting wild stocks for the sake of sport and commercial fishermen—in spite of the well-documented fact that hatchery programs degrade the genetic makeup and consequent fitness of wild stocks.

The idea of using the knowledge gained through commercial and sport fisheries' enhancement programs to create an egg-to-market seafood production system first arose in the heady days of the first blue revolution: the 1960s and '70s, when fisheries promised to feed the world.

In 1967, the United States Congress established the Commission on Marine Science, Engineering, and Resources, commonly known as the "Stratton Commission," after its chairman, Julius Stratton. The commission's report, published in 1969, called for more research into aquaculture, particularly high-value species such as salmon and oysters.

Under the mantra that the new industry would create jobs, reduce the trade deficit in seafood, and make the United States a world leader in aquaculture, the U.S. Aquaculture Act passed

Congress in 1980, and intended to foster a rapid expansion of the fish farming industry.

But in 1980 Norway already had a burgeoning salmon-farming industry, bound to become the largest in the world. Norway's cod stocks had fluctuated sporadically all through history, but dropped precipitously following World War II when new technologies were used to exploit the fishery. Older boats sat at the docks, waiting for repairs they would never get.

In order to slow migration away from coastal communities in the northern regions, those that depended most heavily on fishing, the Norwegian government began to grow salmon in net pens in the protected waters of its northern fjords. The Norwegians initially limited access to the new enterprise to fishing families. The government helped eager entrepreneurs to set up numerous small farms, while providing loans for feed and other inputs. Again, early efforts, though challenged, met with financial success. And similar programs quickly began in nearby Scotland, and later on the east and west coasts of Canada and the United States. Ireland, the Faeroe Islands, and other North Atlantic–rim countries entered the lucrative business, as did Chile, which would become the world's largest Atlantic salmon producer in the Western hemisphere.

By the early 1990s, salmon fillets dyed an alluring orange color appeared in supermarket seafood cases for six dollars or less a pound. Farmed shrimp from Asia, piled on ice alongside the salmon, sold for half of the cost of domestic shrimp. Middle-class consumers in the United States, who had watched wild fish prices rise above ten dollars for once-common species such as cod and flounder, breathed a collective sigh of relief. Aquaculture enabled them to eat luxury seafood at bargain prices.

While shrimp and salmon hardly appeared as candidates for feeding the world, both species offered those interested in experimenting with aquaculture the opportunity to glean a profit from their risky ventures. The science and technology associated with seafood farming were advancing, and that was the important thing.

New economic growth was occurring in some of the poorest regions of the world and the industry was attracting new investors. Because of their high returns, shrimp and salmon farming encouraged more research; research that many believed would lead to sustainable seafood farming on a large scale. Expansion into other species could come later.

Subasinghe believed that aquaculture was of vital importance to world food security. Fish-farm production needed to increase by fifty-four million pounds between 1997 and 2030, according to the FAO 2002 outlook. The money the industry generated and the adventure of solving the problems of opening the blue frontier attracted the best and brightest: optimists like Subasinghe.

4

THE BOYS

THOMAS POWELL—FLORIDA

In 2002, Thomas Powell of Jacksonville, Florida, advertised for potential investors in his land-based shrimp farms. He did not promote job creation or a chance to feed the world; instead Powell saw a chance to meet demand in the high-end shrimp market. "In a worst-case scenario," he speculated on his website, "exotic disease will wipe out 80 percent of the wild shrimp stocks, leaving the market open for aquaculture products."

In a later interview, he qualified the assertion about massive die-offs of wild shrimp. "It's a guess, based on what we've seen in Mexico," said Powell, referring to an outbreak of IHHNV (infectious hypodermal and hematopoietic necrosis virus) in the upper Gulf of California that wiped out wild stocks of blue shrimp for almost a decade. "But I'm not into shrimp anymore," Powell added. "Now we're looking offshore."

Powell and several partners had applied for an offshore lease to raise fish in submerged net pens, but ran into trouble when regulators found out that most of the partners had criminal records, including Powell, who had served time in prison on a drug conviction. The U.S. National Marine Fisheries Service (NMFS) denied the lease.

Powell appeared as a caricature of the avaricious businessman looking at aquaculture as the next place to score a quick buck. Other aquaculture entrepreneurs took a longer term view of the industry as a sustainable source of income, as well as food security.

BOB ROSENBERRY—SAN DIEGO, CALIFORNIA

Wearing khaki shorts and a white shirt, Bob Rosenberry leaned against a pillar at the San Diego airport. He had a thin, wiry build, in good shape for a man nearly seventy. I recognized his bright smile from a photograph on his Web site.

Later, sitting in his condo on Scripp's Ranch, overlooking the city of San Diego with the fog-shrouded Pacific in the distance, I asked Rosenberry if he thought shrimp farming would fulfill the altruistic promises of governments. "What are you talking about?" he said, incredulous. "I don't remember anything about creating jobs. All I heard was that it was a great way to make money." Rosenberry had been writing about the aquaculture industry and publishing the *World Shrimp Farming Report* annually since 1976, and while he often risked the ire of shrimp farmers by reporting honestly about the disease and pollution problems of the industry, like Subasinghe he fundamentally believed those problems had solutions waiting for discovery. "Of course this industry is going to grow," he said. "We'll figure it out." When offered the label of "techno-optimist" Bob latched onto it. "I like that," he said as we headed out to visit the leading shrimp aquaculture entrepreneurs in San Diego.

"This is perfect California weather," Bob said as we walked outside into the bright sunshine. We got in his car and drove down a palm tree–lined avenue on our way to the offices of Ocean Garden Products (OGP), and a meeting with operations manager John Filose, one of the key people Rosenberry wanted me to meet.

JOHN FILOSE—SAN DIEGO

We arrived at 10:00 A.M. and waited a few moments for Filose, who came into the lobby smiling. A tall, trim man with graying hair and a receding hairline, Filose appeared every inch the successful executive at the top of his game. He walked us through an expansive room full of people looking very busy in their respective cubicles. Pictures of brightly colored boats hauling nets full of shrimp hung on the walls beside aerial photos of shrimp farms, large arrays of rectangular ponds bulldozed out of the coastal plain.

In Filose's office we sat down at a large conference table and were joined by Manuel Puebla, a consultant from Sonora, Mexico. Filose had a lot on his mind. The Mexican government, which started Ocean Garden back in 1957, had decided to sell the company. Several prospective buyers, including representatives from Cargill and a consortium of Mexican shrimp farmers, had been in the offices inspecting the books in recent weeks. "It's tough, because the Mexican government is looking for the right buyer, somebody who will be willing to look out for the social sector, the cooperativas and ejidos."

According to Filose, OGP does roughly two hundred million dollars in business every year, handling 60 percent of Mexico's shrimp exports. It once handled 100 percent, but since the early 1990s increasing privatization of the shrimp industry and the ejidos has led to a more diversified market.

Nonetheless, OGP had endured. The market hadn't changed, said Filose. But the the competitors had. He gave an example of what a tough game the seafood business can be. "Tyson chicken got into the seafood business. And the numbers go something like this: they bought three companies and paid about seven hundred million dollars. They wrote those companies down to zero, and then in selling them back to the original owners they essentially became the bank, and lost another two to three hundred million dollars. So they lost almost a billion dollars over a five-year period trying to organize the seafood business. I remember John Tyson saying to me, 'We're going to make it like the chicken industry.' Well, a billion dollars later they hadn't made it like the chicken industry—because you can't."

Even working with farmed product, Filose pointed out, the business remained unpredictable. "Just last week we got in a shipment that was supposed to be a mix of sizes, and it was all one size." Such uncertainties put Filose in a position similar to that of a wild product salesman, who seldom knows from one day to the next what he will have for product. And the stable prices supposedly associated with farmed product did not always apply to suppliers. "I've changed prices three times already this week," said Filose.

While disease outbreaks continued to stifle production on Mexican shrimp farms, particularly in northern Sinaloa and southern Sonora, Filose remained buoyantly optimistic. "Good management practices, GMPs, that's what will keep this industry going." He pointed out a number of farms, including one owned by Daniel Gutierrez of the Mexican Shrimp Council, which produced consistent quantities of large, high-quality shrimp. "And we're working with the Natural Resources Defense Council and fishermen in the upper gulf of California to manage their fishery sustainably," said Filose. Maintaining healthy fisheries mattered as much to OGP as maintaining healthy farms, according to Filose. A third of the shrimp Ocean Garden sells are wild caught.

Filose thought that nongovernment organizations, and radical movements such as the Zapatistas in Chiapas, presented a greater obstacle to shrimp farm development than biological or market factors. "Sub-comandante Marcos, this Che Guevara–type radical, has driven off a lot of investment in the state of Chiapas," he said, referring to the masked leader of the peasant uprising in Mexico's southernmost state. "And it's sad, from our perspective, because they have an ideal climate."

Filose also took issue with the contentions of various NGOs. "You've got people sitting in their condos, driving hybrid cars and going to meetings in nice places, complaining that shrimp and salmon don't feed people, they only generate hard currency. Well, what is wrong with that? What is wrong with somebody in the third world earning hard currency? These companies can pay their employees, who can then live better. That's a sin? I don't get it."

Filose, a former Navy fighter pilot, exhibits the élan of a gallant warrior. He is learning to speak Spanish.

"I saw you make a presentation in Spanish," Rosenberry said to Filose. "I was very impressed."

"I do okay as long as my listeners are patient," said Filose. "Luckily, Mexican people are very patient."

HENRY CLIFFORD—SAN DIEGO, CALIFORNIA

A week later, back at Rosenberry's condo, we met with Henry Clifford, a man who has worked in the shrimp business virtually since its inception in the Western Hemisphere. While Filose ran a company very much into producing shrimp, Clifford remained on the sidelines, selling his problem-solving skills to shrimp farmers. Leaning back in Rosenberry's sofa on a Sunday afternoon, Clifford stretched out his long legs and recalled his entry into the shrimp farming industry of the late 1970s.

"I graduated from Texas A&M with a degree in shrimp nutrition and landed a job with Purina," said Clifford. "It was the job I wanted. I bought a house in Florida and settled down, thinking I would live there the rest of my life working for Purina. Two years later they closed the lab and laid us all off."

Clifford traded a sedentary life to become one of the visionaries of the largest single seafood commodity in the world. "Some of the people from Purina went to Asia," said Clifford. "I went to Latin America." Beginning in 1981, he moved to Brazil, then Colombia and Ecuador, setting up shrimp farms and hatcheries for the fledgling industries of these and other countries.

"Brazil, Colombia, and Ecuador have all put millions into their industries," said Clifford. "The local governments offer the industries financial support, subsidies, tax write-offs, you name it. They want these industries to grow."

In spite of government benevolence, Clifford believed the industries pulled their own weight. "I think they bring in foreign exchange far and above what the governments put into them, and that's what these countries want."

As the problems of the shrimp farmers changed, so did Clifford's expertise. After working on feed formulas, he switched to breeding disease-resistant shrimp, as viruses wiped out hundreds of thousands of acres of shrimp farms in the mid-1990s. When the viruses mutated faster than breeders could produce resistant shrimp, Clifford moved into therapeutics, and in 2005 joined a San Diego lab owned by Aqua Bounty Technologies, a Massachusetts-based biotechnology company known for creating genetically modified salmon.

Clifford had just returned from a trip to Ecuador where he conducted field tests for the company's new antiviral drug. Clifford had spent days on his knees in a flat-bottom boat with a couple of shrimp farm workers who paddled around various shrimp ponds, periodically casting an *ataraya* into the murky waters to catch samples. "I keep them in a bucket and sort through them quickly, looking for shrimp showing signs of disease." Clifford has a good sense of shrimp health. "It's not an innate sense. It's based on years of experience and looking at thousands of shrimp," he said.

Nonetheless, Clifford has refused to invest any of his own money in a shrimp farm. "I'm much too conservative an investor," he said.

CARLOS PARADA—NAVOPATIA, SONORA

For Carlos Parada, struggling to establish a shrimp farm just north of Navopatia, on Estero Bamocha in southern Sonora, Clifford's warning would have come as an understatement. In late February of 2003 I parked my car outside the gate of Acuiacola Clej, and walked across the arid soil toward an isolated brown hut built of plywood. People came out and watched me cross the 200 yards of open ground. A tall, graying man stood near a white pickup truck. The way the others glanced at him it seemed he was the boss, and I headed towards him.

Camera slung over my shoulder, notebook in hand, I arrived within hailing distance. In Spanish I introduced myself as a journalist working on a story about shrimp farms and asked him if he was in charge. He looked at me skeptically.

"I am the owner," he said in English.

"You're Carlos Parada?"

He nodded, and asked me if I was an environmentalist come to make more trouble. I told him the name of the obscure Washington, D.C., publication I was writing for and showed him some of the articles I had written about fisheries. He glanced at them perfunctorily and handed them back to me.

"As you can see, the ponds are empty," he said. "Why don't you come back next month?"

I explained my schedule problems and told him this would be my only chance. "How's it going?"

"Not so good," he said. "They told us this would be a good place, but we're having a lot of problems."

"Disease?"

"No, water. Hopefully we have them solved," he said as he

got into his truck. "I have to go but you are welcome to look around." He called to his foreman to act as my guide.

"Can I get in touch with you later?" I asked, and he gave me his office number in Obregón.

"Come by and we'll have lunch," he said.

Manuel Mendoza, the foreman, was twenty years old; he came from Obregón and had seven years' experience shrimp farming. We went up to the hut for a moment to get out of the wind and have a cup of coffee. I talked to the workers about where they came from and how much they worked and what they got paid.

Ten men and one woman cook worked the farm in the off-season; all of them came from the surrounding ejidos: Las Aguilas, Melchior Ocampo, and Juan Escucha. They said they worked eleven days on and then got three days off. They wouldn't say what they were paid, but the standard rate was about six dollars a day.

"When the PLs [shrimp post-larvae] arrive, the workforce will increase to sixteen," Mendoza said. On March 10, the minuscule shrimp would arrive from the Super Shrimp hatchery. The certified pathogen-free shrimp would be stocked in the ponds at a rate of about eighteen per square meter of surface area, and hopefully yield an average of twenty-eight hundred pounds of shrimp at the end of the five month growing season. "How many harvests had they had so far?" I asked. "One," he told me. "But it was a poor one."

The foreman passed me on to Samuel Guardo, one of the other workers, for a tour of the farm. Guardo and I walked down the low hill to the massive pumps used to flood the ponds. "How many gallons a minute?" I asked.

He didn't know. *"Mucha aqua."* A lot.

I looked at the four intake pipes, all about two feet in diameter. Parada had leased five hundred hectares from the Agiabampo ejido. His primary plan was to develop two hundred hectares, but at the time I visited, the farm consisted of sixteen ponds ranging from four to ten hectares each, with a total of sixty hectares available for production. So far, Guardo said, the farm had taken three times longer to build than they had expected. Erosion scarred many of the dikes, which required constant repair. "We are in the process of changing the screens on all the gates," said Guardo, pointing to the fine-mesh screens that allowed water to pass from pond to pond, but not the shrimp that often carried viral pathogens.

Bulldozers sat idle in the distance as we walked down the long dikes that separated the shallow ponds, only a meter deep. The ten-hectare ponds, Guardo said, were the ones that gave them problems. Dissolved oxygen levels had fallen too low and they had to put aeration pumps into the ponds. He said it was amazing to see the shrimp crowding in around the pumps.

Fortunately they had not fallen victim to the diseases that had ravaged the industry in central Sonora and Sinaloa. Four shrimp farms drew water from, and flushed their ponds into, Bamocha Estuary, the northern arm of the larger Agiabampo system, and they existed to each other's peril. With all exchanging 10 percent or more of their water daily, if one got the virus it would easily spread to the others. I looked at the eroded outflow canal, where some scraggly looking pelicans stood among the litter of plastic feed bags and other detritus from the farm.

A FISHERIES HERITAGE—RALPH DEWITT

Parada, Filose, and Clifford were just three of the thousands of entrepreneurs, managers, and consultants kept who kept the food production system in the developed world awash in salmon fillets and endless shrimp. Behind them stood thousands of hardworking people, most of them faceless laborers operating behind the scenes. Though the laborers in shrimp and fish farming may have caught only a glimpse of the expanding universe they help create, most expressed a passionate belief in the future of aquaculture.

Ralph DeWitt, for instance, came from a fishing family in Eastport, Maine. In the early '90s he rose from deckhand to captain of one of Maine's venerable old sardine carriers, the *Medric*, owned by Peacock Canning of Lubec. Built in the 1950s, the *Medric* was a classic wooden boat, seventy feet long with a twenty-foot beam. He ran the boat for only two years before Peacock switched from packing wild herring to processing farmed salmon.

DeWitt looked at his options. If he wanted to work on the water he realized he would have to become a fish farmer. "By the time I started looking around, all the fisheries had gone limited entry [no more permits were available]. Aquaculture was all that was left."

Bobby Peacock gave DeWitt another boat to run, the new *Medric*, a plastic barge built to deliver feed to the various salmon pens around the bay, including some in Canada owned by companies whose operations straddled the border.

"We call her the Clorox bottle," DeWitt said disparagingly of the new *Medric*.

In 1999, the Maine Sea Urchin Zone Council, an industry advisory board for the state's sea urchin fishery, received an application for an aquaculture lease to grow sea urchins.

Ralph and his crewman Cecil Cates went down to the Orland, Maine, town hall to speak in favor of the aquaculture project. Amid the Formica tables and folding chairs, Cates talked about the benefits of working for a large aquaculture corporation. "I have a 401K plan," said Cates. "I never had that fishing."

"You never fished," said one of the council members who knew him.

Many council members argued that aquaculture would privatize the industry, and eventually consolidate it in the hands of a few big players as had happened with salmon.

DeWitt talked about the privatization issue. "You guys with your limited entry have a private ocean, and I'm not too impressed with what you've done with it. Aquaculture is the only opportunity I have to keep working on the water." DeWitt wanted access to the same resources that had sustained his family for generations, but he was shut out. "I was doing other things when all the fisheries went limited entry, by the time I looked around they was all closed. Leasing a piece of bottom is the only way I can stay in business."

DeWitt is not alone: Washington County has been steadily losing population since 2000. The biggest group leaving consists of people aged twenty to thirty. The region is an exporter of labor, people with a strong work ethic who cannot find work.

THE WORKING WATERFRONT—SEBASTIAN BELLE

Sebastian Belle, executive director of the Maine Aquaculture Association, pointed to DeWitt and Cates as prime examples of what salmon farming brought to the coast of Maine: a chance to maintain a traditional working waterfront.

"Here in Maine the population is growing not by people being born here, but from people moving here from other states," said Belle. "Ninety percent of those people move to within ten miles of the coast, and do you know what? Most of them have no connection with the sea. They don't give a damn about a working waterfront." The way Belle saw it, fishermen and fish farmers had common cause in a culture war between waterfront residents looking for a pristine environment, and those who earned their living in that environment.

Belle's argument had an appeal to fishermen who faced the same conundrum of being run off the waterfront. At a fish health workshop in the wake of a massive disease outbreak among Maine salmon farms, he passed out bumper stickers reading: "This family is supported by Maine's working waterfront."

"A working waterfront is part of the Maine tradition," said Belle. "And aquaculture is part of that tradition."

I had first met Sebastian Belle over the phone, in the summer of 2000. He heard I was writing an article about aquaculture for *National Fisherman*, and called to make sure I got the industry side of the story.

In his new position as executive director of the Maine Aquaculture Association (MAA), he believed that given the correct information, most people would come to the same conclusion he had: that aquaculture was the logical evolution of fisheries development, from hunter gathering to farming.

"I was the same as you," he told me. "I started out as a fisherman, but I could see where that industry was headed and that's when I made a decision to get into aquaculture. Farming is the answer to the fisheries problem."

Belle learned the techniques of salmon farming from the masters, the Norwegians. "Most of the fish farmers over there are fishermen," Belle said. "They run their operations the way you would run any livestock operation, and with full support from the communities because they know that this is the future."

Belle brought his Norwegian perspective to Maine in the '90s. He initially landed a job with the state, promoting salmon aquaculture and reviewing lease applications, but quit after a year and went to work as the executive director of the Maine Acquaculture Association.

Belle avoided prosecution under Maine's revolving door law—which prohibits state employees from going to work for the industries they had been charged with regulating—and continued on his mission to sell aquaculture to the Maine public.

❧

"People need to know what we're doing," said Belle. He went on to list the progress the industry had made in operating in an environmentally conscious way. "We have cut antibiotics use by 90 percent since the 1980s," he said. "And our feed conversion ratios [the amount of processed feed used to grow one pound of salmon] has reached less than two to one, which is far more efficient than any land-based livestock. I think pigs have a ratio of about five to one."

Belle played up the economic benefits of salmon farming, claiming the industry brought thousands of jobs to the region. But by 2000, three foreign-owned companies: Stolt Sea Farms of Luxembourg, Fjord Seafood of Norway, and Heritage Salmon of Canada, controlled Maine's salmon industry. The three companies operating in Maine were among the top ten in the world at that time, and together produced 12 percent of global supply of farmed salmon.

Once the salmon farms reached a threshold in the bay, they started shrinking their payrolls, automating many jobs in order to cut costs. All through the industry, as production skyrocketed in the late 1990s, employment decreased. In the most advanced countries, such as Norway and Scotland, the poundage produced per worker jumped from 20 tons in the early years to 151 tons by 2004. "Increasing efficiency is the logical progression of any business," said Belle.

So is growth, and Belle realized the only way for the industry to grow was geographically, and felt an educated public, particularly those with a connection to the sea, would welcome the industry wherever it offered to set up shop.

But most of Maine's coastal counties did not share the Cobscook Bay area's desperation for economic development. Even given a clear picture of the industry, other coastal counties rejected the farms in favor of the pristine views that invited tourism, and Belle faced the difficult prospect of promoting growth in an industry, within limits. Suddenly salmon farmers had another thing in common with commercial fishermen.

MANIFEST DESTINY—JILL FALLON

Others in the industry looked for ways to defy limits. In 1996, Jill Fallon, president of the Aquaculture Coalition, spoke at the Open Ocean Aquaculture conference held in Portland, Maine, that year. Fallon advocated the expansion of aquaculture into the waters off the U.S. coasts. "Manifest Destiny," she called it, and exhorted her colleagues: "If we [the United States] are to maintain a dominant position in the watery world, in marine biotechnology . . . and in sustainable environmental technology that will set the worldwide standard for open-ocean aquaculture, we must open the blue frontier."

In her speech, Fallon, a former Environmental Protection Agency official in the George H. W. Bush administration, compared fishermen to Native Americans who, she said, "had to be removed, warred against, and eventually forced onto reservations to make room for new settlers. . . ."

THE RACE—JAMES McVEY

While short on funds to promote offshore aquaculture, Jim McVey, the visionary director of the National Sea Grant College Program, contended that fish farms in the open ocean offered the only future for the U.S. marine aquaculture industry. McVey had watched the shrimp and fish farming industries unfold since 1969. He was among those attending the FAO's Kyoto conference in 1976, and like the FAO, he repeatedly called for government to play an ever-greater role in opening the way for aquaculture. He attributed the slow growth to the work of anti-aquaculture NGO's. "We need friends in Congress," he said.

Since 1984, when he started work with Sea Grant, the program has become a major promoter of aquaculture in the Exclusive Economic Zone, U.S. waters from three to two hundred miles offshore. "Coastal pollution means that inshore areas will continue to lose productivity," said McVey. "Past problems with salmon farms show that in some cases they are already straddling the line of what is acceptable. We have to go offshore."

Beginning in 1999 the Sea Grant Program received an extra thirteen million dollars, about half of which went directly into offshore aquaculture development, not only in New Hampshire, but also in Hawaii, the Gulf of Mexico, and Puerto Rico. "We've got two farms permitted in Puerto Rico and two in Hawaii as a result of our program," said McVey, referring to the company Snapperfarm. "Their combined value of production could reach ten million dollars per year in the near future." He also raised the prospect of floating fish farms that would be set adrift within the EEZ.

"But this is a very sensitive time," said McVey. "We are in a race, and we're losing by doing nothing."

THE VOICE OF REASON—JOHN FORSTER

In the 1960s, John Forster began making his living in the aquaculture business. In 1994, he started a consulting firm analyzing the feasibility of aquaculture projects. Soon he gained a reputation for frank appraisals. While remaining a strong advocate for the aquaculture industry, Forster did not gloss over or ignore potential problems, nor did he put blind faith in the power of human technology.

Speaking at the Open Ocean Aquaculture conference in Maine in 1996, Forster startled industry leaders by calling them to look at market realities. He pointed out that the financial picture for offshore aquaculture looked less than promising, as did future availability of feed. Referring to the projected seafood deficit and unfulfilled demand for fish, Forster suggested that a scarcity of fish did not mean people would pay any price for them.

"They won't," he said. "They'll switch to chicken, or lower cost processed meats, or just reduce their consumption of animal protein generally. There is no law that says people have to eat a certain amount of seafood. They will, as they do now, shop for value, and if future aquaculture offerings do not provide competitive value, they will not sell."

Forster pointed out that salmon production, at five hundred thousand metric tons in 1996, was a small fraction of the projected seafood deficits and the production costs might be too high to allow for the industry's continuing expansion. In order for salmon farmers to contribute to the world's seafood supply, "they will have to do so in a way which allows them to compete in the mass market environment, and that can only happen if fish are produced at a cost which allows for wholesale prices no higher than what we are now seeing for salmon [$2.00–$2.50/pound], and preferably lower still."

Forster warned as well that future input costs such as fuel and feed would likely rise, giving economy-of-scale operations an advantage. "This means growing millions of tons, not hundreds of thousands, as the salmon farming industry does today."

PART II

HITTING THE LIMITS

5

THE SPIRAL PATH

We're dumb and dumber, and we don't get paid enough for it.
— Bernard Raynes, commercial fisherman

All over the world, governments big and small strove to grow their aquaculture industries, but something went wrong at a hearing for a new salmon-farm lease in Perry, Maine, in April 2002. Expected to last no more than four hours, the hearing had lasted three days, as local residents brought Maine's Department of Marine Resources (DMR) to a standstill. Exhausted, state bureaucrats Andrew Fisk and Laurice Churchill called off the battle and scheduled another session.

My phone rang the morning of the second meeting. "Get down there," said Bill Crowe, editor of the *Fishermen's Voice*, a monthly paper for, by, and about fishermen, as the masthead said. "Get that story." Crowe hated salmon farms and didn't want to miss what looked to be a feeding frenzy on the DMR's aquaculture promoters.

I drove down U.S. Route 1, a narrow two-lane road that rolled through the empty stretches of Washington County, hemmed close on both side by bush spruce and pointed firs. In Perry's drab community building, a steel box that housed the town office and a pair of fire trucks, low-level bureaucrats from Maine's Department of Marine Resources took on representatives from every sector of the local community, all standing firm against the new lease.

At the first meeting, John Foster, an attorney from Eastport, punched two big holes in the legality of the lease application, pointing out that the site had not been marked and that local fishermen had not received adequate notice, as required by state law. "It's a total waste of time to go forward," said Foster.

But everyone who wanted to make a statement had a right to, and at the second meeting a broad cross section of the surrounding communities signed up to have their whack at salmon farms. The list included shorefront property owners in Perry, some of whom had engaged the formidable Conservation Law Foundation (CLF); Ken Shorey, a Republican senator in the state legislature; the Quoddy International Pilots Advisory Group, the pilots who conned freighters into Eastport and Bayside, New Brunswick; numerous members of the Passamaquoddy tribe; and members of all fishermen's associations operating in the bay. Sebastian Belle sat in the back of the room, realizing that what started out as a lease hearing had become a media circus in which aquaculture was on trial. "This isn't the place for me to speak," he told me during a break.

To many people voicing their opposition, something seemed wrong, but they could not say exactly what. Native and white fishermen alike had seen the bay's resources diminished from overfishing, and they lived with increasingly stringent regulations aimed at rebuilding depleted resources. While the fishermen cut back, three foreign-owned corporations controlled the salmon farming that capitalized on the remaining natural wealth of Cobscook Bay.

"At first it [salmon aquaculture] seemed okay," said Buddy Ritchie, a Perry lobstermen. "But it seems like they've gone too far and the bay is starting to suffer."

"Enough is enough," said Leo Murray of the Cobscook Bay Fishermen's Association. Murray reiterated the points about the sacrifices fishermen made to rebuild fish stocks and from that experience he added a note of caution. "In addition, we feel that the environmental impact of aquaculture sites has not been investigated thoroughly enough. Long-term effects of nutrient loading, chemicals, and antibiotics used to treat disease and parasites, and aquaculture waste are not yet known." Murray, who spent most of his working hours dragging a one-ton steel dredge through various bay habitats, may not have been on the best footing to voice environmental concerns, but traces of the pesticide "Slice," (Emamectin Benzoate) used against sea lice, had been found in Cobscook Bay scallops, and his point was well taken.

"If only the fishermen had the right information, they would understand what salmon farming can do," said Jorn Vad, representing the lease applicant, NorWest Fish, a Norwegian owned company. But the Cobscook Bay fishermen had lived alongside salmon farming for over fifteen years, and felt they understood what it had to offer them and their communities.

Most fishermen at the hearing had used powerful boats purchased with borrowed money to push the bay's fisheries beyond sustainable levels. They believed in the resilience of nature, and most would continue to use technology and capital when it suited them. But watching their traditional resources exploited by foreigners with more sophisticated technology and more capital did not sit well with the locals. Their determined stance made a limited impression. The hearing ended, the state denied the lease, but the fish farms did not go away.

❧

A year and a half later, two stacks of books and files sat side by side on my desk a few miles from the shores of Cobscook Bay. The low winter sun slanted through the window onto the taller stack: thick government reports, books documenting the development and collapse of the North Atlantic fisheries, along with the policies that drove that development. The slighter stack, mostly files and government publications on the rationale for developing the marine aquaculture industry, sat in the shadow of the other. Both stacks could have been much shorter, since they all reiterated similar themes: "The capacity for economic growth is so great that it need not be considered." "This industry will feed the world." "We must develop in order to meet increasing demand." The newest documents invoked the notions of precaution and sustainability, and in fisheries regulators imposed belated requirements to support rhetoric.

Patterns of Development

Most of those in the forefront of aquaculture relied on neoclassical economic models. They believed that privatizing the seafood industry would enable the market to determine the best course for development. Entrepreneurs looking for a place to grow their money and their allies in government pointed to aquaculture as the way to meet the unfulfilled demand created by the decline of capture fisheries. Yet they seemed to miss the lessons that decline offered.

The rationale of feeding the world and increasing employment through the unlimited capacity of the sea first was heard in the 1960s and 1970s to justify the expansion of capture fisheries. I was there, and so were many of the entrepreneurs and regulators who have used the same rational, verbatim in many instances, to promote aquaculture.

Among my files was a clipping from the *New York Times*, June 12, 2005, featuring a quote from fleet owner Danny Cohen, whom I worked for as a young fisherman in Cape May, New Jersey, in 1978.

"Mr. Cohen is optimistic," said the *Times*. "For one thing, he pointed out that regulation in commercial fishing along the East Coast dates back just thirty years and is nearing the point where the supply of seafood is in balance with what commercial fishermen are taking. 'How do you get growth?' Mr. Cohen asked. 'You use aquaculture.'"

While Danny's spin on the state of fisheries is worthy of note, the salient feature of the quote was his assumption that growth must continue.

The biggest obstacle to growth, many businessmen like Cohen agreed, was the environmental community. Fish farmers and their bureaucratic supporters saw gold in the waves of blue, but the NGOs would not let them at it. James McVey of Sea Grant and many others in the government believed big-budget environmental organizations had stunted the growth of aquaculture.

$\backsim$

In the span of thirty years, the commercial fishing business went from a dynamic growth industry to a ghost of an industry. The fisheries' trajectory started with overestimation of resource capacity, followed by overcapitalization in an effort to cash in on largely imagined wealth, followed by a long string of reactive "fixes" that maintained the status quo until it was too late.

Niaz Dorry, a former Greenpeace activist and one of *Time* magazine's 1998 heroes of the planet, had no patience for it. "They are demanding of the ocean what it cannot provide," she said of both the industrial commercial fishing fleet and industrial aquaculture. "And putting us on an irreversible course for destruction."

Dorry noted that after World War II, the impact of fishing increased, primarily due to the use of superior technology and policies aimed at competing in the global economy. International trade agreements proliferated, and global finance moved increasing amounts of capital into fishing fleets around the world.

Margaret Dewar described the regulatory climate of fisheries in the 1950s in her book *Industry in Trouble*. According to Dewar, fishing-industry representatives sought protection from Congress by requesting tariffs on cheap imports from subsidized fisheries in Iceland and Canada—subsidized with U.S. aid, in the case of Iceland. However, President Eisenhower rejected the request, citing the need for free trade and expanded markets that would grow the industry out of its trouble. But he did suggest the industry seek other forms of help from Congress.

Rather than raise tariffs to help the fishing industry, Congress passed the Saltonstall-Kennedy Act, which provided funds for fisheries' research. In addition the government launched several fishing vessel subsidy programs over the next decade, all aimed at creating a new advanced and efficient U.S. fleet. As Russia, Japan, and many European countries expanded their fishing capacities, the United States strove to keep up.

Fishermen and regulators seldom worried about resource capacity. The people of the world needed protein, and the oceans teemed with fish, they believed—and the best minds of the world supported that notion with irrationally optimistic predictions about the oceans' potential largess.

In the stack of my fisheries files, a report from 1966 sat near the bottom. In the introduction, Donald L. McKernan, director of the Bureau of Commercial Fisheries, wrote, "It has been estimated that the world's population may double in the next twenty five years or less with the fastest rate of growth in Asia, Latin America, and Africa." McKernan speculated that worldwide demand for seafood would increase, but expressed optimism about the seas' ability to meet that demand. "That the seas offer hope of providing more food to meet the world's growing needs is indicated by various experts whose predictions of the potential sustainable annual harvest range as high as five hundred million metric tons." He added a somewhat prophetic caveat, however. "When a harvest of this magnitude can be taken on a practical basis is not foreseeable. There are other problems in utilizing the sea's resources wisely which are—even now—compounding rapidly."

McKernan also made the case for national pride and the need to overcome the seafood trade deficit, noting that three years earlier, the United States crossed the benchmark of importing more than half the seafood it consumed.

The 1966 report admonished the nation with its rich fisheries resources to rapidly improve its ability to share "equitably in the expansion of the world's seafood harvest."

"Never before has the need for knowledge been so acute," it said.

"The United States must search out and define the fishery resources in terms of quantity and distribution, expand its capacity to produce and develop new processing techniques, and at the same time reduce the costs and risks of production." New efforts would rely on new technology, the report stressed, which would enable the United States to increase its utilization of fisheries' resources. Among other efforts, the Bureau of Commercial Fisheries subsequently launched a program to locate stocks of broadbill swordfish in the Gulf of Mexico, and helped fishermen learn to use long lines to harvest what seemed like abundant resources.

❧

Rep. Edward Garmatz, chair of the House Committee on Merchant Marine and Fisheries, made the case. "We are now outranked by Peru, Japan, Red China, Russia, and Norway,

respectively. In view of this deteriorating situation, it is impera-
tive the Fishing Fleet Improvement Act be extended." Between
1964 and 1969, the program subsidized 50 percent of the cost of
thirty-two modern fishing vessels, all in excess of one hundred
tons. While the program aimed to replace the entire offshore
fleet, it made no provision to retire the vessels being replaced.

Growing alarm at the decline of the U.S. position in world
fisheries prompted Congress, in 1966, to establish a panel of the
nation's experts: the Commission on Marine Science, Engineering, and Resources. Commonly known as the Stratton Commission, after its chairman, Julius Stratton, the panel was
created to increase the competitiveness of the U.S. fleet. The
Stratton Commission repeated the prediction that the sea could
produce five hundred million metric tons of seafood annually,
and enshrined the previous recommendations of the Bureau of
Commercial Fisheries as recommended government policy. The
commission repeated the Bureau of Commercial Fisheries' call
for more information about the sea, and called for intensive
upgrading of the U.S. fleet. "Fisheries will create jobs and alle-
viate global hunger," said the pundits of the day, as fishery after
fishery became overcapitalized.

In 1976, Congress passed the Magnuson Steven Fishery
Conservation Act, which established federal jurisdiction over
the resources of what became the Exclusive Economic Zone
(EEZ), the ocean waters from three miles off the coast out to two
hundred miles. Some foreign fishing continued in the EEZ, but
the two-hundred-mile limit, as it was known, gave U.S. fishermen
exclusive rights to the resources off the nation's shores. The opportunity for sustainable fisheries appeared briefly championed by

advocates of strict quotas. But by 1982, indirect conservation measures such as minimum mesh size and target landings, which could be exceeded without penalty, replaced strict quotas, and new boats continued to enter the fishery.

To a degree, NMFS sought to rein in the industry. But inflated estimates of the ocean's abundance, along with the agency's conflicting mission to expand the industry, undercut its efforts.

In the mid-1980s, the signs of resource depletion could no longer be ignored. The average size of fish and catch per unit of effort had declined in many important fisheries. Fishermen attributed these troubling omens to natural fluctuations, and regulators were slow to respond in the absence of conclusive scientific evidence that a problem existed.

The U.S. was not alone in failing to deal with declining fisheries. Canadian regulators also maintained unreasonable expectations. In his book *Fishing for Truth*, Christopher Finlayson cataloged the Canadian government's difficulty in managing the Newfoundland cod stocks when confronted with the economic needs of communities and the lobbying power of large fishing companies. In setting its total allowable catch in the late 1980s, the government relied on the Kirby Report, which assumed that Canada's northern cod stock was rebuilding, and predicted annual landings of 550,000 metric tons. Finlayson pointed out that the report based its assumption on modeling done in 1978, and the modelers had warned that any predictions beyond three years would be highly unreliable.

"Based upon the belief that the Kirby Report was valid and 'real,'" wrote Finlayson, "and with the active support of the provincial and federal governments through various incentives, individuals and corporations involved in the fishery made heavy capital investments to update and expand their harvesting and processing capacities."

In 1992, Canada declared a moratorium on the Newfound-land cod fishery. In spite of the Kirby Report's findings, Canada's Department of Fisheries and Oceans (DFO) realized cod had been fished at 60 to 80 percent exploitation rate rather than the intended 20 percent. Beginning in the 1990s, at painful meetings in Canada, the United States, and elsewhere in the world, regulators started admitting that they had overestimated the limits of the sea's bounty. Thirteen years after establishing the moratorium, Canada's northern cod fishery remained closed with little sign of coming back. Many feared that ecosystem shifts, primarily the influx of other less valuable species into the cod's historic range, would prevent the cod from ever reclaiming their niche.

Many species such as swordfish, groundfish, and bluefin tuna were also overfished. Habitat destruction had altered the marine landscape, often permanently, compromising its ability to produce fish. Scientists at the International Convention for the Conservation of Atlantic Tunas (ICCAT) frankly stated in 2000 that the historical levels of bluefin tuna abundance could not be reached due to habitat destruction. Off the coast of Maine, MacArthur Fellow and longtime fishermen Ted Ames documented the loss of spawning habitat for cod to nearshore pollution and trawling.

The loss of ecological function and healthy fisheries that resulted from a global race to exploit existing fish stocks led to further problems in coastal communities that historically relied on those resources. Flurries of activity brought on by technological leaps forward preceded slumps that became chronic as options diminished.

In 2000, thirty-four years after U.S. experts predicted a seafood yield of 500 million metric tons, world seafood production from fisheries peaked at 95.5 million metric tons. Global Landings leveled off at around 90 million tons, and scientists wonder whether that amount can be sustained. As engines of economic growth, most fisheries haves lowed to idle or gone into reverse.

〜

The cycle of decline had repeated itself often enough. I saw it from beginning to end in Maine's last "virgin" fishery: sea urchins. I had worked in several collapsed fisheries including New England groundfish, and had become familiar with the pattern of destruction.

After urchin landings dropped 50 percent between 1993 and 1996, I went to a regulatory meeting. "I just got back from Ireland," I told the sea urchin council. "They had an urchin fishery there. But they fished it out in twelve years, and we're on the same track."

"That's true, I was working there before I came here," said one of the Japanese urchin buyers in attendance.

"When you see a 50 percent drop in landings you're eating up your brood stock, and whittling down your resources," I said, and suggested cutting the annual harvest by at least two-thirds.

Council member Blair Pyne became slightly annoyed. "We're not in crisis management here," he told me. He considered it a maturing of the industry.

By April 2000 I had a seat on the council, and we were in crisis management.

Waiting for the monthly meeting to begin, a mixed group of fishermen, scientists, and state regulators stood outside the door of the Orland town hall, savoring the end of an early spring day. Some smoked cigarettes, others held coffee in travel mugs. Steve Cowles, one of the original council members, walked up to me. "You know," he said. "When I heard you speak at that first meeting I thought you were a crank. Now I think you were a prophet."

"Thanks, but a hell a lot of good that does us now." I shook my head. "I mean, you've been in fishing long enough to have seen how things go down. What the hell made you think urchins would be different."

At five thirty everyone filed in to the hall and took their usual seats. The council's science subcommittee had already been meeting for an hour, discussing areas of research for the future. Chairman Pyne opened the meeting; the secretary read the minutes; the council voted on issues of no great weight. But as business progressed, the chairs in the audience section began filling up. Two important votes were scheduled for that night. One would set the season, the fixed number of days that fishermen could fish, which was the primary management tool the council used to control effort. The other proposed minimum and maximum legal sizes for sea urchins.

When the first topic came up, the room had shifted from its early somnolence to buzzing. Pyne put a few different options on the table: maintain the status quo—110 days, or scale back to 80. Council members fell into three camps that largely reflected the competing worldviews of the day. Several wanted to maintain the status quo, if not increase the number of days, and let the market regulate the fishery. "As the number of urchins goes down, people will get out of the business," they suggested, although the history of fisheries argued the contrary. Others expressed willingness to scale back the number of fishing days, but skip the size limits that would decrease daily production. A very small minority wanted more severe cutbacks.

In a convoluted discussion, one council member, arguing for genuine sustainability, proposed establishing a target quota and limiting the daily catch of each fisherman so as to meet that quota. One fisherman in the audience revolted. He stood up. "I've heard about enough," he said. "Let me tell ya, I don't mind regulating the fishery, but I don't want anybody telling me how much I can catch. I want bigger boats and bigger engines, that's just the way I am and that's why I make $70,000 a year in this business. If other guys don't want to work that's their problem. They're lazy. But don't tell me I can't work."

He sat down to a general round of applause. Inspired, a fisherman from the Milbridge area stood up and argued against any new regulations at all. "Let's wait and give what regulations we got time to work," he said. "Down our way the urchins are comin' back."

One intrepid fisherman, with no high regard for the views of his fellows, accused the council of pandering to the interests of the big producers among its members and former members, and failing to protect the industry. "From what I've seen, things have gone downhill fast. By the time you people get around to doing anything effective there won't be nothing left. An eighty-day season? I think we need to cut back to a forty-day season." A bunch of divers from the Milbridge area sneered at him. "We still got plenty where we are," said the one who had argued against any new regulations.

By the end of the night the council voted to cut the season back to one hundred days and forego any changes in the size limit. While claiming the middle ground, the council actually came closer to maintaining the status quo. The members did not have the political will to control an industry that so many people relied on for their own short-term interests.

The rare fishermen who considered their long-term interests were treated like traitors to the cause.

❧

Anyone observing the meeting might see clearly that the path the industry chose took it further down the road to its own collapse. But the council, in spite of undeniable evidence, refused to acknowledge the limits of the urchin resource or take appropriate action. The worldview guiding the meeting stemmed directly from the dominant view of the economy, which sees it as functioning outside the finite limits of the environment. The majority of council members were content to continue overharvesting: they reaped the benefits in the short term, while conservation-minded fishermen and future generations paid the long-term costs. This could be called a "screw you" system. It made perfect sense if you didn't look too far ahead.

Sitting in a urchin council meeting in 2002, we looked at data that showed urchin landings continuing to slip. Faced with the imminent demise of the fishery, one group of fishermen advocated getting it over with and moving on to the next new thing. "Let's just harvest until they're gone," they said. "Then we'll find something else to do."

Instead, the council finally arrived at the eighty-day season, but coming two years late, it was not enough. The short-term interest consistently prevailed over the long-term until 2003, when George Lapointe, Maine's commissioner of marine resources, ignored all council recommendations, and cut the season in half. But for all intents and purposes, Maine's sea urchin fishery, like many others before it, had collapsed. The sea urchins that might have sustained many fishing families and communities at moderate levels had been turned over to the most efficient harvesters, and they wiped them out very efficiently.

For some reason fisheries seemed caught in a vortex; the collapse of the Newfoundland cod in 1992 mirrored the collapse of the Atlantic herring in 1972, Maine's groundfish in 1998, and Maine's sea urchins in 2003. But in spite of the similarities in each disaster, fishermen and fisheries managers appeared incapable of pulling out of the downward spiral that destroyed one resource after another. The economic models driving development demanded economic growth, and failed to register many variables that had become critical to sustainability. In addition the myth of abundance never died; preventing regulators from establishing cautious policies ahead of resource exploitation.

While fisheries struggled, the FAO, international development banks, and others, generated a new sense of urgency. They called for accelerated development of aquaculture as a matter of global food security. Resource economists advocated aquaculture development as the next new thing to maintain growth. As Danny Cohen said, "Where you going to get growth? Aquaculture." Fish farming would become the new economic engine on the high seas. The prospect that new technology and capital investment would solve the problems created by the technology and capital investment that had led to overfishing, condemned another generation to a continuation of the cycle.

Even the rhetoric sounded dubiously familiar. The 2002 report "A New Initiative for Marine Aquaculture" by NOAA and NMFS repeated most of the upbeat prediction in preceding fisheries reports. In the "New Initiative," NMFS, which succeeded the Bureau of Commercial Fisheries, expressed its readiness to become the lead government agency in marine aquaculture. "This is not the first time that NMFS has had the opportunity to step up and support a new fishing industry," the report boasts. "In 1976, the agency started cooperation with stakeholders to develop offshore fishing for underutilized species within the Exclusive Economic Zone (EEZ)." Some of those species included swordfish, monkfish, red crab, and sharks, which all ended up on strict rebuilding plans due to overfishing.

❧

The document and others like it, produced by governments of hundreds of countries, largely echoed the aquaculture development rationale of the FAO, and the fisheries rationale that preceded it: the world's expanding population needed protein, and if not protein, then export earnings to buy food.

In its "New Initiative," NMFS repeated the Bureau of Commercial Fisheries call for the United States to become an industry leader:

"The small size of the United States marine aquaculture industry is not commensurate with its potential given the country has an abundance of natural and intellectual resources ideally suited to aquaculture production."

Again, Congress supported growth in the U.S. seafood industry by passing the Aquaculture Act of 1980:

(3) Although aquaculture currently contributes approximately 13 percent of world seafood production, less than 6 percent of current United States seafood production results from aquaculture. Domestic aquaculture production, therefore, has the potential for significant growth. (2)

(b) PURPOSE—It is the purpose of the Act to promote aquaculture in the United States by—
(4) encouraging aquaculture activities and programs in both the public and private sectors of the economy; that will result in increased aquacultural (sic) production, the coordination of domestic aquaculture efforts, the conservation and enhancement of aquatic resources, the creation of new industries and job opportunities, and other national benefits.

(c) POLICY—Congress declares that aquaculture has the potential for reducing the United States trade deficit in fisheries products,

> *(5) for augmenting existing commercial and recreational fisheries and for producing other renewable resources, thereby assisting the United States in meeting its future food needs and contributing to the solution of world resource problems. It is, therefore, in the national interest, and it is the national policy, to encourage the development of aquaculture in the United States.*

Calling for a fivefold increase in the value of the U.S. aquaculture industry by 2020, NMFS's New Initiative for Marine Aquaculture pointed out that "while global production has grown at an annual rate of 10 percent, the growth of aquaculture in the United States has been only 1 percent. . . .

"Countries like Canada, China, Ecuador, New Zealand, Norway, Taiwan, Thailand, and many others like them, have developed their aquaculture sectors specifically targeting the rich markets of the United States, Japan, and the European Union. Moreover, almost everyone of these countries has achieved their success in less than two decades through focused government leadership and development policies which have attracted international investment.

"Clearly NMFS needs further Congressional support to implement this broad-based initiative for marine aquaculture and build its foundation in stone."

While the American fish farmers claimed a lack of Congressional support, the U.S government poured funds into the aquaculture industry.

The U.S Marine Shrimp Farming Program collected $65.7 million between 1985 and 2006. The Commerce Department's $1.4 billion Advanced Technology Program (ATP), a little-known office of the Department of Commerce aimed at funding high-risk research, put many millions into aquaculture research from 1990 to 2006. In 2003, a $1.7 million dollar ATP grant helped fund an Aqua Bounty research project into creating sterile versions of the company's transgenic salmon. Another eight million dollars went to a team led by the Hawaii-based Oceanic Institute to develop superintensive shrimp farming in land-based tanks.

Sea Grant put an increasing share of his budget a year into expanding the marine aquaculture industry. NMFS continued to aid research into marine aquaculture, and beginning in 1993, over a million dollars a year of Saltonstall-Kennedy Fund money, originally intended to help expand fisheries markets, went into aquaculture research and development.

⋖

While employing aquaculture policies plagiarized from decades-old policies, NMFS hoped to avoid the pitfalls fisheries had encountered. "We don't want to make the same mistakes we made with fisheries," said Edwin Rhodes, former chairman of the joint subcommittee on aquaculture (JSA), established in 1985 to oversee the emerging industry. To that end, the United States Commission on Ocean Policy Preliminary Report, released in 2004, revealed a theoretical consideration for sustainability

"Recommendation 22-2. The National Oceanic and Atmospheric Administration's new Office of Sustainable Marine Aquaculture should be responsible for developing a comprehensive, environmentally sound permitting, leasing, and regulatory program for marine aquaculture." The system would, among other things, "reflect a balance between the economic and environmental objectives consistent with national and regional goals."

But aquaculture, a generally good idea promoted by dedicated people, seemed to be caught in the same policy snafu as the fisheries before it. The scales used to balance the interests of communities, the environment, and economics were tipped in favor of economics. It is generally accepted among U.S. regulators, as several important policy documents state, that gaining "the highest net profit from fisheries, and aquaculture, is in the best interest of the Nation."

Net profit provides a concrete number, easy to grasp, whereas the values of communities and ecosystems remain difficult to measure. As they had in fisheries, the economic models used to plot the course of aquaculture heavily discounted both social and ecological function.

THE PRECAUTIONARY APPROACH

Delegates to the first Earth Summit, held in Rio de Janeiro, Brazil, in 1992, strove to bring some sense to the way humankind used the earth's resources. "Technology has outpaced man's ability to use it wisely," someone said, almost within earshot of the largest shantytown in the world, in a country where loggers and poor farmers had devastated the rainforest at an accelerating rate. But nothing in any nation's accounting tallied the long-term costs of plundering the environment.

The Rio Declaration, the final product of the summit, was signed by countries including the United States, Mexico, and the European Union; it established the "precautionary principle" and the "precautionary approach" in an attempt to rein in runaway technology and capital. The Precautionary Principle stated, "Where there are threats of serious or irreversible environmental damage, lack of full scientific certainty should not be used as a reason for postponing measures to prevent environmental degradation." Since then, countless policy documents, including the FAO's "Code of Conduct for Responsible Fishing," nominally embraced precaution.

In situations where scant scientific information existed, the experience of fisheries had demonstrated a need to err on the side of caution. The precautionary principle offered a form of risk management that put the burden of proving sustainability ahead of development, rather than waiting for things to go wrong. Throughout the 1990s, the precautionary principle became the watchword of the environmental community, which used it like a sword. But on a practical level it proved unwieldy, and was reduced to a debating point.

University of Rhode Island Resource Economist Jim Anderson called the Precautionary Principle "dysfunctional."

Anderson, a strong proponent of most forms of privatization, including aquaculture, wrote a paper entitled "Aquaculture and the Future: Why Fisheries Economists Should Care." In it, he laid out his perspectives on why aquaculture would dominate the future of seafood production. Precaution played a role, but the precautionary principle does not. "It's a meaningless concept," said Anderson. "Resulting in: if you don't know everything, you can't do anything."

According to Anderson, an enterprise first had to be economically sustainable, which in the long term included being ecologically sustainable. "The problem with fisheries," said Anderson, "is that institutionally it breeds a short-run mentality." Anderson believed property rights in fisheries and aquaculture would instill a long-term view, leading to greater investment, increased efficiency, and better stewardship.

Anderson used the Amish as an example of people who held a long-term view. "They own their property, they take care of it so they can pass it on to their children," he said.

Sebastian Belle argued that the very nature of fish farming incorporated precaution. "The feedback loop is working all the time," said Belle. "If a farmer pushes his fish too hard, then it shows in his production." Belle held that farmers have a stronger motivation to solve problems than NGOs that get their income from fighting those problems.

"I'll bet the CLF [Conservation Law Foundation] made ten or fifteen thousand in contributions from coming down to Perry to fight that lease," said Belle. Indeed, environmental organizations, in order to generate funding, often focused on fighting problems rather than developing solutions, and Belle pointed out that many of the most high-profile proponents of precaution had never worked on the water. "They really don't know anything about aquaculture," he said.

But longtime oceans activist Niaz Dorry remained wary of those who want to charge forth in developing the fish farming industry. "People ought to be worried about anybody who disregards the precautionary approach," said Dorry. "Every time the precautionary approach is disregarded, it is because somebody said I can't deal with these limitations and still make money."

Dorry argued that applying the precautionary principle to development would build on the foundation of stone the NMFS called for. "These people who want to pioneer aquaculture need to remember the Hippocratic Oath: first do no harm."

California fishermen's advocates Zeke Grader and Molly

Thomas, of the Pacific Coast Federation of Fishermen's Associations (PCFFA), expressed their views on the precautionary principle adroitly. "This is really no different than traveling through uncharted waters or jumping into murky waters not knowing where the rocks or logs may be—it pays to be cautious," wrote Grader and Thomas.

"It should be obvious that the precautionary principle calls for greater caution where less is known. This to us, again, seems straightforward and is not much different than the way navigation would be conducted." The authors noted that when steering a boat in the dark with no radar a sensible captain would slow down.

"In the case of piloting," they said, "caution is used to protect the vessel and the safety of the crew. The precautionary principle focus is on the safety of the resource fishery."

In striving to protect its social sector, the fishing cooperatives and ejidos, Mexico might be considered to have had a better record of adhering to the precautionary principle than most other signatory countries, the United States included. But once the country turned from protectionist to liberal economic policies, the environment and fishing communities, while still protected to some degree, took a back seat to shrimp farm development.

❧

Daylight comes slowly through the fog in Navopatia, a sleepy Mexican fishing village on the Bamocha Estuary, the northern arm of the Agiabampo system. The tide flows in from the Gulf of California and the fishermen's long, lean skiffs, pangas, line the shore. The wild lament of a loon, a winter visitor, echoes from beyond the gray shroud and carries on into the surrounding desert.

Although dotted with extensive mangrove islands, the two hundred-square-mile Agiabampo estuary reaches into a rare environment known as fog desert. Thick columns of organ pipe and hetcho cactus—virgin stands estimated to be almost two hundred years old—tower above thorny mesquite bushes on Sonora's coastal plain. Although the region averages less than fourteen inches of rain a year, Sonora's fog desert thrives on moisture from the sea, and has been documented as the most biologically diverse desert environment in the world.

But the bulldozers of shrimp farm developers are roaring along the coast, and like the panga fishermen who work the estuary, the fog desert is disappearing fast.

❧

At 6:30 A.M., a worn-out Nissan pickup pulls into the parking lot near the bodega, a flat-roofed, white building where the Navopatia fishermen store their nets and crab traps. A burly, mustachioed man wearing black rubber boots, white pants cut off below the knee, and a University of Arizona sweatshirt gets out of the cab. He pulls a bucket of bait and a gas can out of the back, carries them down to his panga, and sets them in the bottom of the boat.

His name is Juan, he says, as he unties the painter, and shoves off into the channel. Like many Navopatia fishermen, Juan does not live in the village, now dominated by vacation homes. Instead, he drives five miles across the rutted washboard road every morning to check his fifty crab traps.

As the incoming tide carries him north, Juan works on starting his engine, a twenty-five horse Johnson. He disappears into the fog, but his position can be marked by the sound of his pulling on the Johnson. After many tries, it starts . . . dies . . . and starts again. Juan has little to worry about as he guns he engine: the estuary has no ledges, only sand bars and mud bars.

Most of his traps lie in less than five feet of water, and the tide in the estuary rises a mere two or three feet, because the tide changes only once a day, rolling slowly in for twelve hours and out for another twelve. Juan finishes hauling at around ten in the morning and returns with a bushel of crabs—a small species; swimmers with back legs like paddles, similar to the blue claws of the Chesapeake.

By eleven the fog burns off. Juan has headed back to the arid flatlands, but more fishermen appear at the bodega. A father and his two sons arrive from one of the sparse desert towns, all marked by tall, rusting water towers, some of which have never seen a drop of rain.

The boys flake a four-hundred-meter-long gill net from a flatbed pickup into their panga and head out with their father in search of mullet. Once they spot a school of the small herring-like fish, they will use the gill net like a purse seine: circling the mullet with the net, and drawing it in like a lasso.

Before they are out of sight, another mullet boat comes in with its catch. The two fishermen aboard pull their panga broadside to the shore and start to flake their net onto the beach, untangling the mullet as they go and tossing the fish into a plastic crate that holds about forty pounds. The captain, a small, stocky man of about forty, says his name is Armando. His crewman introduces himself as Juan. They have about eighty-eight pounds, says Jorge; and they will get twenty cents per pound. After deducting for two gallons of gas, that leaves a grand total of thirteen dollars for two men for a morning's work.

"The fishing has been getting bad for the last fifteen years," Armando says. "Too many pangas, and the big boats offshore taking all the fish." These two continue to eke out a living in a variety of fisheries. In May and June manta rays move into the estuary and the fishermen harpoon them in the shallows.

"Juan is one of the best harpooners in the bay," says Armando. Juan shakes his head humbly.

Nonetheless, Kenny Dessain, a former Texan, now living year round in Navopatia, says he sees fewer and fewer fishermen coming to the shore. "They used to get all excited about shrimp season, now nobody even goes," says Dessain. "Our friend Joaquin made a shrimp net this year and I asked him how he did. He said, 'Great! I sold the net.'"

🐟

Just north of Navopatia, thousands of acres of desert have been bulldozed to create shrimp farms. Sonora has the highest rate of shrimp production per acre of any region in Mexico, and the dikes of raw, red earth pushed into the estuary hold a promise of wealth. But few of the local fishermen will see it.

Dessain and many others believe that the rampant shrimp farm development in the estuary has ruined the fishing, but there is no way to prove it. "We managed to stop them building a farm just north of here," he says of Carlos Parada's farm. "They didn't have the equivalent of an environmental impact statement. Two days later they had it, and the bulldozers started up again.

"I ask the fishermen if they still go oystering up near the shrimp farms, and they say, 'No, it's all muck up there now,'" says Dessain. "Then I ask if they think the farms are having a negative impact on the estuary and they say no."

⋑⋐

In spite of experiences in natural resources industries, shrimp and salmon farming surged ahead with double-digit growth, driven either by "pathological optimism," in the case of business and governments, or panic, with the FAO and development banks reacting to perceived food/economic growth crisis without considering long-term consequences.

The precautionary principle was meant to give the pessimists the upper hand in debates on development, caution being the operative word. But when faced with the gamble of shrimp and salmon farming and the prospect of mass starvation, or migration, desperate people took the gamble. China, having experienced the largest famine in the world in the last half of the twentieth century, became the world leader in aquaculture. After expanding its freshwater fish farms, Chinese shrimp farms may soon eclipse Thailand, the industry leader. Countries one step ahead of famine or economic meltdown embraced any technological advance in the race for survival. They could not afford the luxury of contemplating the future when they had to survive the present.

⋑⋐

The Amish culture that Jim Anderson cited to illustrate how private property could instill a long-term view might just as easily have been cited by aquaculture opponents. The nineteenth century lifestyle of the plain folk is an example of a very cautious approach to technology.

Nonetheless, after years of making bad decisions in the fisheries, the precautionary principle became an indelible feature in regulatory language. But with so much disagreement about what, if anything, precaution meant, implementation became difficult.

The problem arose when scientists tried to model the effects of aquaculture on the environment. The industry had no database, nowhere to measure from. Shrimp and salmon farming moved from a standstill to high gear without ever establishing a baseline—a clear understanding of the ecosystem, with consideration of important issues such as diseases and the dynamics of plankton communities that served as the foundation of ocean life. Indeed, the prospect of predicting and measuring the important variables seems to have appeared so costly and daunting that it was simply ignored.

The state of Maine attempted to establish a limited baseline, requiring photos of the bottom of a lease site prior to operation, and sampling of the bottom and water column beneath the pen. While Maine managed to set a benchmark from which future changes could be measured, the state's effort missed a great deal. The studies ignored the fact that water columns beneath pens often changed in a matter of minutes. The DMR did not document the status of the pelagic herring and mackerel, the anadromous salmon and alewives, the catadromous American eels, or any of the many other noncommercial species inhabiting the bay.

David Bengston, an aquatic veterinarian and professor emeritus at the University of Rhode Island, advocated risk assessments before aquaculture projects began, but pointed out the difficulty in forecasting so many unknowns. "You use common sense," he said. "As we collect data we learn more and we can adjust to what we learn, but for now every new aquaculture project is an experiment."

Those businesses and governments driving the new ocean economic growth vehicle—aquaculture—and their science community seem to believe they have it under control. They may have failed with fisheries, but they believe they can keep aquaculture on the road. Others who have watched the rise and fall of fisheries saw disturbing similarities in the trajectories of both. Considering the rapid growth of shrimp and salmon farming, coupled with the poor understanding of the ecological parameters, and the fact that the engineers of the world's collapsing fisheries are in charge, it came as little surprise when these two industries started to hit their limits.

7

THE PLAGUES

Show me a drop on the graph of shrimp [or salmon] production, and I'll show you a disease event.
—Rohana Subasinghe, senior fisheries officer
of the United Nations Food and Agriculture Organization

There will always be plagues, we'll get over them with shrimp the same as we did with pigs and chickens.
—Cristina Chavez, scientist at CIAD,
(Center for Sustainable Development) Mazatlán, Sinaloa, Mexico

In late October 2001, a barge loaded with containers of dead salmon plowed across the choppy waters of Cobscook Bay. As the cumbersome craft slowed and pulled in alongside the public wharf in Lubec, Maine, a crewman clad in an orange survival suit against the chill wind glanced up and found himself looking into the lens of a photographer leaning over the wharf. "Hey, who said you could take pictures?" the crewman shouted.

I was the photographer and I snapped the shutter. I had every right, and if the crewman was ashamed on behalf of his employers, the Norwegian-owned company Atlantic Salmon of Maine (ASM), he had every right to be. The infectious salmon anemia (ISA) outbreak that began in ASM's pens had spread throughout Cobscook Bay, leading to the destruction or early harvest of 2.6 million farmed salmon. The dip in Maine's production graph was steep: from thirty-six million pounds in 2000 to fifteen million pounds in 2002. By 2005, a new management regime cut harvests to a little over eleven million pounds.

≈

The viral epizootic—an epidemic in an animal population—cost an estimated twenty-five million dollars in lost fish alone, and brought the sixty-million-dollar-a-year industry to its knees. According to the Maine Aquaculture Association, the three salmon farming corporations operating in Cobscook Bay—Atlantic Salmon, the Luxembourg-owned Stolt Sea Farms, and Canadian-based Heritage Salmon—laid off roughly 400 of the state's estimated 1,200 salmon farm workers that year. Maine's labor department put the number of aquaculture workers at a meager 214 for the year 2002. Only a sixteen-million-dollar bailout package kept the big producers from abandoning Maine.

Temporary workers unloading dead salmon from a hired barge at the same wharf showed no misgivings about being photographed. Like many aquaculture workers, they blamed the disease problem on poor management practices, mainly what they considered overstocking the cages. "Take all the pictures you want," said their foreman, Gene Greenlaw. "Just don't mention my name."

"It's their own damn fault," said Gene Blake, one of the hired barge crew in Lubec. He lifted the lid of a tote filled to the top with the limp forms of decomposing salmon. "Look at that," he said. I could see patches of dull red meat where the skins had torn off the once beautiful fish. "They knew this was coming but they still overstocked their pens."

No one could say the ISA took the fish farming industry by surprise, and it would be unfair to lay blame solely at the feet of ASM. The virus first appeared in Norway in 1984 and had been present in nearby Canadian pens since 1996; it seemed to crop up all around the north Atlantic, by turns devastating the industries of Scotland, the Faeroe Islands, and Canada, where four million fish were killed between 1996 and 2001 in efforts to control the spread of the virus. Animal husbandry has seen many such battles in its long war with disease. From hoof-and-mouth and bovine spongiform encephalitis (BSE) to avian bird flu, producers have fought pathogens that run rampant among animals held in crowded conditions.

Disease is a fact of life for farmers. Like many factors of production, its a numbers game: a question of when the costs of disease exceed the profits generated by intensive production.

Early in its history, salmon farming contended with a host of bacterial diseases, and the farms had plenty of mortality prior to ISA. In the late 1980s, Lubec salmon farmers commonly disposed of morts, as the dead salmon were called, at the local dump, which drained into the sea. On Saturday mornings salmon farm workers backed their trucks up to an embankment and tossed down plastic boxes overflowing with rotting salmon and marked with the names of the companies: Lubec Sea Farm (Stolt), Connors Brothers (Heritage). At the time, I joined other fishermen in picking the boxes from the dump. We found the small boxes very useful; each held about fifty pounds of fish, or sea urchins, or salmon cuttings used for bait, and were easily handled by one man. We emptied and cleaned the gray and blue boxes by the hundreds until they became a common sight aboard boats around Cobscook Bay. Based on their value, the free boxes amounted to handing each of us a hundred-dollar bill, and they represented the nicest thing the salmon farmers ever did for Maine's fishermen.

Ten years later, vaccinations brought many bacterial diseases under control, but ISA spread through a wide range of environmental vectors, such as sea lice that can carry and transmit the virus, gulls that have eaten infected fish, and numerous other pathways. The sloppy disposal practices of dead fish and boxes added to the risk.

I asked Sebastian Belle, executive director of the Maine Aquaculture Association, if he thought ISA might be the biofeedback he had mentioned before. "No. This was a natural disaster," he said. But most of the locals who worked in the industry blamed the ISA outbreak on the hypercompetitive practices of the big companies operating in the bay.

I had not seen Cecil Cates since he came to the urchin council to argue in favor of aquaculture. I ran into him again after he had lost his job and his 401K plan due to the 2001 melt-down. "Goddamn pencil pushers figure if they can crowd twenty thousand fish in a pen and get 50 percent mortality they still do better than if they put in five thousand and get 50 percent. Then they're surprised when they all get sick." he said.

FISH HEALTH

"Stocking density had nothing to do with it," said Belle, who believed that ISA actually broke out in New Brunswick as early as 1992 and was misdiagnosed, or unreported, until 1996. "What amazes me," he said, "is that we had this disease raging clinically in Canada for eight years before it reached us."

Belle pointed out that the industry put its own biosecurity measures into place, which included cleaning boats and equipment with iodine, and having all sites monitored through semi-annual audits by the state. "I think if you look at this epidemically, it's a strong testimony that we were able to stave it off as long as we did," said Belle.

~

The biosecurity audits Belle referred to began in the winter of 1997–98. In 1999, Dr. Peter Merrill of Micro Technologies, based in Richmond, Maine, took over the state-funded program. Merrill notified companies prior to his visits, and kept their identities confidential in his reports to the state. In 2000 he conducted only one audit of ASM, and in 2001 the state discontinued the program, leaving the companies to monitor themselves.

In 2002 the U.S. Department of Agriculture took over and established an ISA Indemnity and Control Program in Eastport, Maine. The USDA promised to reimburse farmers for up to 60 percent of the cost of fish lost to ISA, claiming the indemnity program would encourage faster reporting of disease outbreaks.

Program director Dr. Stephen Ellis had been working on an ISA response building on experiences in Norway and Canada, where salmon farming continued to grow in spite of continuous ISA outbreaks. "Julia Mullens in Canada brought the Norwegian ISA experts over and ran seminars for ISA control," said Ellis. "We got the basic virology from them and a whole list of risk factors, including vessel traffic and disposal of blood water from processing."

ISA is a flulike virus, and as anyone who has ever had the flu knows, it can be treated, survived, but not cured. Viruses display a number of traits that make them the biggest threat to life on earth. Neither alive nor dead, viruses travel light in the world without the baggage of complex cell structure and reproductive systems, instead they commandeer them from host cells. A master of efficiency, a virus enters a cell by copying the chemical signals of molecules the cell's receptors recognize. Once inside the cell's cytoplasm the virus "uncoats" and releases viral nucleic acid, which essentially takes over the cell's generative processes and material, in order to replicate more viruses: as many as fifty thousand from a single host cell. While in the uncoating and replicating stages, the virus is undetectable, making it impossible for the immune system to combat it until target cells learn to recognize the virus and change the password for entry. The virus in turn has the ability to mutate rapidly, and learn the new password. It is a deadly game.

"We don't know what's out there," Ellis said, as the program got under way. "We've identified over seventy viruses so far, but we still don't have a clue about the parasite and pathogen relationships with fish. After seven years' work we're still in the dark."

According to Ellis, ISA behaved like a typical flu virus and would prove as impossible to eradicate. "It changes identity, it quiets down for periods of time, then comes back," he said.

In July 2003, in a small lab built at Eastport's Marine Trades center, Theresa Robinson, daughter-in-law of salmon guide Jimmy Robinson, prepared to examine a dead fish taken from one of the pen sites in Cobscook Bay. The fish, lying on a stainless-steel table under fluorescent lights, had a white swollen area behind the head, a winter sore as the farmers called it, the external sign of a common bacterial infection. Robinson donned the rubber gloves of a surgeon. Taking a scalpel, she made an arching incision around the fish's belly, peeling back a flap of skin to expose the internal organs. "I'm looking for any abnormalities," she said, "discoloration or lesions on the organs." Robinson proceeded to cut various organs out of the fish and place them into test tubes, labeling them for further testing at the Micro Technologies lab.

Program director Ellis put his faith in new technology. "We're looking at improving the immune systems of the fish," he said, referring to the increasing interest in what essentially amounts to health foods for fish. "And labs are working on vaccines," he added.

In June 2003, Micro Technologies and another company, Maine BioTek, received a $218,000 Saltonstall Kennedy grant to conduct tests of a live ISA vaccine. Because of the mutable nature of ISA, however, developing an effective vaccine would be difficult, and held the potential of creating additional problems.

"One thing people don't talk about is how much protection the vaccine gives the transfer of disease," said Dr. David Scarfe, assistant director of scientific activities for the American Veterinary Medicine Association (AVMA). "A vaccine prevents any animal from developing clinical signs and symptoms of diseases, versus preventing them being infected by the virus," he said. "It's a common misperception that all vaccines will both protect an individual from showing diseases, and from being infected with pathogens like viruses." Consequently, Scarfe warned, vaccinated fish could become carriers. "You could have salmon swimming around shedding the virus."

In June 2003, Heritage Salmon alerted Ellis that they had increasing mortality in one of their pens. Micro Technologies identified ISA by cell culture in six fish from the site. In accordance with a state order, Heritage Salmon "destroyed the fish," as the local paper said. Actually, the company harvested twenty-eight thousand small salmon from the infected pen and sent them to market at a loss. Clearing infected pens became a regular part of growing salmon, as it had in Norway and every other affected country. If the fish showed no gross symptoms, they went to market.

By 2005, Ellis reported that most companies harvested around 10 percent of their fish early, due to ISA infections. "But they've established markets for the small fish, so it is not the economic disaster it used to be."

LOCAL STRUGGLE IN A GLOBAL ECONOMY

Bobby Peacock's office at Peacock Canning Company in Lubec overlooks the Lubec narrows, where the cold waters of the Bay of Fundy surged in and out of Cobscook Bay, essentially flushing the toilet for the salmon. But this massive movement of water, which made the bay so attractive to salmon farmers, also spread pathogens.

Peacock, who laid off seventy-eight workers in the wake of ISA, made a simple assessment of aquaculture's future in Maine. "Getting a handle on disease is going to be the defining issue for the industry here," he said.

In fighting ISA, Peacock looked across the border. "What we have is essentially a Canadian problem spreading into Maine," he said. "I started bitching about the boats coming across five or six years ago," he added, citing a Center for Disease Control (CDC) report that identified vessel traffic as the primary mode of disease transfer. "But I was told by the state that the CDC report was bad science." (In its report on Scottish ISA, the CDC had identified shipping as a significant pathway for spreading ISA. Nonetheless, Stolt Sea Farms and Heritage Salmon regularly transported fish and feed by boat between their Maine and New Brunswick sites, some of which operated within half a mile of each other in the transboundary waters of Cobscook Bay and the St. Croix River.)

❧

In June of 2003, Cooke Aquaculture, which did not expect to receive indemnity for salmon it destroyed, reportedly ignored a provincial fish kill order after ISA was found in its pens. "You wouldn't kill your fish, either if you weren't going to get paid for them," said industry spokeswoman Nel Halse. At the same time, vessels continued to move from New Brunswick to Maine; Heritage Salmon ran feed from Blacks Harbor, New Brunswick, over a hundred miles down the Maine coast to a salmon farm in Blue Hill Bay.

"What do you think I think about that!" said Peacock, alluding to the continued risk. "It all depends on how well the guys are taking care of biosecurity," he said. "Hopefully they're doing a good job."

While aquaculture vessel traffic came under control of the industry's Bay Management Plan and state regulations, fishing boats moved freely through the area, and Eastport had a deepwater port visited by ships from around the world.

According to a 1994 report from the Harvard Working Group for New and Resurgent Diseases, the multinational economies of scale, and their transportation needs, as exemplified in salmon aquaculture, created new pathways for emerging diseases such as ISA. For several years salmon farm apologists claimed that the local strain of ISA had existed in Canada for at least a century. But new studies revealed that the European strain also occurred on the Canadian side of Cobscook Bay.

"In my opinion, the European strain came from herring," said Mike Beattie at the Huntsman Marine Lab in St. Andrews New Brunswick. "The salmon feed manufacturers imported herring from Norway and if you look at where the European strain popped up it's in the areas where those fish were first processed."

The World Trade Organization (WTO) and the Office International des Epizooties (OIE)—also known as the World Organization for Animal Health—both established guidelines aimed at limiting the spread of pathogens while encouraging international trade. "Countries experiencing a disease like ISA very quickly implement a control and eradication program," said Scarfe. "Under WTO rules, other trading countries that believe they are at risk of importing a disease have discretion on banning importation of salmon products, as long as they can justify it with sound science." In situations such as the outbreak of mad cow disease, biosecurity systems that include depopulation, quarantines, rapid diagnostics and continued surveillance have apparently proven effective.

Unlike their U.S. counterparts, however, Canadian growers had no obligation to report disease outbreaks. While laws required mad cow disease and other animal infirmities to be reported to the Canadian Food Inspection Agency (CFIA), as of 2006, the country had no list of reportable fish diseases. Although Canada's membership in the OEI obliged it to report outbreaks of ISA, it did so through something of an "in-house" process, whereby growers notified fish health specialists at the Huntsman Marine Lab, which in turn notified the CFIA, which then passed the information on to OIE.

"That's all going to change soon," said Beattie. "The CFIA just received fifty-nine million dollars [over a five-year period] to develop a monitoring and control program. Listing some of these diseases will undoubtedly be a part of that."

≈

Veterinarians like Ellis, Beattie, and Scarfe live comfortably with the realities of disease on earth, and express no alarm. "The veterinary profession deals with disease outbreaks all the time," said Scarfe. "With an emerging industry like aquaculture comes recognition of new disease problems; it's inevitable. As with all disease, the target is always prevention and, when necessary, control and eradication; we do this daily with all animal diseases. When situations arise, you put the appropriate systems in place and carry on."

But working around disease has a price. According to Mike Beattie, health monitoring and biosecurity measures such as washing of feed barges and other equipment cost New Brunswick salmon growers around forty thousand U.S. dollars per site, per year, in addition to losses from ongoing disease outbreaks.

Farmed fish are unique among livestock in that they share the ocean with wild resources that still provide most of the world's seafood. The fates of the salmon farms, coastal communities, wild fish, and ultimately, world food security depend to a large extent on whether or not open water fish farmers can control disease, protect wild stocks, and still make a profit.

THE MICROSCOPIC WORLD OF SHRIMP DISEASE

Baceran Shrimp Farm, Estero Bamocha, Sonora, September 2004
As Mexican shrimp production surged in the 1990s, the only thing that slowed development was disease. At a typical small scale shrimp farm in southern Sonora, a veteran of the industry watched the muddy ponds, unable to determine the condition of his growing crop. Dressed in jeans and a Western shirt, he sported a pair of designer sunglasses and a baseball cap with the logo NASA—a local feed manufacturer —emblazoned on the

front. He scuffed the dirt under his leather boots and looked back at the ponds.

As he had since 1994, the farmer had purchased disease-free, post-larval white shrimp, *Panaeus vannamei,* and stocked his ponds in April. For eight years he had made money on his shrimp.

WSSV was first found in Asia in 1992. In spite of Mexican efforts to control the international movement of shrimp, the virus struck there in 1999. In Ecuador, the virus cut production by 70 percent. Through international trade, it spread to farms and wild stocks around the world.

In 2004, a cool spring led to an outbreak of white spot disease in the neighboring state of Sinaloa, and the epizootic spread north, wiping out hundreds of shrimp farms along the way. The shrimp farmer watching his ponds had managed to escape the 2004 first bout, but his worries returned as the waters began to cool in the fall of 2005, and the virus again spread north from Sinaloa.

Other farms in the bay system suffered new outbreaks, and, much as he hated to, the shrimp farmer had drawn water from the bay and circulated it through his ponds. He hoped to keep his shrimp disease-free for one more month, harvest a decent crop, and sell it to Ocean Garden Products for a profit. If white spot struck, he would have to harvest early and at best break even, more likely, lose money.

If he could have seen beneath the waters the farmer would have witnessed the first signs of trouble: in a scene reminiscent of a science fiction movie, long slender shrimp paddled their translucent bodies through the murk with ten pairs of legs. Some had become lethargic, they had already ingested the virus, perhaps after cannibalizing the earliest victims, or from eating infected bacteria on contaminated bird droppings, or from the processed feed Larraguibel bought by the ton from NASA.

Panaeus vannamei, the most commonly grown shrimp species in the world, have a high-speed digestive system: food passes through an adult shrimp in eight minutes. Once disease takes hold, it spreads rapidly. The white spot virus targets many of a shrimp's cells, everything from connective to nervous tissue, muscles, and the shell, leaving characteristic white spots on the inside of the shrimp's carapace. As it progresses, the virus severely damages internal organs as well as the antennae and eyes of the shrimp. None survive once the infection takes hold.

The farmer's ailing shrimp began to approach the surface of the pond in growing numbers, and masses of gulls appeared overhead. When the birds show up, shrimp farmers say, you know you have a problem.

A day after visiting his ponds, the shrimp farmer received an urgent call from his workers, and immediately ordered an emergency harvest in an effort to cut his losses. Trucks arrived loaded with tanks and a conveyor system. Some workers set up the conveyor while others began draining the ponds and herding the shrimp into a densely packed holding area near each drain. There the conveyor lifted the dying shrimp into a hopper and sorting machine. Workers picked out individuals that showed gross symptoms, and, if they were not too bad, took the rejected shrimp home to eat. The rest of the product went to market.

"I need to harvest close to three thousand kilos per hectare of twenty-eight gram shrimp in order to make money," said the farmer. "I got about two thousand kilos per hectare of twenty-gram shrimp." Like many others, the shrimp farmer sold his shrimp domestically through Guadalupe Buen Rostro, a man in Guadalajara who controls 80 percent of the domestic shrimp market in Mexico. "If you have export quality, you sell to Ocean Garden," said the farmer. "If not you sell to Guadalupe."

Because of their northern location, Sonoran shrimp farmers had a shorter growing season than their counterparts in Sinaloa. While the Sinaloans usually get two crops of small product, the Sonorans usually tried for one crop of large shrimp. They faced higher risks, but have the highest monetary return per hectare of any state in Mexico, and closer proximity to their main market, the United States.

In 2005, however, the shrimp farmers of southern Sonora lost the gamble, and lacking a technological breakthrough stood little chance of defeating white spot. In addition, a host of other major shrimp viruses stood in the shrimp farmers' way: the highly mutable Taura virus appeared in Ecuador in 1992 and spread to shrimp farms around the world, as well as IHHNV, which arrived in Sonora from Asian shrimp farms in 1990 and then passed to wild shrimp in the Gulf of California.

According to Dr. Donald Lightner, a world renowned shrimp disease expert based at the University of Arizona in Tucson, the IHHNP virus arrived with some shrimp feed imported from Asia. "It never existed here before the shrimp farms arrived," said Lightner. "It spread to the wild blue shrimp and they virtually disappeared from the upper Gulf of California for the next eight years." Not counting the socioeconomic impact on small, non-mobile fishermen, Lightner commented that the event was not a major disaster because the shrimp have since bounced back, but not to predisease levels.

✎

White spot has proven too complex, Taura too mutable, and IHHNV too ubiquitous to eradicate. As with salmon, the best scientists in the shrimp world sought ways to enable their industry to live with disease rather than eliminate it.

Aqua Bounty, for instance, continued field testing its antiviral drug on shrimp in Ecuador and elsewhere. Early results looked promising, according to Clifford, who had toured shrimp farms all over Latin America in the summer of 2005. But, he pointed out, white spot and a new mutation of Taura virus continued to inflict losses throughout Latin America. "I think you'll see production for Mexico drop by about 20 percent this year," said Clifford.

Mexico represents the rule rather than exception in twenty-first century shrimp farming. By 2001, the major shrimp viruses had caused at least ten billion dollars in losses, not counting the destruction of wild stocks in the Gulf of California, and possibly China.

In 1976, the FAO called for international safeguards to keep emerging diseases in check. But the diseases spread globally through international shipment of shrimp broodstock and post-larvae, as well as uncooked frozen product from infected farms and infected feed such as Artemia; and locally through a variety of vectors such as escaped shrimp, bird guano, and a long list of wild carriers.

In 2003, twenty-seven years after the warnings at Kyoto, Subasinghe expressed hope that the worldwide monitoring system the FAO was working on would prevent the further spread of existing and emerging aquatic pathogens. Among other strategies the FAO established protocols for testing shrimp at various exit and entry points of trading countries. Though Subasinghe noted that developing countries lacked the technical and financial capacity to implement such a system, saying it might take as long as ten years.

To its credit, if not its benefit, Mexico has consistently acted ahead of the curve. In March 1999, Mexico enacted emergency laws governing the movement of shrimp, and three months later experienced its first outbreak of white spot. In 2000 growers established networks to promote best management practices up and down the coast, increasing each other's awareness about white spot and how to it might be controlled. But with the number of known and unknown vectors for disease transmission however, the job proved impossible.

White spot was so well established in wild and farmed populations that in 2001 Donald Lightner found white spot virus in 70 percent of the shrimp he pulled off supermarket shelves in Hawaii. "That was higher than previous studies that we ran in Tucson [Arizona], where prevalences were around 40 to 50 percent," said Lightner. "Then there was another study done in Massachusetts where the prevalence was lower, around 30 percent." Under the circumstances, any consumer disposing of uncooked shrimp peels became a vector for spreading a pathogen that Lightner believes originated in one location. "Regardless of where they were obtained, isolates of WSSV have shown little genetic or biological variation," Lightner wrote in 2005, "suggesting that the virus emerged and was spread from a single source."

In 2004, Lightner identified another emerging virus, infectious myonecrosis (IMN) in Brazil. "I expect it will be everywhere in a few more years," he said. After two years, IMN had caused several million dollars in losses. In spite of the damage, Lightner believed that the diseases had forced shrimp aquaculture to become "far more sustainable than it was before the emergence of the virus-caused diseases."

Early harvest of diseased salmon and shrimp kept healthy animals alive long enough for growers to capitalize on their investments. But aquaculture's troubles did not stop with viral disease.

A Drug Problem

In the late 1980s, I went out to the pens with a friend who had a job feeding fish. I helped him open up plastic sacks of feed, and joined him in tossing great scoopfuls of the pellets as far out into the pens as we could. We knew the pellets were made from herring, and held synthetic coloring to make the salmon's flesh an alluring red. Another friend had once showed me a color chart he used to pick the color of the fish he wanted. But it never occurred to us to wonder what else the pellets contained. Years later, I learned that the feed contained antibiotics that worked against the numerous bacterial diseases that the fish came down with: salmonicida, furunculosis, various vibrios. It also had pesticides to protect the fish from sea lice.

I watched as the fish boiled the surface eager to gobble it up. When the feeding slowed and pellets drifted down out of the pens uneaten, we quit tossing. "Show's over," said my friend.

As we picked up the empty bags, the uneaten feed sank to the bottom and began to break down. Almost ten years later, I had a chance to see what it looked like under there.

In November 1995 Peter Hilyard, a part-time longshoreman in Eastport, anchored his small motorboat near an Atlantic salmon farm in Cobscook Bay, Maine. He cut the engine and invited me to go find some sea urchins; maybe they'd be think under the salmon pens. Wearing a dry suit and scuba gear, I rolled over the side and splashed into the cold water. I sank below the surface, drifting down through the jade green into the murk. I sank past the mooring lines that held the vast net-pen system to granite blocks set in the mud. Underwater, the heavy wires streamed long ribbons of black kelp that wrapped fleetingly around my legs and then slipped off as I descended.

As I sank into the gloom, the pressure increased and I lost touch with any spatial reference points beyond the light above and the darkness below. I became aware of a terrible noise, an intermittent electronic ratcheting like the amplified scraping of fingernails on a blackboard: a sonic seal deterrent, meant to keep seals away from the fish. Unexpectedly, I hit bottom. The visibility had been less than six feet, but when my flippers touched the sediment it exploded into a cloud that blinded me.

Keeping off the bottom, I swam out of the cloud into a desert smothered under fine silt. A scattering of sea urchins and polycheate worms, the last holdouts in a stressed environment, dotted the sparse landscape. If I had spent any time reading

Centers for Disease Control reports on what they were finding under salmon farms I might have gotten out of there sooner, but as it was I spent a half an hour under the two-acre cage system.

＆

According to the CDC, antibiotics used on the farms to treat various bacterial diseases accumulated in the sediment. Oxytetracycline, one of the most commonly used drugs, did not break down. It entered the food chain where, according to the CDC, it increased the prevalence of disease-resistant bacteria.

"Use of antimicrobial agents in aquaculture also selects for antimicrobial resistance among bacteria that are not fish pathogens," wrote veterinarian Frederick Angulo, DVM, PhD. "Several studies have assessed the impact of use of antimicrobial agents in aquaculture on the bacteria in the sediment and within fish in the local environment. For example, bacteria resistant to antimicrobial agents used on specific fish farms have been isolated from sediment beneath the fish 'netpens' on those fish farms. In another study, bacteria resistant to antimicrobial agents used on specific fish farms were isolated from the intestinal contents of natural and commercial fish species captured on those fish farms; in contrast, no resistance was present among bacteria from the intestinal contents of fish from untreated areas."

＆

I didn't see any fish in the barrens beneath the pens, but some folks I knew said they caught lots of flounder near the salmon pens every summer. I refused those flounder even before I read the CDC paper. Angulo warned that the bacteria could pass antibiotic on to diseases that effect humans and pointed out that the 1991 cholera epidemic in Ecuador began among shrimp farm workers.

☙

I had gone below looking to make a day's pay, not to become part of an unofficial science experiment. Above me hung the net pen, densely packed with farmed fish swimming in circles. The roughly seventy-foot-wide, fifty-foot-deep net moved in the current, a vast black mess ready to tangle in my tank and regulator, possibly drown me. I made my way carefully out from under its shadow and slowly ascended toward the light, the seal deterrent ratcheting incessantly. I broke the surface near the boat and I spit out my regulator. "Let's get out of here," I said to the skipper.

Salmon farmers initially used a host of antibiotics against vibrio, furunculosis, salmoncida septicima and several other nasties, but switched to vaccines as red flags went up from the CDC. Shrimp, with their rudimentary immune systems incapable of creating immunity, lacked the vaccine option. Growers took two strategies to deal with bacterial disease: they tried low stocking densities and the use of probiotics (health food) to raise healthy shrimp, or they treated their animals with common antibiotics such as chloramphenicol and Oxytetracycline.

"We don't use antibiotics in Mexico anymore," Ocean Garden's John Filose told me when I visited him. "Our farms don't use them." While Mexican farmers appeared to be moving

away from antibiotics and moving toward better health management as a way to cope with disease, according to Bob Rosenberry, farmers in other parts of the world, particularly Asia, have
a deep-rooted antibiotics problem. "They're addicted to the
stuff," said Rosenberry.

Much of the shrimp coming out of Asia would not pass the
equivalent of a urine analysis, and Europe, Japan and the United
States have all condemned container loads. Chinese growers,
who have the worst reputation for antibiotic overuse, have tried
shipping through other countries to avoid scrutiny. Others have
sought to mask the traceability of chemicals.

NGOs dogging the industry have had a field day with the
antibiotics issue. Adding to the contamination issue, the report,
produced by Norway's Institute of Nutrition in 1999, advised
people, particularly pregnant women, not to eat farmed salmon
due to high levels of organic pollutants found in the fish. The
report blamed the high levels of organic pollutants on contaminated feed. Knowledgeable sources within the salmon industry
reported that Chilean salmon growers use antibiotics that cannot
be detected.

Disease was the first of many bottlenecks the growing
shrimp and salmon industries have encountered on their paths
toward dominating the seafood markets of wealthy nations.
Antibiotics create risks for the environment and consumers, and
as the industries grow, so have problems outside the farms.
Escapees interact with wild fish, the feed supply has tightened,
and a host of other issues have imposed limits on the growth of
aquaculture.

Regulators, environmental organizations, courts, and regular citizens increasingly call on salmon and shrimp farmers—the moneymakers who account for 5 percent of aquaculture volume and 20 percent of the profits—to account for problems outside the pens and ponds.

PART III

THE COLLAPSING UNIVERSE

8

THE GREAT ESCAPE

I needed to go to Mount Desert Island for a job interview in August 2002, and I hitched a ride with my neighbor Jean-Noel Ragot. We left before dawn on the eighty-mile commute he made every day to his job on a salmon farm near the island. "I can get there in an hour and a half," he said as we raced along the dark empty road: U.S. Route 1—a two-lane highway that hugged the coast. The gray light of the emerging dawn revealed fir and spruce trees interspersed with gaps where bays and estuaries reached inland from the sea.

On our journey we crossed the Machias River, the Narraguagus, and the Pleasant, three of the eight rivers in Maine with salmon runs listed under the Endangered Species Act. The biggest single threat to their survival, according to the U.S. Fish and Wildlife Service, came from salmon-farm escapees, but I did not raise the subject on that ride.

Ragot and I lived a half a mile apart on the same road, our children played together, and our wives were good friends. We had once worked on the same fishing boat, shucking scallops for Benny Crocker of Bucks Harbor. Twelve years later, after Ragot found a job with Atlantic Salmon of Maine, and I became a journalist, we knew where the other stood on the salmon aquaculture issue. He was a company man very sensitive to criticism, and I wrote articles sometimes critical of the industry. In a story for the *Fishermen's Voice*, I had quoted our former captain, Crocker, saying, "I wouldn't exactly call 'em [salmon farmers] liars, but they play pretty loose with the truth."

I knew, though, that Ragot had risked his life during the largest single escape event in the history of Maine salmon farming, and I asked him about it one evening at a party. Ragot refused to talk. "There were so many incidents like that I can't even remember," he said. ASM laid him off in 2005, before selling out to Cooke Aquaculture of Canada. But he remained loyal. "I still have a lot of friends in the business," he said. "I don't want to say anything that might hurt them."

I called Ragot's former boss, Bob Hukki, of Machiasport. "I'm not saying nothing," he said. But reluctantly he recalled the events of Christmas 2000, when a fierce storm destroyed a set of pens in an exposed location, releasing thousands of salmon.

"It was the site out near Stone Island," said Hukki. "The wind was out of the west. They clocked it at a hundred miles an hour over in Cutler [a sheltered harbor five miles from Stone Island]. The tide was running out against the wind making some awful steep seas."

Hukki and his crew remained trapped onshore, watching helplessly as the storm tore apart the cages full of fish. "We could see 'em from shore," he said, "eighty-foot-wide cages disappearing under the waves. I guess the worst came in the night."

The winds diminished to gale force the next day, Christmas. Hukki and his crew, Ragot among them, made it out to the cages and started to recover what they could. They approached the tossing wreckage with no set plan. "It was just a mass of twisted steel and tangled nets," said Hukki. "We got on there any way we could and started chaining things together." Hukki noted that half the men struggling with the cages that day had been fishermen at one time. "They knew how to work on the water," he said.

For forty-eight hours straight, Hukki's crew risked all on the tossing wreckage, pumping what fish remained in the torn nets into the company's well boat the *New Ferry*. "Butch Harris brought his boat, the *Christina M.*, around and helped us take out what was left," said Hukki. They managed to get half the fish out of the pens. "They say that a hundred thousand fish escaped," said Hukki. "But that's how many we lost, a lot of them died from the stress and were still in the nets. I was so busy with the live ones I can't remember how many dead fish we took out."

George Lapointe, Maine's commissioner of marine resources, did not report the Atlantic Salmon of Maine escape incident to the National Marine Fisheries Service (NMFS) until February 2001. It slipped his mind, he said. NMFS and other federal agencies had been in ongoing negotiations with the state to protect wild salmon, and would soon put them on the endangered species list.

In 2000, federal agencies broke off negotiations with the then–Maine governor, Angus King, a major supporter of salmon farms, and placed Atlantic salmon runs in eight Maine Rivers on the endangered species list. Maine senator Olympia Snowe called for an investigation by the National Academy of Science to determine whether Maine's listed salmon runs were, after years of stocking, distinct species. The NAS found that Maine's salmon were, in fact, distinct species as defined under the ESA.

Angus King, the governor of Maine, the only state in the United States with wild Atlantic salmon populations, took immediate action and sued the federal government over the listing. In a 2002 World Wildlife Fund rating of various countries' efforts to protect wild salmon, the state scored a meager half point out of a possible ten.

The state needed some arm-twisting to get protections in place, and it came from a federal judge. In 2002 Judge Gene Carter of Maine District Court handed down a decision against two Maine salmon farming companies: ASM and Stolt, both of which had refused to stop using European strain fish in their pens.

In order to curb nutrient loading in the waters used for salmon farming, Carter imposed extensive restrictions on how often growers could stock their pens and with how many fish, but he focused his harshest words for escapees. He ruled that growers could no longer use fish of European origin, noting that escapees could crossbreed with wild fish, causing irreversible genetic pollution. "The end result of repeated interactions with farm escapees could ultimately be the extinction of these wild populations," said Carter. "Escapees from the defendant's farms can negatively affect the endangered wild salmon by spreading pathogens and parasites, and by competing for food, habitat, mates, and spawning sites. Without regulation," he said, "salmon farming operations present an imminent threat of irreparable harm to the wild Atlantic salmon populations in Maine."

I mentioned the genetic thing to Sebastian Belle in one of our many phone conversations. "That's bogus," he said. "There is not one study that shows that escapees have had a negative impact on Maine's wild salmon. Ask the National Academy of Science; they did a study on it."

It had been a few years since I spoke with David Policansky at the NAS, but I sent him an e-mail regarding Belle's assertions. He replied the next day: "I think what Sebastian was claiming, which is probably legitimate, is that our report says that we can't document adverse effects of escaped farm salmon on wild salmon in Maine. However, our report also says that adverse ecological effects of escaped farm salmon on wild salmon have been documented elsewhere, and there's no reason not to expect similar [results] in Maine."

In spite of the potential harm escapees could cause, large and small escapes continued to occur. In another incident of note, disgruntled scuba divers who had been laid off from Cooke Aquaculture are believed to have swum out to the company's sites in New Brunswick in the spring of 2005 and slashed open the nets. An estimated two hundred thousand fish escaped. No one knew the exact number, because under Canadian law Cooke Aquaculture had no obligation to disclose the information. The company only acknowledged the escapes when record numbers of farmed fish showed up in Maine Rivers in the summer of 2005.

"We didn't have the weir in," said Jimmy Robinson, referring to the weir intended to capture every fish entering the Dennys River, allowing Maine Department of Fish and Game personnel to release wild fish and remove salmon farm escapees. Robinson, who owns a sporting camp on the Dennys River, another one of the eight listed under ESA, recalled that it became impossible to stop the escapees from entering the river. "The water was too high, they were coming right over the weir. After that, they had to take the weir out and then they just swam right in. You could watch 'em comin' up the fishway, and right over the damn. I counted at least five hunnert below Gardner's rips," said Robinson. Most years, only twenty-five or so wild salmon return to the Dennys.

The escape events represented just a few among many, and since the industry began in earnest in the 1980s, an estimated ten million salmon have escaped into the wild. While most breakouts occur on a grand scale, the industry also tolerates what it calls leakage: slow-growing salmon simply swim out through the meshes when larger nets are put on the pens to accommodate the bulk of the fish.

While the state of Maine avidly supports fish farming as a form of economic growth, the state's fish and wildlife wardens do not.

Of all the salmon rivers in Maine, only the Penobscot gets significant returns. Hundreds of fish make it up the river and into a weir on the Veazie Dam, where wardens weigh fish and take fat samples before releasing them to continue their upstream journey. On a late September day in 2003, I climbed aboard a small skiff in Veazie, Maine with Mitch Simpson and two interns, and motored out to a salmon weir. Simpson pushed a button on an electric winch and the weir, an iron cage about five feet square and six feet high, with a gate that allowed the fish to enter but not to exit, rose until all but a foot of it cleared the water.

Three fish swam trapped inside. Quickly, without ever taking the fish out of the water, Simpson and his workers measured each fish and took a sample from the adipose fin. Each fish slipped back into the water and vanished.

"Do you find many escapes?" I asked.

"There's always a few," said Simpson, betraying contempt in his voice. "You can tell them right away 'cause they're ugly and beat up."

"The fins are usually all chewed up from swimming around in the pens," chimed in Coley Powers, one of the interns.

"You don't like farmed fish?"

"We hate them."

Simpson noted that two fish tested positive for ISA the year before. "The farms have a leakage problem they need to fix," he said. "And they should tag every fish."

❧

Jim Ostergaard, a former commercial fisherman, drove to Bucks Harbor, Maine, not long after the great escape in 2001 to work with Bob Hukki. Ostergaard had left the industrial groundfish fleet in 1987 around the same time I did, and became involved in the international Hazard and Critical Control Point program (HACCP), known as hassip.

"I went up there to see how they could reduce or eliminate the number of escapes," said Jim. "We looked at how to control the flow of fish through the system and set up a monitoring system that I could audit unannounced. What they really need, though, is a way to mark the fish."

UNNATURAL DISASTERS

Shrimp weren't the powerful swimmers salmon were, but they, too, "leaked," through various minor mishaps, and when hurricanes and tsunamis hit in tropical areas, farmed shrimp escaped not by the hundred of thousands, but by the hundreds of millions. Hurricane Mitch, for example, sat on Honduras from October 29 to November 1 in 1998, dumping fifty inches of rain in some areas.

By the second day, workers at a Honduran shrimp farm owned by the U.S.-based Seaboard Corporation reported that the ponds were completely flooded and the water was still rising. According to Jack Crockett, the general manager, he could not reach the isolated farm, but told the crew by radio to abandon efforts to save the shrimp and save themselves.

The region supported fifty thousand acres of shrimp farms, and water rushing down off the mountains inundated pond after pond. The floods flushed as many as half a billion domesticated *P. vannamei* into the Gulf of Fonseca, home to the wild version of the same species.

Mariculture Solutions, a report by the FAO-sponsored Center for Bio-Diversity, later warned, "Farmed native species may cause a decrease in intraspecific genetic variability when released into the environment." With eight thousand people dead or missing and five billion dollars in damage, Hondurans did not focus much on the storm's impacts on wild shrimp. But three years later, Steven Travis, a geneticist with the U.S. Geological Survey in Louisiana, went to Honduras to try and find out if the mass escapes had had any effect on the genetics of nearby wild *P. vannamei*.

In May of 2001, Travis and his assistants flew to the Gulf of Fonseca—the most intensely farmed body of water in the Americas—to collect samples of wild post-larvae. Travis reasoned that the wild shrimp would show a homogenous mix of similar genetic markers unless they had crossed with highly inbred farm escapees: domesticated stock from hatcheries in the United States, Panama, and Ecuador.

Indeed, Travis found what was, for him, compelling evidence of crossbreeding between wild and farmed shrimp, and raised the possibility that such mixing could reduce the overall fitness of wild stocks. But when he tried to publish his results in peer-reviewed journals he hit a wall.

"One reviewer for *Conservation Genetics* focused almost exclusively on our use of dominant genetic markers, stating numerous statistical reasons why they are unreliable and how they could/should have been handled differently," said Travis. "Other than my shrimp paper, I have never had a paper focusing on population structure in natural populations rejected on the basis of the type of marker or statistical analysis used, and I have published a total of eight such papers in high-impact journals such as *Ecology*, *Ecological Applications*, *Journal of Ecology*, and *Molecular Ecology*. This reviewer also proffered the opinion that without samples from the local shrimp farms, all of our conclusions about escapees were mere arm waving. She even went so far as to rank the quality of the science presented in our paper as a two on a one-to-ten scale, and the originality of the research as a three!" Travis said, a bit pained.

"A third reviewer for *Conservation Genetics* (deemed necessary because the second reviewer was enthusiastic about the paper and thus in direct opposition to the first) felt that our sample sizes were too small, that our genetic markers were potentially unreliable, and that simple family cohorts could have produced similar results."

Unaccustomed to such a harsh reception, Travis attempted to publish in other journals, but found consistent rejection, though inconsistent criticism.

"I had a rather chilly conversation with a leading shrimp researcher at Tufts, Dr. Acacia Alcivar-Warren," said Travis. "She felt that there was essentially no point in conducting the research in the first place, since the release of captive shrimp into native estuaries surrounding shrimp farms is inevitable and at any rate should be quickly diluted via genetic mixing in the open ocean."

Travis sought publication in two other journals, *Molecular Ecology* and *Estuaries*, to no avail. Inconsistent but constant criticism eventually drove him to shelve the paper, though the experience continued to rankle. In spite of concerns that an influx of hatchery-raised species would have a negative impact on wild stocks—voiced by the FAO in 1976 and thirty years later by the Center for Bio-Diversity, Travis's work remained unpublished, sending a strong signal to researchers not to waste their time generating negative science on the impact of aquaculture on the environment. In 2004, a European conference on aquaculture featured papers by over four hundred scientists, only two of which looked at the industry's impacts on the surrounding environment.

"My guess—and I stress that I have absolutely no concrete evidence for this," said Travis, "is that, since the majority of researchers who work on penaeid shrimp probably receive most if not all their funding from the shrimp farming industry, they are likely to be biased against research that has negative things to say about it."

For Cristina Chávez, a prominent shrimp biologist at Mexico's CIAD lab in Mazatlán, the issue boiled down to funding. "Research in the wild is very expensive," said Chávez. "And the results are unreliable." Chávez also noted that most research institutions were deeply tied to the aquaculture industry.

"That's where the money is," said Dr. Leobardo Montoya, also at CIAD. Nonetheless, he was one of the few scientists to study the incidence of white spot disease in wild shrimp. "We've only done two studies," he said. "We found the white spot virus in some shrimp in the estuaries, but only a few exhibited symptoms of the disease, and they were close to an infected farm. On the high seas we didn't find any virus."

Montoya felt that wild shrimp had a natural resistance to pathogens. "They have been living with viruses for thousands of years," he said. He also noted that viral disease outbreaks only occur under a unique set of circumstances: a high amount of pathogens in contact with a susceptible population under stress. While intensive aquaculture systematically created stress conditions for farmed animals, events such as Hurricane Mitch created them in such a random way that Montoya expressed little concern about epizootics occurring in the wild.

In the United States, a white paper on aquaculture from the state of Massachusetts noted the institutionalized nature of Monoya's views. "It is not uncommon to find resistance to [disease] assessment and control," the report said of research on wild stocks. "This attitude is due, in part, to the 'old school of thought' that significant epizootics rarely if ever occur in wild populations."

Most prominent aquatic veterinarians admitted that precious little money had gone into risk assessment and monitoring of wild stocks; yet, in my first conversation with Rohana Subasinghe, he said that contamination of wild stocks posed a significant problem. "It could come back to haunt them," he said of the negligent shrimp industry, pointing out that breeding programs for farmed shrimp often needed to bring in new blood from the wild. "When they start looking for broodstock, they need uncontaminated shrimp."

The rapid expansion of the early days of shrimp and salmon farming led to decisions that were already coming back to haunt the industries. But while the shrimp and salmon farmers sought solutions, their respective problems contined to multiply.

9

GROWING PAINS

While shrimp farming and salmon farming exhibited meteoric growth in the 1980s and 1990s, moving into the unknown at such breakneck speed, speculators and regulators inevitably made mistakes.

Photographs of sea lice–infested salmon appeared on the Internet along with descriptions of how the farms, when sited near the mouths of salmon rivers, spread lethal numbers of the parasites to wild salmon smolts swimming out to sea. Early shrimp farmers sometimes built their ponds in mangrove jungles and lagoons, the nursery grounds of numerous tropical fish species, including the valuable red snapper. Aquaculture, in particular shrimp and salmon farming, quickly came into conflict with the numerous artisanal fishermen who supplied local communities with fresh fish and income.

At every setback shrimp or salmon farms encountered, the environmental community moved in, enlisting commercial fishermen as allies. The Suzuki Foundation, in Canada, accused salmon farmers of taking more fish protein from the ocean than they generated, and of destroying the ecological balance that supported wild stocks and fishing communities.

In 1990, the state of Alaska, which borders British Columbia, banned salmon farming. But escaped Atlantic salmon from British Columbia farms continued to show up in Alaskan rivers. Although Alaskan fishermen relied heavily on aquaculture in the form of hatchery-reared smolts, most saw the farms as threats to wild salmon in the environment and in the market: salmon prices had plummeted in the early 1990s, putting many communities on the ropes. The combined concerns of its northern neighbor, fishermen, and environmental groups such as the Suzuki Foundation led the B.C. government to declare a temporary moratorium on further expansion of the industry in 1996.

But shrimp farms also continued to increase. They required less capital and encountered less resistance in less-developed countries like Thailand and China. Nonetheless, Greenpeace took on the shrimp industry in 1997, before the outbreak of white spot, with the publication of "Shrimp: The Deadly Delicacy." The report focused on the use of wild post-larvae to stock shrimp farms and the destruction of mangroves, two situations that had been resolved in Mexico, but are reported to continue in other parts of the world. In 2001, Public Citizen, the consumer lobbying organization, picked up the ball. Along with Food and Water Watch, another such NGO, Public Citizen raised the issues of continued environmental destruction, as was occurring around Agiabampo; antibiotics and other contaminants in shrimp; as well as social concerns regarding the fates of coastal people in shrimp farming regions.

Journalists picked up numerous stories about aquaculture's battle for ascendancy in the world of seafood production. On one of my first assignments, I traveled from my home to the College of the Atlantic on Mount Desert Island, Maine, to hear Father Thomas Kocherry and Harikrishna Devnath discuss the impacts of shrimp farms on fishing communities in India.

According to Devnath, in 1998, Indian police had opened fire on a demonstration by fishermen against further shrimp farm expansion around Chilika Lake, killing four and wounding twenty-five. The fishermen claimed, as did the Greenpeace and Public Citizen reports, that bulldozing shrimp farms along the estuary silted the riparian waters and destroyed the local ecology. The harvest of post-larvae to stock the ponds was also taking a large number of fish species as bycatch. "The small fish are then unable to grow and recruit to the fishery," said Devnath.

The social impacts of shrimp farming became difficult to ignore as incidents of violence occurred all around the world. In British Columbia, activists destroyed a salmon hatchery. Protesters were shot in Ecuador, Nicaragua, Chile, Thailand, and elsewhere. In Mexico, too, several people were killed in reprisal for their anti–shrimp farming activities, but no concerted opposition formed in Agiabampo. In places like Alaska and Chilika Lake where fishermen felt they had something to protect, they tried to do so, but many of Mexico's estuaries already suffered from pollution and overfishing. People on the coast had few options. Shrimp aquaculture at least promised a future to the local ejidatarios, even if it didn't deliver.

❧

Kenny Dessain, an American who now lives in Navopatia, and I drove the back roads through the desert on our way to meet Lalo Mendivil, *un voz abandonado*, a voice in the wilderness. As we bumped along the rutted road, jackrabbits, roadrunners, and quail all darted in front of us. Approaching the ejido, we encountered the usual array of domesticated animals, and I slowed down for Brahmin cattle, burros, and horses.

"When the shrimp farms first came, Lalo fought them," said Kenny. "He tried to organize the other fishermen, explain to them what the shrimp farms had done to communities up north, but they all had dollar signs in their eyes."

Meredith de la Garza, from the Mexican environmental group Pronatura, spent a year interviewing residents around Tobari, a large bay eighty miles north of Agiabampo. I had spoken with de la Garza one morning in Tucson and she described a level of abject poverty seen in the most desperate parts of Mexico, noting that the handful of jobs on the shrimp farms had done little to change that situation. She added that besides being poor, the people were sick. "They were sick in ways they said they'd never been before," she said.

The Agiabampo ejidatarios did not want to hear about it. They said they would do better and ignored Mendivil. "It was discouraging to watch him get discouraged," said Dessain.

❧

Lola Mendivil and his family could not have expected us; they had no phone. They welcomed us regardless, and invited us to come in and sit down. They were about to eat. Mendivil's wife put a full plate in front of me. I looked over the contents: refried beans, rice, and boiled mixed vegetables dotted with chunks of *panela*, a homemade cheese. She put a bowl of warm corn tortillas on the table, and after a short prayer we all dug in. It was good food and not having had lunch, I ate it up. "*Quiere más?*" Mendivil's wife asked. Did I want more?

"Yes," I answered, and she filled my plate again. I could tell by the way the grandmother watched the food going onto my plate that this was precious stuff. Kenny refused seconds. We finished, and the women collected the empty plates already mopped clean with the last of the tortillas. No bycatch here. Nothing wasted.

Outside we sat in the dark and watched the lights of the shrimp poachers in the bay. Mendivil offered me a *refresco*, a Coke, and I accepted. In my mind, it was better to accept his hospitality gratefully than refuse it.

Kenny asked about the shrimping, and Mendivil said it was all done. The bottom was all smothered from the eroding shrimp farms and surrounding desmonte.

What about the poachers?

They weren't getting much, a few pounds.

Mendivil was an independente. The poachers came from the Agiabampo *cooperativa*. They would not let him fish even if he wanted to.

What about the shrimp farms?

Disease. They are not growing anything.

So how was he feeding his family?

By working in the campo picking chiles for six dollars a day. But they were starting to use machines for that.

❧

Shrimp farming took over the estuary. Lalo Mendivil became a part-time fisherman and moved to a landlocked ejido, effectively surrendering his legitimacy as a fisherman activist. But while he was silenced, support for his assertions came from a respected biologist in Mazatlán.

In 2001, Dr. Federico Páez Osuna edited a 450-page book entitled *Camaronacultura y Medio Ambiente* (Shrimp Farming and the Environment), which detailed the impacts of shrimp farms on the environment. The day after meeting with Rohana Subasinghe in Mazatlán in 2003, I took a bicycle ride to the south side of town to talk to Páez, who spoke and wrote in English, making my life a bit easier. He met me at the UNAM campus, located on a spit of rock at the entrance to Mazatlán's harbor, and we walked up to his office. I started off by buying a copy of his book, and he gave me a file of his papers written in English.

Among other things, Páez had found that shrimp farms contributed only slightly to the pollution of the estuaries overall, accounting for just 5 percent of nutrient loading; agriculture and industry accounted for the rest, with agriculture being the worst culprit. "But the nutrient loading around shrimp farms can be very concentrated, depending on how a farm is managed. On a local level, it can be much worse than other sources," he said. "But shrimp farmers can address this issue through polyculture," he said, referring to the practice of growing mollusks and seaweed near shrimp farms in order to absorb nutrients.

Páez' research documented most of Mendivil's contentions. Páez proposed general solutions, some of which were slowly adopted by the industry. He blamed reduced commercial catches on loss of habitat and recommended better siting of farms. Escapes, he warned, would cause biological pollution, and he recommended that farmers "optimize management and include new technology, though he did not explain those amorphous terms." He also identified saltwater intrusion into freshwater aquifers and the conversion of agricultural land to shrimp farms as problems and made general recommendations on how to ameliorate them.

While Páez attempted to guide the shrimp industry in a sustainable direction, Devnath and Kocherry toured the world on behalf of the World Forum of Fish Workers and Fish Harvesters, an organization determined to establish a global system of sustainable seafood production that did not include semi-intensive shrimp farms stocked with wild post-larvae.

BREAKING THE BANK

According to Thomas Kocherry, who took the podium after Devnath that night at the College of the Atlantic, fishermen, aquaculture developers, and coastal people needed to step back and look at industrial aquaculture within a very broad context. "We cannot destroy natural capital," he said. "Destroying natural capital takes down communities with it."

Sitting in a folding chair in a school auditorium after having driven eighty miles in a rush, I was a little foggy. Kocherry repeated the statement with the force of the preacher—a Catholic priest. "We cannot destroy natural capital!"

Though I did not understand the concept completely, something in Kocherry's statement resonated with me and many others. Niaz Dorry explained it to me in more detail after the lecture.

"You have renewable natural capital in the form of fish stocks and ecosystem function," she said. "And that pays dividends in terms of resource generation and harvestable stocks. If you use up capital by overharvesting, destroying ecological function, or both, you destroy the resource base."

Natural capital amounted to money in the bank that paid interest, but destroying estuaries or overharvesting forage fisheries for feed, for example, could lead to irreversible damage and deplete the interest generating capital.

While we spoke, on the other side of the continent ecological economist Peter Tyedmers, then a graduate student at the University of British Columbia, was gathering data for his thesis, a look at the ecological cost of salmon farming versus the costs of fishing. He was particularly interested in aquaculture's use of forage fish—herring, sardines, anchovetta—as feed, and the cost of feed production. His investigation looked at sustainability, based on the ecological footprint of salmon farming: its use of natural capital, renewable and nonrenewable. Unlike the aquaculture and fisheries promoters of the past who counted on technology such as genetically engineered corn to replace vanishing resources such as forage fish, Tyedmers defined sustainability as using resources at a rate that would leave future generations with sufficient amounts of those same resources—what the growing discipline of "ecological economics" referred to as "strong sustainability."

Tyedmers had accumulated a staggering amount of data with which he could measure the energy use and ecological footprints of salmon production methods in British Columbia. He calculated the solar energy needed to produce the forage fish and added that to the energy costs of harvesting, transporting, processing, and delivering the feed, to farmed fish, and the costs of producing other ingredients in feed, as well as infrastructure and other costs of salmon farming. He compared those to all the costs of fishing, including boat construction and maintenance, fuel use, ice, etc., and found that fish farming in the worst-case scenario used more than three times the resources commercial fishing used per ton of fish produced.

In the best-case scenario, when compared to the trolling fishery for Chinook salmon, which comprise less than 4 percent of the wild salmon catch, farmed salmon production still had a slightly larger ecological footprint per ton.

Tyedmers' research gathered momentum over the years. It did not come from an NGO with an agenda, but from the new ideology that supported the increasingly relevant field of ecological economics.

Not long after Tyedmers' work gained attention among the antiaquaculture forces, COMPASS (the Communication Partnership for Science and the Sea), an organization serving conservation groups, invited him to help them deal with an impending problem: how to grow industries that depended on wild fisheries. As many as five million metric tons of 2005 aquaculture production used fishmeal and oil to one degree or another. While some forms of aquaculture, including shrimp farming, showed promise of cutting their dependence on wild fish, salmon and carnivorous-fish farmers could not easily replace wild fish in the diets of animals. As Tyedmers said, "These are the Hummers of aquaculture." They burned up a lot of oil, and technology had yet to replace the source: wild fish.

The shrimp fleet has sailed from Yaváros, Sonora, and only a few boats remain at the dock. Drifting in and out on their mooring lines, the idle boats all have their long outriggers pulled up. Each has a net drying above deck. In each net hangs a round grate, the turtle excluder that they must use by law.

A white and blue sardine boat, the PROPOMEX T-3, *sits at the dock waiting to unload. Its power block, a large hydraulic pulley used to haul the net, hangs from a boom above deck, and the purse seine net forms a mountain of twine on the stern. A small seine skiff sits on a ramp aft of the twine, ready to be launched. The hatch covers are off, and a green hose hangs down into the hold. Several fishermen move around the deck, and I start snapping pictures.*

I ask if I can come aboard and take some pictures. They nod. Two guys are tending the hold. For an hour I snap pictures of their work and in a mix of Spanish and sign language they tell me about their industry. They introduce themselves: Filipe Corral, the bigger of the two, and Rosario Duarte.

Duarte guides a hose shooting water into the hold to loosen up the fish, while Corral handles the big green hose that sucks the fish up and into the reduction plant. The pump stops intermittently and they have time to talk while they wait. It's the same for deckhands everywhere, I say: waiting and then working like crazy. They laugh and nod in agreement.

There are five types of sardines, says Filipe: charro, zrinuda, japonesa, monterrey, *and* macarela. *The charro are used for animal feed. The plant reduces them to bags of dry fishmeal and barrels of fish oil, which will be used to varying degrees as components of livestock feed and feed for the shrimp in the surrounding aquaculture ponds.*

Corral has been working on purse seiners for seventeen years, and Durante about ten. Both live in Yaváros and come from fishing families.

The eighty-foot boat has about 120 tons of sardines aboard, says Durante, not a great trip. Overall landings have been down about 30 percent this season from an average of about 1,000 tons a month. The season runs from October to June and he hopes things will pick up, though he says it is not likely.

Lots of people along the coast sense another El Niño in the offing, bad for fishing, and Corral agrees. "Scientists say the stocks are declining," he says.

Nonetheless, the sardine boats are among the most profitable on the coast, and are coming off some of the best years in history. An El Niño event in 1998 cut fishmeal production by 20 percent, driving prices up. When the fish stocks bounced back in 2001, the seiners made a killing. But those high times have gone by.

By midnight, Corral and Durante will be casting the lines to head out again for another trip. They steam for twenty-five hours along the coast, either north deeper into the Sea of Cortez, or south to the Pacific off Sinaloa.

"We caught these off Sinaloa," say Durante, "in about four sets of the net."

The sardine boats do not set their nets until they find fish. They hunt at night when the fish rise off the bottom. Using sonar, they cruise along watching the screen until it shows a large mass of green blips that represent a bunched school of fish. When they hit a school, the boat moves downwind of them. The deckhands cut loose the seine skiff with one man aboard and one end of the net. They then run their 360 horsepower Cummins at full throttle as the boat circles up around the fish, a third-of-a-mile-long net streaming out behind it until it comes back to the seine skiff, lassoing as much of the school as possible. A line of floats marks the top edge of the twine, two hundred feet below the surface. A rope runs through rings on the lower edge like a drawstring, and as soon as the boat and skiff bring the ends together, the men hook the rope to a winch and purse the bottom, creating a giant sack before the fish find their way out. With the fish securely in the net, the men begin the process of drying the twine. They feed the fine mesh up into the power block, a hydraulic-driven roller hanging from the boom; it pulls the twine up and drops it on deck. Soon the water in the net boils with frantic fish, flashing silver in the decklights.

The men sink a pump into the midst of the fish and begin to pump them aboard, filling the separate holds evenly so as to keep the boat trim. Once the net is empty and back aboard, they begin the hunt again.

"Sometimes we make eight sets for nothing, other times we load the boat in one set," says Corral.

I leave them and walk around the plant. Palettes loaded with *sacks of fishmeal sit in the sun, ready to be loaded onto trucks. While I wait for my ride, a middle-aged man and woman and a teenage girl arrive at the wharf on bicycles. The man carries an ataraya, a cast net; the woman, a bucket. He walks up to the edge, looks out at the water and without much ado lets fly. The net spreads out into a fifteen-foot-diameter circle and splashes flat on the water. It seems to hesitate, then sinks quickly. The man hauls it back and shakes out a few tiny fish that his wife and daughter race to put in a bucket. They are not waiting for aquaculture to feed them: they still count on fish close to shore.*

❧

From the sardine boats in Yaváros to the menhaden seiners in the Gulf of Mexico, reduction fisheries increasingly supported aquaculture. The limitations of relying on wild fisheries were clear. According to research by Stuart Barlow and Ian Pike, by 2010 the aquaculture industry would take 79 percent of the world's available fish oil and 48 percent of available fish meal, provided supply remains constant at 6 to 7 million tons of meal and 1.1 to 1.4 million tons of fish oil annually.

BAD PRESS

The 2002 scallop season in Cobscook Bay was a bust. Late in the afternoon on November 1, the boats started coming to the docks with pathetic catches. A few years earlier the small fleet of draggers, mostly forty-foot boats bought used in Canada, had rafted out from the public wharf until midnight and hired extra hands to help shuck the mountains of scallops they had on their decks.

But that, as they say, is history. In 2002, the boats arrived with two or three five-gallon buckets of scallop meats all shucked out. Some of the scallops tested contained traces of Slice, the pesticide salmon farmers used against sea lice.

Earlier that year, a commission of scientists, fishermen, and government officials funded by the Pew Charitable Trusts had released a report calling for a moratorium on further development of carnivorous fish farming until scientists better understood its impacts. If Maine's salmon farms had trouble before the ISA outbreak, it mounted steadily in its wake as NGO funded researchers aired more and more of the industry's dirty laundry.

National Geographic ran a story by Fen Montaigne in July 2003 which dwelled at length on the sea lice issue and other impacts salmon farming had on wild stocks. In 2004, *Science* published a paper by R. Hites warning consumers, particularly pregnant women, not to eat farmed salmon because it contained high levels of PCBs. Newspapers gave considerable coverage to the story, and followed it up with more revelations. Excessive levels of PCBs were blamed on contaminated feed.

"We're trying to accomplish in thirty years what the agriculture industry did in three thousand," said Sebastian Belle. "And the press and NGOs are watching our every move. We're the most heavily monitored industry on the water."

The most powerful salmon farming corporations operating in the United States, Canada, and Chile attempted to get out their side of the story. In 2003, they formed a promotional group called Salmon of the Americas (SOTA), and contracted with the publicity firm Market Share to develop a publicity campaign. In November 2005, SOTA paid for a six-page advertisement in the

New York Times Magazine, refuting what it felt were unfair accusations against farmed salmon.

The ad featured a photo of a smiling pregnant woman, and in big red letters, "Her doctor told her to eat farmed salmon." It also featured some major stretches in truth that Belle, who sat on the board of SOTA, defended by saying the other side had stretched the truth pretty far in the other direction, so it all balanced out.

❧

Not long afterward, David Carpenter, and a coauthor of the 2004 *Science Magazine* paper, wrote that in addition to PCBs, farmed salmon had levels of at least thirteen organic pollutants more than ten times higher than their wild counterparts. "The half-life of these compounds in the human body is on the order of ten years. Therefore if a ten-year-old girl eats a contaminated salmon, when she gets pregnant at age twenty she will have half of her contaminates still in her body to pass on to her child." On December 20, the National Environmental Trust ran an op-ed in the *Times* that responded to claims made in the SOTA ad, and ended with the statement, "Ocean-farmed salmon is definitely not what the doctor ordered, especially if you are pregnant or ever expect to be."

❧

Shrimp farmers, too, faced problems beyond the confines of their ponds. Most critics focused on habitat destruction and traces of antibiotics in shrimp. Others looked at the socioeconomic effects. The shouting match was almost as intense as the salmon debate. Mexico tried to rise above the fray with the Mexican Shrimp Council's three-million-dollar "naked shrimp" campaign.

The glossy brochure discussed farmed and wild shrimp as one homogenous product, and showed palm trees and clear-watered tropical oceans, claiming that the waters Federico Páez said were contaminated by industry, agriculture, cities, and aquaculture were "great for growing shrimp." The clear tropical water and palm trees gave anyone who had ever visited a shrimp farm a chuckle: even if Ocean Garden's anitbiotic-free Mexican shrimp were indeed a cut above the competition, the reality of their origins was muddy ponds surrounded by bulldozed dikes of raw earth scattered with pelican shit.

10

TECHNO-OPTIMISM

I sat in my office—the wheelhouse of an old fishing boat set out in the field behind my house in Maine, and wired with telephone and broadband—and listened with one ear to a white-throated sparrow singing outside my window: *pure sweet Canada Canada*. With the other ear I listened to Sebastian Belle again.

"We do a lot we don't get credit for," Belle said over a bad cell phone connection, insinuating what he sometimes said to my face, that journalists had failed to give the industry a fair shake. "I ask you," he said in the rhetorical style of a salesman. "Who has a greater motive to solve problems, the farmer or the environmentalist who makes money from those problems?"

Belle was on the defensive. "Didn't you ask me that before?" I said, not wanting to argue. I wondered if he, too, got tired of the struggle. I recalled seeing him at a fish health meeting in Bucks Harbor, red eyed, pale, looking completely played out, but he never gave up. *Surrender* was not in his vocabulary, he had too much of his life invested in establishing salmon aquaculture in the waters of Maine.

In 1996, when Jill Fallon called the open ocean the Manifest Destiny of aquaculture, she invoked a sense of entitlement that in turn bred tenacity. She and Belle believed and fought fiercely for the scientists and entrepreneurs who promised to solve aquaculture's problems. They had an almost religious faith in technology.

"We'll figure it out," as Bob Rosenberry said. It was a common refrain, and not just among shrimp farmers. To their credit, the most controversial sectors of the aquaculture industry made great strides in problem solving. They were the pioneers, on the cutting edge of an industry seen as the hope of the world. From the laboratory scientists to local managers, shrimp and fish farmers learned how to work around disease, negative publicity, and the escape issue. Beautiful red fillets of salmon continued to fill seafood cases in grocery stores at under five dollars a pound, and Red Lobster never took endless shrimp off their menus—although the price went up.

Governments, private investors, and international lenders continued to pour millions of dollars into solutions-oriented research, most of it aimed at addressing the problems inside the pens and ponds through biotechnology, disease control, and what some might refer to as "the geographical cure."

For carnivorous finfish, that meant moving from the protected bays and fjords to exposed offshore locations. "Coastal pollution means that inshore areas will continue to lose productivity. We have to go offshore," said Sea Grant's James McVey.

The only thing needed, he and many other offshore aquaculture proponents believed, was a streamlined system for leasing the open ocean. Efforts to put such a system in place took a great leap forward in 2005, when Senators Ted Stevens (R-AK) and Daniel Inouye (D-HI) introduced the Offshore Aquaculture Act (S.1195). The legislation would set up a leasing process for the entire EEZ, a three-million-square-mile area—equal to the size of the continental United States. Not that aquaculture would fill all that space. According to McVey, a mere 1 percent of the EEZ devoted to aquaculture, an area the size of the state of Indiana, could supply the United States' seafood needs.

As assistant director of aquaculture at NMFS, Linda Chaves helped draft the Offshore Aquaculture Act. "We're not reserving huge areas," she said in a brief telephone interview. "Just a handful." While she felt that adequate safeguards would be provided, Chaves preferred to implement them via regulation rather than legislation. The offshore aquaculture legislation addressed jurisdiction and process and omitted any environmental standards. The offshore waters provided so much diluting power that environmental impacts seemed negligible. "We don't see it [offshore aquaculture] as a huge problem for the environment," said Chaves.

The door was opening, and the lure of manifest destiny and an open frontier had already attracted some of the best minds in the country.

❧

FRIDAY, JUNE 13, 2003, ISLE OF SHOALS, NEW HAMPSHIRE
Marine biologist Michael Chambers had been involved in open ocean aquaculture for twelve years before he arrived in New Hampshire in 2003, having worked on Sea Grant Projects in the

Gulf of Mexico, Hawaii, and eventually in New Hampshire. While Chambers held a degree in biology, he also worked with technical experts in the design of mooring, monitoring and other systems that made open-ocean aquaculture possible.

The technology took years to develop. Fish pens off the coast of New Hampshire had to withstand the strong tides of the Gulf of Maine dragging on the nets twenty hours every day. Winter gales battered the moorings all winter, and the occasional hurricane mounted thirty-foot waves that wracked the cages.

The UNH team opted for six-hundred-square-meter submerged Sea Station cages. In profile, a fifty-foot-deep, eighty-foot-diameter Sea Station cage resembled a diamond; from above, a circle. Designers believed submerged pens, moored twenty feet below the surface, would provide a safer, more stable growing environment. For the pilot project, they stocked one pen with halibut in October 2001, and the other with haddock in December 2003, while a three-thousand-square-meter cage sat empty, awaiting stocking with Atlantic cod.

❧

At eight o'clock on an overcast morning, Chambers and his crew boarded UNH's *Gulf Challenger*, a fifty-foot research vessel moored at the Portsmouth Fishermen's Co-op, and headed out to the Isles of Shoals. A half hour later the boat arrived on site, six miles from shore, but still within state waters near the islands. Small buoys that marked the cage site, surrounded a large cylindrical buoy sprouting antennae—the automated feeder that had broken down a week earlier. It bobbed on the surface above the cages. A stretch of bad weather had kept the crew ashore and for several days the fish went hungry.

"The fish haven't eaten since Monday," said Chambers as he and two enthusiastic graduate students suited up in dive gear. "The haddock are more fragile than the halibut or cod," he added, looking pensively at the surface and wondering how many dead fish he would find. Carrying bags of feed, he and the grad students slid off the stern and disappeared under water, where haddock and halibut swam slowly round in the cages.

After half an hour, the crew returned. "The halibut were so hungry they were biting at us through the nets," said Chambers. He emptied a bag of eight dead haddock on deck and began to inspect them, peeling back the gill covers. He set aside five that appeared to have had parasite infections. "Looks like a common ectoparasite," he said. "We'll have to take them back to the lab to be sure." Chambers noted that algae grew on the nets and entire ecosystems evolved in the farm system. Monitoring would be crucial, and part of Chambers' work entailed developing a remote video system to keep an eye on the fish.

The day's work also included some harvesting. Chambers took a net bag below and returned with a dozen small halibut, each about five pounds. "We have to send these down to Washington for a NMFS picnic," he said.

GOING COMMERCIAL

In September 2003, UNH stocked its three-thousand-square-meter cage with cod. "We're almost at a commercial scale," said Chambers, as he described his vision of groups of pens spread throughout the Gulf of Maine.

But the economics of open-ocean cod farming continued to challenge private companies such as Great Bay Aquaculture, which supplied the juvenile cod for the UNH project. Cod's low ratio of edible meat per body weight—40 percent compared to salmon's 60 percent, made it all the more difficult for any aquaculture venture to recover the costs of offshore cages and still make a profit. Speaking at an industry meeting in St. Andrews, New Brunswick, Great Bay manager Chris Duffy outlined a dual harvest strategy that he believed would make the venture work.

"In nearshore experiments we plan to stock each cage with thirty thousand juveniles," Duffy said, twice the level of salmon stocked in similar cages. But he planned to harvest half the fish halfway through the twenty-month growing cycle. Duffy's proposed final stocking density, eighteen kilos per cubic meter, is lower than salmon's twenty-plus kilos per cubic meter, but utilizing the total capacity of the cage over a prolonged period of time is a novel experiment. In the open ocean, where U.S. developers foresee minimal disease and pollution problems, Duffy hoped to push densities even higher.

"What about disease?" someone from the audience asked.

Before Duffy could answer, another panelist sharing the stage chimed in.

"We're scared to death of it," he said.

In an earlier telephone interview, Duffy had brushed aside the issue. "We're not worried about it," he said, certain he could cope with whatever came up. When he spoke at St. Andrews, however, Duffy had already been dealing with cod disease for three years. A virus, nodavirus, had wiped out his first two years of cod fingerling production.

While Duffy waited to see what diseases arose, Scottish researchers Ian Bricknell and Rob Raynard had found that cod were susceptible to a variety of known pathogens, including Infectious Pancreatic Necrosis Virus (IPNV), which like nodavirus caused high mortalities in juvenile fish, and some strains of viral hemorrhagic septicemia virus (VHSV).

The fanfare with which Duffy and his Canadian partner Ivan Green launched the stocking of pens near the island of Grand Manan, New Brunswick, was not repeated a few months later when the project folded. Green died not long after, and people on the island still wonder what happened to the farmed cod.

"Disease is a bottleneck every aquaculture industry has to go through, and they all know that," said Dougie McIntosh, a microbiologist from RPC, a Fredericton lab, voicing an opinion held by many aquatic veterinarians. "They're kidding themselves if they think they can get around it.

"The models that they're using are very small and controlled," said McIntosh, who had worked on fish health in Scotland and Canada since 1987. "When they get to commercial scale and you've got several fish shedding viruses in different ways, it's going to be a different situation, and they can't predict that."

McIntosh and many others pointed out that U.S. farmers lacked the same level of government support that the Norwegians and Canadians had. Developing strategies for hypothetical problems would cost millions of dollars, money the fledgling industry did not have. In order to jumpstart offshore aquaculture and avoid costly research, the NMFS gave the industry what looked like a free ride on environmental review.

The agency had once imposed stiff requirements. In 1993, when the Norwegian American Aquaculture Company tried to lease an area of the EEZ off Massachusetts, NOAA demanded an extensive baseline study and a costly environmental impact statement. By 2005, requirements for an offshore lease amounted to an Environmental Assessment. If the assessment found "no significant impact," no environmental impact statement would be necessary. The Offshore Aquaculture Act contained no environmental standards, but NOAA promised to regulate the industry when necessary.

~

The Pew Charitable Trusts picked up the ball where NOAA dropped it. In 2005, together with the Woods Hole Oceanographic Institution, Pew established the Open Ocean Aquaculture Task Force to consider the future of aquaculture in the United States and what regulators and legislators should consider in terms of the environmental and social effects of an extensive industry. Chuck Fox from Pew described the task force's mission. "We're not against aquaculture," he said. "We just want to be sure it is done right."

The Task Force invited Peter Tyedmers to speak at the opening meeting in Woods Hole, and he gave me a heads-up. I called the director Chris Mann to find out if I could attend. It took him a while but he finally okayed it. "You can come to the presentations, but not the executive sessions," he said. "You can use the material the presenters offer, but nothing the panel members say. If you want to talk to panel members outside the session you're welcome to, and you can use whatever they want to give you. Can you work with that?"

I rode my bicycle seventy miles from Boston to Cape Cod, slept at a campground in Falmouth, Massachusetts, and drove down to the meeting with Tyedmers the next day. On a cool, sunny July morning we found our way across the extensive parking lots near WHOI's Clark laboratory. As we entered the building small cardboard signs guided us down a long enclosed walkway with windows looking out into the spruce woods that surrounded the campus. Panel members, Pew staff, and presenters mingled outside the meeting room. Chris Mann introduced Tyedmers and me to some of the panel members: Bruce Anderson from the Oceanic Institute in Hawaii, Bill Dewey of Taylor Shellfish in Bellingham, Washington, and another presenter, Biliana Cicin-Sain from the University of Delaware.

Mann hoped that Tyedmers would introduce the panel members to some ecological economics ideas that would make it into the group's final recommendations, but that would come later. The point of the initial meeting was to identify areas of concern, one of the most interesting of which came from Cicin-Sain.

"We are advising Congress to make it explicit that the National Environmental Protection Act [NEPA] applies to the EEZ," she said.

It seemed a minor point, but many people in the environmental community counted on using NEPA as a way to maintain some control over offshore aquaculture. At the meeting with Michael Rubino, NOAA's aquaculture coordinator, activists asked why the agency failed to deliver an environmental impact statement with the Offshore Aquaculture Act, as required under NEPA. "If we need to do one, we'll do one," Rubino reportedly responded.

Without specific standards in the Offshore Aquaculture Act, NOAA would call the shots on environmental regulation. According to Cicin-Sain, considerable doubt existed whether NEPA actually applied to the EEZ, and if it did, whether a pro-offshore aquaculture administration would enforce it—sobering news.

Tyedmers spoke after Cicin-Sain, and in his unassuming style he gave the panel members their first taste of ecological economics by explaining what he considered a widely held misconception about salmon feed. Many of the people in the room shared his view that farmed salmon offered the most efficient use of fishmeal and fish oil, the critical components of aquaculture feeds. With a feed conversion ratio of around three pounds of wet fish to one pound of edible meat—compared to five to one or more for chicken, beef, and pigs, and ten to one for wild salmon—most believed farmed fish utilized the valuable forage fish better than any other type of livestock, or wild fish for that matter.

"I find this fallacy everywhere," said Tyedmers standing next to a power point projector. "Even in Department of Fisheries and Oceans [DFO] literature. The assumption is that all fish feed is equal, and that is patently false." According to Tyedmers, most salmon are 85 percent plankton-feeders, acting as grazers of the oceans' primary production, much as cattle eat grass, the earth's primary production.

On the other hand, he pointed out, the pellets fed to farmed salmon fingerlings are made from fish equal to or higher on the trophic level than the salmon themselves. "The pellets are made primarily from South American forage fish, sardines and anchovetta, and Gulf of Mexico menhaden," he said. "But they also include fish like blue whiting and pollock: fish that could be eating these salmon in the wild."

Tyedmers, a big man with close-cropped hair, stood in the middle of the room. Panels members looked at him and a Power-Point image that showed the trophic levels of fish that went into fish feed. He waited for them to make the next logical mental leap—that the issue was more about the quality of feed than the quantity. Feeding high-trophic-level fish to farm fish turned the food pyramid upside down, and, depending on the amounts of fish used, could increase the ecological footprint of farmed fish exponentially. But it would be a long time coming. Most people, even in the industry, stuck with simple interpretations of crude numbers.

"Farmed fish are more efficient feeders" Bruce Anderson said out loud. True enough, within the narrow scope of farmed salmon requiring three pounds of wild fish for every pound of weight gain, versus the ten pounds needed for one pound of weight gain in the wild, where salmon swam for their feed and to escape predators. Agencies like the DFO regurgitated the salmon industry's stand on the feed debate because it looked like simple arithmetic.

Tyedmers, on the other hand, looked at salmon aquaculture in terms of its ecological footprint, and that changed the picture dramatically. "Feeding farmed salmon with fish from equal or higher trophic levels requires an area of primary production far greater than that needed to sustain wild fish," he said, watching the panel members to make sure they understood.

Tyedmers strove to educate people about the economy of money instead of the economy of dollars. "I like to get them to think in terms of carbon fixed by the envioronment," he said later. "So they can grasp what it takes to create a pound of farmed salmon versus a pound of wild."

Tyedmers wrapped up his talk by explaining that feed made from higher-trophic-level fish, such as carnivorous sand eels and whiting, required a greater area of primary production, carbon fixed initially by phytoplankton. In a nutshell, he argued, using pellets with a high content of fishmeal and oil increased the ecological footprint of salmon farming.

"I hate to be the one to say this," ventured OI's Bruce Anderson, "but maybe we shouldn't be growing these fish at all." Tyedmers smiled until Anderson added, "maybe we should concentrate on developing the technology and selling that to other countries."

Tyedmers had ventured as far as he could go. The paradigm shift from measuring sustainability by net profit to measuring it by ecological footprint would have to wait.

If nothing else, however, Tyedmers kept his eye on the ball. "I don't like to call anything unsustainable," he said to me that evening. "But I would say that growing carnivorous finfish offshore is heading in an unsustainable direction." The solution, he believed, was to grow other species. Carnivorous fish producers already knew that a shortage of feed fish was imminent, but the feed production system itself also used large amounts of fossil fuel energy that Tyedmers foresaw as being less and less plentiful. "Fossil fuel availability per capita has been in decline since 1978," he said. "Petroleum production is peaking or will peak in the near future." What, Tyedmers wondered, was the point of developing a food production system that relied on large quantities of a diminishing resource bound to become more expensive. "They might do better focusing on mollusks," he said of the offshore seafood farmers.

At a picnic held for the task force the next day, I met Hauke Kite-Powell, an economist at the Woods Hole Ocean Policy Center. An innocent-looking blond in his early forties, his bulging calves betrayed his passion for bicycling.

He had spoken to the panel the day before and I had an idea where Kite-Powell stood, having read a paper he had cowritten on access to the EEZ. In it, he stated a standard position that even if aquaculture produced less fish and created fewer jobs than commercial fishing, if fish farmers could reap a higher net profit from an area than fishermen, the area should be turned entirely over to aquaculture. He and many others believed the neoclassical economics tenet that resource allocation should be based solely on profit-generating potential that represented "the highest good to the nation."

We chatted a bit about cycling and our kids. He had missed Tyedmers' presentation, so I summarized it for him, and even knowing his background, his reaction surprised me.

"If it is more efficient to feed them plankton then that is what we need to do," he said. Ignoring the fact that poultry and pig feed manufacturers had directly and indirectly paid for the development of the fishmeal and fish oil industry, and that fish farming essentially took over an existing system, Kite-Powell suggested building an entire new industry that harvested plankton and processed it into feed for millions of tons of cod and salmon.

Rather than invest in turning plankton into fish food, Tyedmers had suggested developing aquaculture that utilized primary production more efficiently.

The systems were not black-and-white however, and many good ideas fit both models. Polyculture for instance, the growing of mussels and scallops in proximity to finfish, capitalized on the high nutrient levels around the cages. The filter feeding mollusks transformed the high levels of fecal matter from the fish into human food, increasing the food output without significantly expanding the ecological footprint.

On our trip out to the Isles of Shoals, Michael Chambers had harvested some mussels and scallops grown in suspension culture near the fish pens. "Look at this," he said opening a mussel from one of the hanging ropes near the fish pens off New Hampshire. It burst open, full of smooth orange-colored meat. "You would never see that amount of meat in a wild mussel." The scallops too, held extremely large meats. I tasted a couple. "What do you think?" asked Chambers.

"Kind of bland," I said, and watched his gears start turning: how could he fix that?

"Maybe it's the time of year," he said.

"Maybe."

Polyculture also gave fishermen a chance to cash in on off-shore aquaculture. According to Kite-Powell, setting up mussel and scallop farms would be within the economic reach of commercial fishermen looking to augment their incomes. "We did an experiment to look at the economic viability of farming blue mussels on longlines," said Kite-Powell, and according to his numbers, a mussel farm consisting of 120 longlines, each 120 meters long and seeded with mussels, would cost about $1.5 million to set up. He predicted the farm would be able to harvest one thousand tons of mussels per year, generating anywhere from $2 to $4 million in gross revenue.

Gradually, industrial aquaculture has realized that grow-out systems need to resemble natural ecosystems and mimic the cyclical dynamics of natural ecosystems where waste from one process became fuel for another. Polyculture had been practiced for centuries in China, where carp were farmed in rice paddies. The fish farmers dried out the ponds and gathered up the gasping fish from the mud, then planted rice that utilized the nutrients, carp excrement, left in the soil.

Closed-cycle systems worked and shrimp farmers, too, took the path of moving their farms to new locations and creating self-sustaining ecosystems within the ponds.

But where salmon and cod growers took their net pens further offshore, shrimp farms moved onshore. Beginning in Belize, on the Caribbean shore of Central America, shrimp aquaculture pioneers started experimenting with advanced techniques that would resolve several of shrimp farming's problems simultaneously. Farmers started growing shrimp in densely packed tanks onshore. Rather than exchange water, these farmers aerated the tanks heavily and recirculated the water.

Russ Allen, one of the pioneers of the Belize method, got started in the shrimp farming business working for four hundred dollars a month in the 1970s. "It was sort of a case of being in the right place at the right time with the right education," he said from his home near Lansing. "I went down to work on a sailboat in the Galapagos Islands and when I got tired of taking care of tourists I got into shrimp farming."

Allen had been trained to set up farm ponds in the United States. "It was basic pond management," he said of those first farms in South America. "Looking at carrying capacity, pH, and things like that."

While he managed to make a living, Allen professed to have been driven by environmental concerns rather than the profit motive. "In the beginning, we thought of it as being better than trawling for shrimp," he said. "Not that we didn't make mistakes in understanding our impacts on the environment." Allen called the outcry about mangrove destruction a myth. "There was so much other land that was open—the salt flats within the mangroves that were much better for growing shrimp that that's where 99 percent of the people went first. Of course there were some mangroves cut down, but those were the farms that went out of business first." The real problem, he believed, was the uncontrolled growth of the industry beyond ecological limits of the supporting estuaries. "I think degradation of the estuaries from the effluent caused some of the diseases we've seen. One of the last farms I built in Ecuador was on the Taura River where Taura virus first appeared and I'd have to say that's something that cropped up from the environmental problem. Everywhere that kind of rapid development went on anywhere in the world they all ended up having their own disease problems," said Allen.

After ten years in Ecuador, Allen moved to Belize, where he helped develop the zero exchange method, where the water in the tanks was recirculated through filters and aerated, offering the shrimp a stable growing environment and protecting them from diseases. "We started focusing on biosecurity and fast growth," he said. But the Belize system, as it came to be known, proved unattractive to many investors. "You go to a grower in a third world country and say I can build you a semi-intensive pond for $5,000 a hectare, or a zero exchange system for $150,000 a hectare: that just sounds like too much to them and they stick with semi-intensive," he said.

Allen gave up on the project in 1994 and moved back to Michigan, where he began growing tropical shrimp on the fringe of the nation's northern rust belt. He built tanks in greenhouses and stocked them with *P. vannamei*. "We've got production costs down to seventy or eighty cents a pound," said Allen. "Nobody can compete with that. And this is probably the most environmentally sustainable form of raising shrimp in the world." Allen foresaw a bright future for his farm. "I think this is the future of the industry," he said. "Right now people eat around four pounds of shrimp per year, compared to sixty-five pounds of chicken. I'd say there is plenty of room for growth."

Allen continues to struggle with moving the project from the experimental to the commercial stage. Among other things, he couldn't get access to the fastest growing shrimp developed by the U.S. Marine Shrimp Farming Program. "I don't know why, but they just won't give them to me." In addition he had diffi-culty garnering support from the state. "What I want to do now is get the environmental community involved. See if I can get them to be less critical and put some of their money behind this. If they did, it could really turn the corner."

❧

Far from the cold gray winters of Michigan, blue waves broke on the shores of Hawaii's Big Island, where the Oceanic Institute pur-sues research intended to wean shrimp off fishmeal diets. With backing from the Shrimp Farming Program and an ATP grant, the nonprofit research institute worked on a five-year, sixteen-million-dollar project to develop what they dubbed the "Bio-Zest" system. Shawn Moss, the lead researcher for the system, felt it would offer environmentally sustainable, biosecure shrimp production, and eliminate the feed problem. In the Bio-Zest system the shrimp would grow in the same sort of recirculating tanks and raceways developed by Allen, but they would feed on a microbial soup called floc.

According to Moss, ammonia-nitrogen could be removed from a recirculating system through assimilation into microbial biomass. Shrimp could feed on the bacteria, reducing the cost of production. "What we're working on is creating a self-sustaining microbial community within the tanks," he said. The Oceanic Institute joined forces with the Pennsylvania-based Ziegler Feeds and Sy-Aqua, a subsidiary of Sygen, a British-owned genetic improvement company that in 2003 bought the largest shrimp hatchery in Mexico.

Moss wrote a paper called the *Greening of the Blue Revolution* in which he, like Russ Allen, saw the shrimp industry of the future as a land-based industry. He, too, wanted to grow shrimp in tanks that would protect them from wild-borne diseases and at the same time protect the wild from effluent. In addition, Moss believed shrimp would eventually be fed on vegetable proteins rather than marine fish, and that genetic engineering would lead to fast growing animals needed to pay for the expensive infrastructure.

Are people working on transgenic shrimp? I asked.

"Yes," said Moss.

"Like who?"

"Me."

The prospects of sustainable shrimp farming seemed far ahead of salmon and other carnivorous finfish, and as the industry moved toward land-based superintensive production, Moss was among the many striving to create fast-growing disease-resistant shrimp. It was a race, as Jim McVey said, and demanded the most advanced technology.

KURT KLIMPEL, AQUA BOUNTY LAB, SAN DIEGO, CA 2005

"Wait 'til you meet this guy," said Bob Rosenberry as we pulled into the Aqua Bounty parking lot on our way to meet molecular biologist Kurt Klimpel. "He's amazing. He'll keep you going for hours." Klimpel, wearing a bright Hawaiian shirt and a thick gold chain around his neck, met us at the reception desk and walked us to his office. On the way, he asked me about my book. I told him that, among other things, it would track the growth of shrimp farming from the boom years to the appearance of disease and beyond. He stopped me in midsentence, sensing my tone. "Is the boom over? I hear it's just beginning."

"How so?" I asked.

Klimpel smiled a knowing smile. "Biotechnology," he said, and we stepped into a windowless room adorned with pictures of his family and race cars—his two loves.

Klimpel sat down and began explaining the challenges he faced and how he hoped to overcome them. In the late '90s, as white spot and Taura ravaged the shrimp farming industry, Klimpel had joined other scientists around the world in attempts to create transgenic shrimp resistant to the major viral diseases.

"The problem with that," said Klimpel, "is that the shrimp egg is so small and grows so fast." He pointed out that while salmon eggs can be a quarter inch in diameter, shrimp eggs are microscopic. "Besides that, in creating a transgenic species you have to introduce new genetic material before the egg cell begins to divide. With salmon eggs, you have as long as sixteen hours to do that, but with shrimp you have only a couple of minutes. The egg's cells begin to divide almost immediately. By the time you physically move eggs from a broodstock tank to the lab you've lost your opportunity."

Aqua Bounty headed in a new direction. "We're moving to therapeutics," said Klimpel, who as of 2006 had spent nine years of studying the white spot virus and how it entered the shrimp. He had identified the proteins on the white spot virus that interact with the proteins in the shrimp's intestines, enabling him to develop a blocker molecule that coated the shrimp's intestines and prevented it from ingesting the virus.

Lab tests had been 100 percent effective. "But that's in the lab," said Klimpel. "We can do anything in the lab; the real world is different."

❧

In a room full of blue light refracted through stacks of aquariums amid the bubbling of aerators, a few white shrimp, *P. vannamei*, paddled patiently, their long translucent bodies bouncing off the glass of their individual tanks. Other shrimp lay prostrate on the bottoms of their tanks, and still other tanks sat empty. Five days before, all held shrimp that were fed the white spot virus. The remaining live ones had been treated with Aqua Bounty's new drug. The dying shrimp had held out due to their own natural resistance, and the empty tanks had held to the shrimp that perished quickly.

In a large room full of incubators, the lab churned out the new drug as fast as possible. "We're going to have expand our production facilities," said Klimpel.

Aqua Bounty's market for the drug existed primarily among semi-intensive shrimp farmers in Latin America, from Mexico to Ecuador and Peru. While Klimpel concentrated on therapeutics, other scientists such as Moss used biotechnology to develop fast-growing shrimp suitable for land-based operations.

Transgenic shrimp may seem beyond the limits of available technology, but genetic markers identified on the *P. vannamei* genome have helped sharpen selective breeding. Moss and other scientist use the markers to identify desirable and undesirable traits.

"We use it to accelerate the selective breeding process," said Moss. "Not to create transgenic shrimp."

❧

Klimpel claimed that delivering genetic material to shrimp eggs was not yet feasible in October 2005. But several months earlier, a patent filed in the name of Dr. Piera Sun, of the Pacific Biological Research Center, claimed she had found a way to deliver genetic material into shrimp eggs. Sun, a diminutive middle-aged woman of Korean descent, apparently succeeded where many had failed. While not willing to discuss details of her method, Sun acknowledged that a patent was filed in her name for a scientific breakthrough that held great potential.

If Sun's technique worked, it would open the door to the possibility of transgenic shrimp immune to the major viruses. Molecular biologists could potentially create rapidly growing transgenic shrimp similar to the fast-growing transgenic salmon Aqua Bounty had unveiled in 1999.

TRANSGENIC SALMON

I met Joe McGonigle at a Maine legislative hearing years before. He had preceded Sebastian Belle as director of the Maine Aquaculture Association, and appeared before the Marine Resources committee to testify against a bill that would have given local communities more control over the leasing process. "They did that in Washington," he warned the Marine Resources Committee, "and there hasn't been a lease granted since." I sat listening, wondering why he would draw such stark attention to the fact that many communities did not want fish farms. But such was Joe McGonigle, a big hulking Irish American with a plainspoken and graceless style that assumed you agreed with everything he said, and he made you want to. I spoke with him again in 2003.

"This is going to radically transform the economics of production," said McGonigle, who has since become Aqua Bounty's vice president of business development. "But right now transgenic salmon are considered an adulterated food. We can't sell them without FDA [Food and Drug Administration] approval."

According to McGonigle, salmon farmers in the United States have expressed a guarded interest in GM fish. Commercialization depended on approval from a variety of government agencies, most importantly the FDA, which required that the mature fish could not breed, an expensive proposition. "The whole process will cost about eight million, two or three million for FDA approval alone," said McGonigle. "Our hope is that we can satisfy government officials that our fish our sterile."

With a $1.7 million matching grant from the Department of Commerce Advanced Technology Program (ATP), the company worked on processes to sterilize the fish so that if some escaped, they would not pose a genetic threat to wild salmon. "We tried a lot of things," said McGonigle. "But there have been trade-offs between sterility and survival." After several failures with chemical treatments and thermal shock, the company began experimenting with creating triploid salmon. Technicians put eggs into a cylinder and pressurized them at 9,000 PSI for three minutes.

"We have consistently had 100 percent sterility," said McGonigle. "We need to scale up the verification process for smolts."

McGonigle believed that GM salmon would be a boon for the environment. He pointed out that most salmon in the United States come from Chile, where environmental controls are lax and production costs much lower. "If we can cut production costs by getting a fish to market in eleven months, that will lead to a radical restructuring of the economics—a leveling of the playing field," said McGonigle, predicting increased production in the United States and Canada, "where environmental controls are tighter."

While McGonigle hoped to use biotechnology to the benefit of the salmon industry, it may have more to offer the nascent cod farms sprouting off the coasts of almost all North Atlantic rim countries as well as Chile.

Salmon yield 60 percent edible meat per pound of whole fish, while cod yield a meager 40 percent. In terms of dollars, a ten-pound salmon selling for $2.50 a pound at a farm, yields six pounds of fillets at a cost of $4.17 a pound, plus processing. A similar-sized cod selling for $2.50/lb. at the farm yields four pounds of fillets at $6.25 a pound. By the time they hit the seafood market, the cod fillets cost over ten dollars a pound and the salmon under eight dollars.

By 2006, the international cod genome project, supported by the United States, Canada, Iceland, and Norway, identified genetic markers to assist selective breeding. But the Norwegian government among others has recommended strengthening programs that would lead to a sequencing of the entire cod genome.

To achieve full genome sequences, Norway should as soon as possible take initiative to form international consortia of stakeholders that can make a common effort towards genome sequencing of selected marine species (e.g. salmon and cod) within five years. Central research environments should get responsibility to work out the consortia in close collaboration with the [Norwegian] Research Council and Ministry of Fisheries to ensure anchoring with the financial institutions at an early stage."

—Division for Strategic Planning,
the Research Council of Norway

In Canada, Jane Symonds took the reins of a $12,706,092 cod genome study at the Huntsman Marine Science Center in St. Andrews, New Brunswick.

"Traditional fisheries provide an important basis of cultural and economic activity in Atlantic Canada, although the fisheries for some species such as Atlantic salmon and Atlantic cod have severely declined," wrote Symonds in her rationale for the project. "The decline in Atlantic salmon stocks served as an incentive to develop today's aquaculture sector, which generates more than $200 million in annual revenue in New Brunswick alone." Fish farmers applied the lessons learned in salmon farming to other carnivorous species in an effort to maintain a growth industry. Estimates showed that cod farming in Newfoundland alone could generate more than $100 million in new wealth while meeting consumer demand for a high-quality food resource. Bad weather bad luck and a parasite, *Loma branchialis,* which killed 63 percent of the fish in one pen, brought Newfoundland cod farming to a halt. Nonetheless, in 2006, Cooke Aquaculture managed to harvest their first crop of cod.

As with shrimp, biotechnology promised to aid in developing vaccines for the viral and bacterial pathogens that have already taken a toll on the salmon, and threaten the developing cod farming industry.

Martha Zarain, Culiacán, Sinaloa 2005

Amid all the multimillion-dollar projects leading towards larger and more intensive shrimp farms, where economies of scale would give companies massive buying and selling power that would lead, theoretically, to lower-priced shrimp, one Mexican researcher took a different path. Biologist Martha Zarain became well known in shrimp farming circles after she isolated the Mexican strain of Taura virus. I had interviewed her at the Centro de Ciencia in Culiacán in 2003, and she had mentioned that the best way to combat shrimp disease was to grow shrimp in net pens in the open water, and that she would soon be launching a test project.

When I met her the second time in Culiacán, Sinaloa, Zarain was dressed in designer jeans, and had her hair down. I had returned to Culiacán with hopes of visiting her pilot project in Bahia Santa Maria. But the timing did not work, so she brought me a slide show, which we looked at while sitting in the restaurant of the hotel in Culiacán, Sinaloa.

Somewhere on the way from wild fisheries to aquaculture, Zarain turned back toward fisheries. The shrimp farming boom had left the small boat fishermen behind. They were being displaced rather than embraced by the new industry. Zarain sought to get them into aquaculture by utilizing floating net pen technology imported from Brazil. In 2005, after completing a pilot project the year before, fishermen from a local cooperative received 225 three by three meter pens, which they stocked at low densities with hatchery stock.

"The fishermen can use their pangas to move the nets around," said Zarain. "That allows them to take advantage of natural food supplies. Because the shrimp have access to clean water and are not crowded, they will be less stressed and less prone to disease outbreaks even if they come into contact with a virus," she said.

The numbers looked promising. The fishermen expressed enthusiasm, according to Zarain, but observers from the mainstream shrimp industry were not impressed.

"It's a social program," said Aqua Bounty's Henry Clifford of the $1.7 million project. "It'll fold as soon as the government money is gone."

"I don't think much of that idea," said Bob Rosenberry. "How much can they supply?"

Social concerns, the idea of fairly distributing the wealth generated by shrimp farming, played an important part in agendas of people like Rohana Subasinghe of the FAO, but did not amount to much in the view of the shrimp farming establishment. As far as Rosenberry, Clifford and others in shrimp farming were concerned, change was a part of life, and those displaced by the industry would adjust.

ECONOMIC GUIDES

Jim Anderson of the University of Rhode Island proposed an economic solution to aquaculture's problems. "Why is it some sectors prosper while others do not?" Anderson asked, and proposed that economic sustainability had to precede social and environmental sustainability. Anderson defined as "economic sustainability" those aquaculture projects that generated profits consistently and could absorb shocks to the system, such as disease events, competition, and natural disasters.

In *Sustainable Aquaculture: What Does It Mean and How Do We Get There?* Anderson wrote: "If there is no expectation that economically viable enterprises are possible, then there are no environmental issues related to aquaculture that matter. There are no social equity or income distribution issues related to aquaculture that matter and there are no aquaculture regulations and policies that matter."

As with fisheries before it, solutions in aquaculture can only go so far; they must enable the enterprise to continue to generate profit. "Zero production might be sustainable," said Anderson, "but not very interesting or relevant."

Within the abstract world of economic models, Anderson argued that "the development and protection of well-defined property rights are the essential first steps in developing a sustainable aquaculture sector."

Strong property rights imbedded in stable governing institutions and policies would create the economic incentives—the assumption that the investor could reap the profit—leading to sustainable aquaculture.

But, Anderson warned, if governing institutions "are unstable, unfair or corrupt, then sustainability is unlikely."

According to Anderson, uncertainty increased the discount rate. When the discount rate went up it meant diminishing prospects of future returns and led to overexploitation in the short term. In a world of diminishing resources, terrorism, and instability, uncertainty seemed to be the one thing everyone could count on.

Since it began as a state agricultural college in 1888, the campus of my alma mater, the University of Rhode Island, has grown to cover twelve hundred acres. Concrete and steel megaliths stretched out into the farmland that once surrounded the original stone buildings at the heart of the campus. The new buildings allowed the university to expand its enrollment and the breadth of subjects it taught, but it was within the walls of those old buildings that people like Anderson and my old teacher Andreas Holmsen preserved the ideological foundations of resource economics.

I can still see Holmsen, a six-foot-tall Norwegian, smoking his pipe in class and explaining in his heavy accent the theories of economic efficiency and maximum sustainable yield: showing us how well the models worked in a perfect world. The ideas all sounded good and I scored well in the tests. But the unfair, corrupt, and uncertain world failed, scoring straight collapsing fisheries. As Kurt Klimpel said: "We can do anything in the lab, the real world is different."

Effective solutions to fisheries and aquaculture problems might have eliminated profits, at which point one could con-clude that the enterprise was unsustainable. Difficulties arose when so much money had been invested in a project that it could not be abandoned. At that point environmental and social sustainability were sacrificed for the sake of short-term economic sustainability—all that mattered.

For Mexican fishermen and ejidatarios facing faltering fisheries and limited opportunities in agriculture—which had long absorbed the rural unemployed—shrimp farms had offered a glimmer of hope. But the region's new industry could not support everyone, and for many former fishermen who once listened to the wild birds that filled the lagoons, that meant making a move, usually to urban areas.

The day Sergio Larraguibel and I drove back from his shrimp farm on Estero Bamocha, in the winter of 2005, he pointed to long rows of cinder- block houses being built on the outskirts of Navojoa. "Those are for the people coming in from the campo," he said. "There is no more work for them there." Larraguibel believed that the North American Free Trade Agreement (NAFTA), globalization, and the neoclassical economic system served these itinerant campesinos well. "NAFTA created the maquiladoras," he said, in reference to the numerous factories that have cropped up along the United States/Mexican border. "They provide the jobs for these people."

Working the glitches out of the system: Offshore aquaculture pioneer Michael Chambers and an assistant carry bags of food for hungry halibut swimming in a net pen ten meters below the surface. The automated feeder (the big yellow buoy) broke down, and for five days bad weather kept the men from reaching the site six miles off the New Hampshire coast. Photo by Paul Molyneaux.

Armando Alcantar tosses mullet into a crate in Navopatia, a fishing village hemmed in by shrimp farms in a part of the Agiabampo Estuary once recommended for designation as a national park. With this catch, a morning's work, Alcantar made less than eight dollars after expenses. Photo by Paul Molyneaux.

As inshore catches decline, small shrimp boats (foreground) give way to the high seas fleet (background) in Yaváros, Sonora. Photo by Paul Molyneaux.

Last of a dying breed: Captain Gary McLeod (on ladder) and the crew of the scallop boat *E.E. Pierce*, owned by Clearwater Fine Foods. These men have worked for a share of the catch all their lives and take pride in their speed when shucking scallops. The few who made it aboard Clearwater's new automated boat received wages and faced the prospect of being displaced by automated shucking machines. Photo by Paul Molyneaux.

Michael Chambers holds a market-size halibut grown in a submerged fish pen six miles off the coast of New Hampshire—part of a pilot project that he and many others hope will lead to increased fish farming in the open ocean. Photo by Paul Molyneaux.

The sardine carrier *Double Eagle* delivers herring from a night's fishing to a lobster wharf on Vinalhaven Island, Maine, where the fish will be sold as lobster bait. Over seventy percent of Maine's herring catch goes back into the water as bait. Elsewhere in the world, fisheries for small pelagic species supply the fishmeal and oil that go into aquaculture feeds. Photo by Paul Molyneaux.

A feed barge at a salmon farm near Deer Island, New Brunswick, delivering a portion of the estimated 1.5 million tons of salmon feed used annually to grow over a million tons of salmon worldwide. Photo by Paul Molyneaux.

Salmon pens in Cobscook Bay, Maine. The pens that once promised a bright future for the fishermen of Lubec and Eastport, Maine, are now owned by one company, Cooke Aquaculture of New Brunswick, Canada. The industry continues to battle disease and re-establish itself after the infectious salmon anemia virus forced growers to clear over two million fish from the bay in 2001. Photo by Paul Molyneaux.

Fisherman Armando Alcantar and his crewman clear mullet from their gill net. The mangrove slough in the background used to teem with shrimp in the summer. Less than a mile to the north, and to the south, shrimp farmers have bulldozed earth dikes into the bay and created ponds where most of the area's shrimp now grow. Photo by Paul Molyneaux.

At the public wharf in Lubec, Maine, Gene Blake lifts the lid of a container containing salmon that died in the outbreak of infectious salmon anemia in Cobscook Bay in 2001. Photo by Paul Molyneaux.

The definition of efficiency, Herb Bishop sits in a dory full of herring caught in a herring weir. These fish traps, first used thousands of years ago, require scant resources to build and maintain. They once lined the coast of Maine and produced as many as 30,000 tons of fish annually. Photo by Paul Molyneaux.

No Trespassing, warns a sign at the intake canal of the shrimp farm Acuícola Clej, near the Agiabampo Estuary. Three years after several hundred acres of virgin cactus forest and shoreline mangroves were cleared in 2001, the farm was abandoned. Older farms in the area have produced consistent crops of shrimp, but almost all succumbed to an outbreak of white spot virus in 2005. Photo by Paul Molyneaux.

11

GLOBALIZATION OF THE OCEAN

Within the context of global economics, the shrimp farms bull-dozed out of Sonora's fog desert represented a solution to stalled economic growth: "a means by which poor countries could exploit their comparative advantage," as the FAO's Rohana Subasinghe had said. Subasinghe did not propose that industrial-scale shrimp and salmon aquaculture would keep aquaculture's promise to feed the world, but he believed that generating export income would benefit small countries. "My son disagrees with me, of course," said Subasinghe. "He's anti-globalization."

As globalization based on the neoclassical model for free trade spread throughout the world, it led to some fundamental debates on everything from ethics to the definition of sustainability—which boiled down to who would benefit. I wanted to hear what that debate sounded like within the Subasinghe family, and made a date to talk it over with Rohana and his son Ruwan in London.

I left the shrimp farms in southern Sonora, and headed for London. On Easter Sunday 2005, the bus hummed along on Mexico's Route 15, heading for the Nogales, Arizona, border crossing. I looked out the window at a sight that many experts claimed was a first, at least since the conquistadors arrived. A freak of nature had sent rainstorms across the Sonoran desert all winter, creating a verdant cactus garden; the various species: hecho, pitahaya, and senita bulged with water, their skins smooth, clean, and deep green. Flowers hung between the thorns and spines, dotting the landscape with bursts of color: yellow, pink, red, and orange. Such was the desert as no white people had ever seen it. An old man in a white cowboy hat, his callused feet in a pair of huaraches, watched me looking out the window. "*Esta un siñal de viene El Niño malo*— it's a sign of a bad El Niño coming," he said, nodding toward the desert.

On my way to visit the Subasinghes I stopped at a conference in New York to hear some of the world's experts share their views on globalization. I arrived within the gray confines of the city on a rainy March morning, and hiked up Amsterdam Avenue to Columbia University's school of journalism. Inside the journalism building a paper sign posted in the lobby said "Covering Globalization Workshop," and gave directions to the event hosted by Nobel Prize winning economist Joseph Stiglitz. The three-day workshop also included presentations by Jeffrey Sachs, the architect of the Russia's transition to a market economy, Thomas Friedman, author of *The World Is Flat,* and other prominent economists. There were no fish experts there, but I hoped at least to get a sense of what the big thinkers and the journalists who covered them thought about globalization and natural resources.

In a large meeting room, journalists from all over the world found their seats and chatted in a variety of languages. I looked at the list of participants and saw only three U.S. journalists in a group of twenty-five, and all of us worked at least part time in other countries. The organizers had done well, and the points of view represented were varied in many respects.

As we washed down bagels and danishes with cups of tea and coffee, Anya Schiffrin stepped up to the podium. In a brief introduction, she claimed that the benefits of globalization were many. "It's better to be working at a Nike factory than bent over in a rice paddy," she said, adding that development could not take place without the media as a watchdog.

On the one hand, Schiffrin made us feel like part of something big, something inherently American: like free speech and democracy. But her assumptions about whether the factory was better than the rice paddy troubled me. I had worked in fields and factories, and if I received a fair price for my produce I would have chosen the fields by a wide margin. Among the Mexicans I knew, the factories of Nogales were the very last resort.

Schiffrin went on. "The free press has a key role to play in helping people think critically. It also limits corruption and guarantees human rights." She urged us to write about other countries, but not about issues we didn't understand. "Some journalists get moralistic and hectoring," she said. "That's not our job." According to Schiffrin, journalists had a duty to dig into stories, to unmask corruption, and unearth facts that might not otherwise see the light of day. "Drug issues for example, are deeply tied to politics and legitimate business."

I had heard from some reliable sources in Sonora that many shrimp farms existed only to launder drug money. Billie DeWalt alluded to it in his report *Shrimp Farming and the Environment*, prepared for the World Wildlife Fund, as did Maria Cruz-Torres in her book *Lives of Dust and Water*. A shrimp farmer I talked to played it down. "Drugs are not that important to our economy," he told me. But at the same time he noted that the road we were on, the trunk road that ran parallel to Route 15 along much of the coast, served as a major artery for drug traffic.

I asked Anya Schiffrin how one went about serving the public in uncovering drug activity, money laundering, and corruption without getting killed. One of the staff directed me to the Committee to Protect Journalists. The New York–based committee worked to get journalists out of jail, among other things, but did not act as a shield in difficult situations. Out on the trunk road, they would do me no good, not that I was going to chase drug stories; those issues looked more like symptoms than root causes.

Stiglitz followed Schiffrin to the podium and cut right to root causes. He explained some of the groundbreaking work that had pitted him against the World Bank, the International Monetary Fund (IMF), and other engineers of globalization. "The IMF showed no evidence that capital market liberalization was good for growth," said Stiglitz. "Their economic models are not based in reality." Stiglitz contended that IMF loans made to float foreign currency in failing economies simply protected the interests of United States "speculators."

Among other things, Stiglitz revealed some intriguing facts

about the workings of international finance. "The United States borrows from poor countries at 2 percent interest," he said, "and then lends the money back at 18 percent. A peculiar situation." Poor countries, Stiglitz pointed out had to repay foreign debt in U.S. dollars, often bankrupting themselves in the process.

Rapid aquaculture development in the 1980s seemed to fit Stiglitz's scenario of speculators determined to get returns on their instruments, even at the cost of global stability. While industrial-scale shrimp and salmon aquaculture might not have served rural fishing communities or the long-term interests of economically depressed regions, its potential to boost export earnings made it a winner in cash-strapped developing nations and the resource-based economies of places like Maine. In light of Stiglitz's comments, the development of the export aquaculture industry looked more like a solution to a financial problem than a path to food security.

But Stiglitz held firmly to the view that human ingenuity would compensate for declining natural resources. "I'm optimistic about our ability to innovate in the long run. The exhaustion of natural resources is not a problem, the main risk is to sinks," he said, noting the rapid decline in the earth's ability to absorb waste. The so-called sinks—the atmosphere and the oceans—could no longer process all the waste generated by economic activity. As they filled up, they became obstacles to economic growth. Stiglitz however, did not seem to dwell on resource issues. He put his primary focus on finance as the trouble spot in globalization that needed immediate repair.

Mark Weisbrot, the codirector of the Washington, D.C.–based Center for Economic and Policy Research, echoed many of Stiglitz's views in the next presentation. But where Stiglitz looked primarily at Asia, Weisbrot searched for an explanation to lagging economic growth in Latin America. Both saw economic growth as an absolute necessity. "If there is no economic growth, it means that any gains for the poor will have to come from somewhere else," said Weisbrot. "It is very difficult to carry out this kind of massive income redistribution without violence."

To illustrate the lackluster growth in Latin America, Weisbrot projected a familiar-looking graph onto a screen above the podium. He intended the curve, which rose steeply on a vertical axis through the years 1960 to 1980 and then fell sharply in the following years, to show the rise and fall of growth rates in Latin America, but to me it appeared hauntingly familiar. The curving line looked exactly like many illustrations I had seen of the expansion and decline of various fisheries, many of which registered meteoric growth during the years 1960–1980 and then plummeted from 1980 to the present.

"Do you think the slowdown in growth has anything to do with resource depletion?" I asked.

"Not at all," said Weisbrot. "There is still plenty of capacity for growth in Latin America." It struck me that his answer, too, was the same used by the most avaricious fishermen: "There's plenty of fish out there," they said as landings sank. Fisheries' managers, eager to maintain a growth industry, kept trying to tweak the system; reacting to each new crisis with regulations that proved to be too little, too late.

Resource decline spurred the redistribution of wealth, but in the opposite direction needed. In the seafood business, the most economically efficient fishing operations gained access to more resources. Increasing forms of privatization, including fish farming, led to consolidation, which sparked new investment in yet more economically efficient technology, creating an illusion of economic growth. The losers in the game tried to point out that there were two definitions of efficiency. But policy makers look only at money. The fact that low-tech fishing gear might land more fish with less energy output did not register, and the old fishing jobs lost were never tallied against the new jobs created.

Like Stiglitz, many of the journalists in the workshop focused on financial policies, and interest rates, as the keys to the economy. Others, coming from developing countries, obsessed over the subsidies the United States paid to farmers and the tariffs that kept poorer countries from cashing in on the benefits of globalization. The heavy-duty economic writers adroitly questioned particular policies guiding globalization, and seldom looked at resources or culture. But few in attendance questioned growth as the soulution to the world's economic problems.

When Columbia professor Amar Bhide suggested that the information technology boom occurring in India's Bangalore region offered limited opportunity for growth—"as an economic engine, IT isn't pulling much in Bangalore; it's unlikely it will pull much elsewhere," he said—he came under fierce attack. Two reporters from India's *Economic Times,* Pooja Kothari and Candice Zacharias, who throughout the workshop had offered congenial and polite questions, demanded a recantation from

Bhide. While Bhide called for India to create an atmosphere more conducive to growth, his comment, and the data that supported it, burst the Indian reporters' illusions of what appeared to them as robust growth.

❧

The economic rationale for free trade did not easily accommodate limits. It worked great driving the engine up the hill of resource wealth as in Weisbrot's graph, but it had no brakes, and zipped right past sustainability on the way down. According to the dominant model, the limit to fisheries' exploitation was extinction.

It was profitable to kill the last great auk, and the last Stellar's sea cow. It was profitable to take cod stocks to levels of economic extinction. Without the intervention of the International Whaling Commission the market would have signaled whalers to kill the last North Atlantic right whale.

Contrary to the dominant view, economic growth appeared to be the basic recipe for disaster in one resource industry after another. It came as a contradiction that well-intentioned people promoting growth as a remedy for world's food security consistently created more problems than they solved. I wondered if they could find solutions outside the economic growth model— solutions demanded in the resource-limited industries of fisheries, and in aquaculture that relied on fisheries.

But no one seemed to walk that road. In his book *Globalization and Its Discontents*, Stiglitz promoted economic growth. What made him a radical challenger of the establishment was his contention that the market needed government controls. He argued for government policies to protect nations, people, and the environment within an economic system he and most of the workshop attendees otherwise kept faith with.

In a running discussion at a cocktail party at Stiglitz and Schiffrin's Upper West Side apartment, Patricia Mercado, editor of Mexico's *El Economista*, Anthony Wilson of *The Trinidad Guardian*, and I discussed the pros and cons of NAFTA.

Wilson had earlier asked, politely, if I was a socialist. I focused my questions on Mercado. "When you make every industry economically efficient what do you do with the displaced people?" I asked.

"The people knew that free trade was coming for ten years," said Mercado. "They didn't do anything to prepare for it."

"They should have consolidated, invested in technology," said Wilson.

"The Mexican government was unprepared for NAFTA, how could millions of campesinos with limited education and resources get ready?"

"People are lazy," said Mercado. "It's a cultural curse."

"The Mexicans I've met have been pretty hardworking, if they have work. That's the trouble, here in the U.S. the economy can still absorb displaced labor, but out in *ejido* country it's life or death."

Mercado shrugged, "That's life, my mama told me," she said.

HUNGER IN THE GLOBAL ECONOMY

In London, I called Rohana Subasinghe, and then Ruwan. We'd meet at a tube stop near Ruwan's apartment, and find a place to chat, preferably without too much background noise. At one thirty I locked my bike at the tube stop near Piccadilly and waited. A crowd came out of the tube exit and I searched their faces. The crowd thinned and a man about my age and another in his early twenties stood on the corner looking around. Rohana and I had not seen each other in two years and we did not recognize each other at first, but our mutual searching looks confirmed who we were. After we shook hands all around, I suggested we go to Starbucks, but Ruwan refused. "I don't go to Starbucks," he said.

We went to a independent coffee shop. We served ourselves and went downstairs where plush furniture surrounded coffee tables. Rohana and Ruwan sat next to each other on a sofa and I faced them, sitting on another sofa. It seemed a bit dark, and there was some music, a little intrusive, but nobody blew horns in our ears.

I put a tape recorder on the coffee table, something I rarely do but I had come a long way and did not want to lose a word. We talked a bit about our lives, sitting there trying to figure each other out.

"What are you studying?" I asked Ruwan.

"I just finished my first degree, in law."

"Gandhi was a lawyer."

"Right, he practiced in South Africa, a great man, one of my idols."

We talked about fair trade, the foundation promoting equitable trade that put more money in the hands of small producers.

"It's logical to us," said Ruwan, who was active in the foundation, "but not to the market. The market puts profit over people."

"Yes, but what is the difference between fair trade and ethical trade? It's all market mechanics," said Rohana. "All of them, fair trade, eco-labeling. Then there is ethical trade, consumers want to know that their products are not made using child labor. But there are no widely accepted standards."

He noted that Pope John Paul II had come to the FAO every year, or sent a message about poverty and hunger. "He came to the world food summit in 1996 and asked us, when you formulate economic policy don't think only of profit. Think of Solidarity." Rohana explained that the word Solidarity had a "big meaning."

Ruwan, who had founded the first social forum movement in the United Kingdom, began to explain Solidarity, but Rohana did not yield. His vision of solidarity took a long time to explain, but seemed to boil down to getting poor people into the expanding universe, on their own terms.

He described the mechanics of global trade, controlled by the United States, Japan and the EU, and arrived at the conclusion that while large corporations dominated many markets, small operations could find a place in the global economy, "if they have the right technology." By that, Rohana meant that small growers had to have the technology necessary to conform to HACCP standards for hygiene and quality. He was working on projects to upgrade management practices of small producers in Cambodia, so that they could market their products globally. On a larger scale, Rohana pointed to the use of antibiotics. "There's no need for this, we need to get people to produce without antibiotics, to understand the benefits."

"I think this is a crucial point," said Ruwan. "The FAO and the UN were well intentioned in promoting industrial aquaculture. But their good intention does not count for anything once you're feeding into the market system. Once you get there, it's all-out profit. The power of the market defeats all the good intentions the FAO had."

"That's his opinion," said Rohana. "Number one, we don't promote industrial aquaculture."

"The World Bank promotes it," said Ruwan. "And the FAO assists them."

"We promote sustainable aquaculture," said Rohana, arguing much as Jim Anderson had that sustainability rested on economic sustainability.

"This argument has been put forth since capitalist societies existed," said Ruwan. "There's always going to be social and environmental costs to satisfy the need for profit. But when you look at fair trade and organic farming, it goes to show something different can be done with this system."

Rohana defended economic sustainability while conceding a need for "balance."

"There will always be risks to society and the environment," said Rohana. "The point is to identify the what level of risk we can take. We look for the best way to produce something with the least environmental harm and the greatest social benefit, and the lowest price to the consumer. In theory this is beautiful; in practice, difficult."

"That's the big problem, isn't it?" said Ruwan, sitting on the edge of his seat while Rohana leaned back. "Every time there's a compromise, it's always the consumer who wins and the consumer is living here in the West."

Rohana walked a narrow line; he illustrated several situations that supported his son's arguments, noting the low price of shrimp and the social and environmental problems of shrimp production. He told of shrimp farmers in Asia who committed suicide because diseases wiped out their farms and left them unable to pay their debts to feed companies, and farms contaminating each other by discharging into the same lagoons they drew water from.

"How do you stop this?" asked Rohana. "Cooperation." Rohana had worked on aquaculture development since the early 1980s. He was the first Asian to head the fisheries department at the FAO, and like a lot of people who had invested their lives into something, he wanted to made it work. "I can see how this can work," he said, sounding every bit as idealistic as Ruwan. "You have to do risk analysis. We do this when we cross the road so we don't get hit. Right? So when we are looking at shrimp farming in west Africa, for example, the important thing is to understand the level of acceptable risks so you can move forward. Right?"

"Maybe," I said. "Depends on who's determining what's acceptable."

We all laughed. "That's right," said Rohana.

We took a break and as we went upstairs to get more coffee and tea I scrambled to put all I had heard into context, maybe come up with an intelligent question or two.

GLOBAL HUNGER

I recalled a quote by Pascal Lamy, director of the World Trade Organization:

"We [the WTO] are in the business of creating wealth. . . . Our member-states remain in the business of distributing this," he said. I wracked my brain trying to figure out how an organization that facilitated trade created wealth. Most observers saw trade as a mechanism for the distribution of wealth. That was indeed one of the bragging points of globalization.

Through economic consolidation and the development of global systems for redistributing wealth, the GNPs of many nations registered what appeared to be economic growth between the years 1995, when the WTO was formed, and 2005. And while abject poverty decreased in that time, the spread between rich and poor increased and more and more people, even in developed countries, slid below the poverty line.

Developing countries accounted for 50 percent of fisheries exports by value throughout the first decade of the WTO's existence. The wealthiest countries accounted for 80 percent of the imports. Per capita seafood production had declined slightly, according to FAO statistics, but per capita seafood consumption in the developing world continued to increase.

The FAO considered food security the "physical and economic access" to food and water, and as budding lawyer Ruwan argued, the shrimp and carnivorous finfish industries use up high-quality forage fish and the best water resources available to feed a relatively small number of already well-fed people. The poor people and the wild species pay the opportunity costs of these development choices, as they attempt to survive in a degraded environment that can no longer produce subsistence foods.

A significant portion of Lubec's population, such as the McCurdys, McConnells, and Murrays had migrated from Ireland during the famine. Their mobility and the ability of the U.S. economy to employ their labor enabled them to survive. A hundred fifty years later, mobility and an economy that could absorb their labor became their saviors once again, as many left the area to find jobs.

"Children under the age of five show the highest percentage of poverty," wrote Deidre Mageean, a research associate in the University of Maine's Smith Policy Center. In her extensive report on childhood hunger in Maine, Mageean continued: "Child poverty rates by county in Maine range from a high of 27.1 percent in Washington County to a low of 9.1 percent in York county."

York County has the highest per capita income in Maine, and salmon aquaculture is banned there, as it is in all but two of Maine's eight coastal counties. Creating food on an industrial scale often creates pollution and aesthetics problems that populations with options opt out of.

"Hunger in the United States appears as a chronic, mild malnutrition with more subtle physical or mental impairments. Examples of such impairments include frequent headaches, fatigue, irritability, inability to concentrate, and increased susceptibility to ill health," said Mageean.

Economically speaking, Washington County, within the borders of one of the oldest states in the union, has experienced the equivalent of a third world colonial history. Its people, according to another study, suffer from a higher rate of obesity than do people anywhere else in the state. The county's children have the highest rate of ADHD and other problems that many doctors consider nutrition-related.

In 2000, Maine Governor Angus King pointed to the two thousand jobs salmon farming created, and the position of salmon as the state's number two seafood. He touted aquaculture as the savior of the downeast Maine coast. But while aquaculture generated money, many Lubeckers had lost their greatest asset: locally produced food, much of it from the sea.

Researchers from Alaska to Mexico pointed to subsistence diets as one of the most nutritious options for the rural poor, and local agriculture and subsistence food once fed the people of eastern Maine. In 1951, hunters in Washington County shot 5,181 deer, not counting what they poached. By 2003, hunters shot a meager 134.

Old folks far inland talked to me about how they used to stock up on salt fish every fall, but the last local seafood dealer, Rick Cowles in Eastport, closed up shop in 1988, and the remnants of the small boat fleet disappeared not long after.

"Can you get me some of that salt pollock?" an 83-year-old farmer named Damon Furlong asked me in the fall of 1989. "They sell something in the store, but I don't know where it come from."

He lived up-country, about fifteen miles north of the Cobscook Bay. I salted some cod for him the next year, but when I took it up there, he was dead. The culture of subsistence diets vanished faster than the food itself.

In late summer, when the mackerel ran in Cobscook Bay, Doug Small would fire up his smoker and put out his sign for smoked mackerel. One afternoon I stopped by and worked with him. We stood in the shade of Small's barn, at a wooden table piled high with fresh mackerel. I watched as Small took a fish, cut off its head, and split it down the back. He flipped it open, scraped the guts into a gurry bucket and dropped the cleaned mackerel into a tub of brine, water salted to the saturation point. "We'll let 'em soak a day or two in the brine, and then smoke 'em," he said as I split open a fish.

I stopped over a few days later with some seasoned apple wood and traded for a few pounds of fish. At home I ate it on a bagel with cream cheese.

When the mackerel started running in 1998, I started looking for Small's sign. It never appeared. I finally pulled into his driveway one afternoon. "What's goin' on? No mackerel?"

Small looked at me. "The state came by and told me I couldn't sell 'em anymore," he said, and shook his head in disgust. "I told 'em I'll be goddamned if I'm going to quit smokin' mackerel," and nodded to the refrigerator in the barn. Inside the fridge he had plenty of product.

He gave me a package and I paid him $2.50. "Business as usual," he said. But his heart wasn't in it. Instead of proudly offering his community a healthy local food at an affordable price, he had to be sneaky, and last I knew he had given it up as a regular thing.

The Underdogs

In 1989, anthropologist Maria Cruz-Torres began documenting the changes that globalization and shrimp aquaculture brought to two typical rural Mexican ejidos: Celeya and El Cerro, in Sinaloa. In her book *Lives of Dust and Water: An Anthropology of*

Change and Resistance in Northwestern Mexico, Cruz-Torres documented the ejidos' histories since their formation in the 1960s and 1970s respectively. In roughly forty years, the Mexican communities went through changes similar to what Lubec had experienced over one hundred fifty years. The shorter time frame for the changes in Mexico made the results all the more apparent.

The original settlers of El Cerro and Celeya received the land after they applied for it under the laws of Article 27 of the Mexican Constitution. In addition to the land, the settlers of coastal ejidos received fishing rights in nearby lagoons. Cruz-Torres arrived in 1989 and found most of the ejido residents living typical rural lives supported by dependable resources. She documented a society where the men worked seasonally in their own fields, and fished or hired out as laborers on big farms to earn cash.

Among other things, the men waded out into the shallows and cast their atarayas, loading up with small shrimp. The women worked at home. In season, they salted and dried the shrimp, which they in turn ate, sold, or gave away. What Cruz-Torres saw was, according to *Nutrition in Latin America*, the best arrangement rural people could have to guarantee themselves a nutritious diet: reliable sources of subsistence foods from land and sea, and opportunities to earn money.

"Some nutritionists have suggested that raising cash crops can lead to deterioration in nutritional status and have strongly advised against farmers shifting to these from subsistence crops," stated the report. "After an extensive review of the literature on this association, the authors noted, 'In many cases nutritional evaluation of agricultural development projects was an afterthought. Impact evaluation was undertaken after the projects were well underway . . . sometimes on the basis of a single survey.' According to these authors, the main limitations of the studies reviewed were lack of baseline data on nutritional anthropometry [the study of the human body over time] and inadequate or nonexistent control groups. They concluded, 'The question of whether agricultural development has a positive effect on nutrition remains unanswered.'"

❧

By 2003, Cruz-Torres found the ejidos in crisis. In 1992, after the changes to Article 27 gave ejidatarios private property rights, many residents sold their meager plots and became full-time farm laborers, or moved north to work in the maquiladoras on the U.S. border. According to Cruz-Torres, in 1989 around 15 percent of the ejido women over the age of fourteen worked outside the home. In 2002, the number had risen to over 60 percent. My limited research in Agiabampo, a community similar to those Cruz-Torres studied, generally confirmed her findings. Shrimp farming was making a few people a lot of money, but as an economic engine it was not pulling much in Sonora or Sinaloa.

Cruz-Torres attributed the downturn in the fortunes of the ejidatarios to the global economy. Poverty fed on itself within the globalization scheme, and driven by neoclassical economics, lead to a loss of social capital and the breakdown of societal function: a culture's ability to produce well-adjusted human beings. In addition to increasing anxiety over food and water supplies, Cruz-Torres found increasing alcoholism and drug use among the ejidatarios, particularly among the young.

Free trade led Mexico to develop more export-oriented crops, including farmed shrimp. She documented how the development of five shrimp farms around Celeya privatized what had been a community resource. The shift put 150 salt harvesters and several hundred part-time shrimp fishermen out of work. And it degraded the ecology of the region's lagoon system, already stressed by pollution and overfishing. Cruz-Torres noted that the rapid changes impinged on the combination subsistence/wage economies of hundreds of ejidatarios, many of whom would, like the people of Lubec, migrated in search of better prospects. Some undoubtedly ended up as part of the low-wage labor force pushing against, and through, the U.S. border.

❧

In Maslow's hierarchy of human needs, the basics, such as food and water, come first. According to hierarchy theory, when people's sources of these simple essentials became unreliable, communities begin to break down. Many of the coastal ejidatarios had been displaced by the type of agriculture development cited in the "Nutrition in Latin America" report. During our discussion in London, Rohana Subasinghe claimed that the rapid development of modern farming since 1940 had caused a great deal of poverty as well as increasing hunger. "Science contributed to industrial production that destroyed communities," he said.

His son Ruwan and I both asked if he saw the same thing happening in industrial aquaculture.

"No. Absolutely not," said Rohana. It seemed the conversation had come full circle. "We need to produce sixty million more tons of seafood by 2030," said Rohana, noting that it would mostly be freshwater species. "Shrimp and salmon will not help global poverty and hunger. We need to produce fish for people. Where there is an opportunity to produce money to buy fish for your people we should proceed, but do it carefully, not at the cost of producing for local people."

"That's great, but that's not what the World Bank thinks, is it?" said Ruwan. "They'd rather use the best resources for profit."

CLEAN WATER: THE BEST RESOURCE

In terms of resources, the most important one for aquaculture is water. Shrimp and salmon aquaculture need clean water above all else. Aquaculture business consultant John Forster expressed this idea succinctly in a speech at the Open Ocean Aquaculture, held in Portland, Maine, in 1996. "If there is one thing that over thirty years of experience has taught me," said Forster, "it is the value of free water."

While free water suitable for aquaculture might have been valuable, its nature did not lend itself to accounting as production capital. With no apparent value, water was not valued. Of the 99,465 square miles of estuaries in the United States, NOAA had assessed 28,687 square by 2004, and found 44 percent "impaired," polluted to the point that ecosystems no longer functioned. Speaking before the U.S. Senate in 2005, Forster supported the idea of moving finfish aquaculture offshore, and echoed his earlier statement. "If you want to grow a lot of things, you need a lot of water," he said.

The cost of building recirculation tanks made the prospect of practicing finfish aquaculture in land-based facilities impractical. The industry's research money went into finding ways to utilize the free water of the ocean.

Forster acknowledged that the production of luxury items destined for developed nations would be a drop in the bucket in terms of meeting future needs. "The millions of tons of projected seafood deficit is predominantly for fish [carp] which sell at much lower prices than those contemplating aquaculture ventures can live with," he said. These low-priced fish, Forster pointed out, were often grown in stagnant ponds "at costs, which, if their product was appreciated by Western consumers, would put growers of salmon . . . out of business."

Nonetheless, the production of the large quantities of shrimp and salmon consumed in developed countries required the best water available. Never mind the best intentions of the FAO or the pope, as Ruwan had pointed out, water's value to coastal communities and wild marine organisms did not register in the market. Shrimp, salmon, and carnivorous finfish farming promised to produce the highest returns on the resources, and won the bidding for access to clean water, lots of it.

In their push to create a privatized ocean, water was the one common property resource that the neoclassical economists seemed to have missed. Perhaps they overlooked water because it had some unique qualities that made it extremely difficult to manage.

In another "tragedy of the commons" scenario it is in the best interests of the users to exploit available water for the highest marginal return. As fisheries' economists had explained before, as long as the marginal return of putting in another fish pen or shrimp pond exceeded the marginal cost, seafood farmers would continue to add units of production. "Growers are going to put as many fish in their pens as they can," noted Sebastian Belle and many others.

In other words, as long as the water was clean enough to produce another fish or shrimp in the short term, it benefited a grower to stock another fish or shrimp. Because the clean water resource belonged to everyone, caring for its long-term health demanded a group effort on the part of competitors acting in their own interests. The market did not signal users to cooperate as Rohana Subasinghe hoped. As competitors, shrimp farmers had to work against the market, to join forces. But as Rohana said, "this is the only way." In London he reconsidered his optimistic view of the capacity of the ocean to support shrimp farming. "I would take that back," he said of his statement two years before, calling capacity virtually unlimited. "I think we are at least two-thirds full."

❧

Watching the tide fill around the mangrove roots, slowly sinking the plants until the tips of the lowest leaves dabbed the water, the fishermen of Navopatia had told of declining catches. The abandoned pangas pulled up high on the beach illustrated an increasingly familiar story. The tales became repetitive, lamentations that sounded the same in Mexican dialect as they did in English with a Maine accent.

It was the sound and hum of deepening uncertainty. Human collapse dropping slowly down the hierarchy of needs, approaching the last and most basic items: food and water.

⮂

"We're living in the age of Empire," said Ruwan, as we wrapped up our conversation. "We're dealing with corporations, it's going to be hard to change. The FAO and people like my dad can't do it."

"Will it require violence?"

"No. That's ridiculous. We can redistribute without violence," said the young man who claimed Gandhi as an idol.

Ecological Economics: Welcome to the Real World

The Subasinghes and I parted company on a London street; Ruwan had already disappeared into a record store when Rohana and I said our final good-byes. The next afternoon, I carried a bundle of disintegrating newspaper through the rain in Oban, Scotland—the paper soaked not from water falling out of the sky, but from grease dripping from the fish and chips inside. I passed a gray stone doorway and stepped inside. Peeling away shreds of paper, I found two piping hot fillets on top of a great pile of French fries—chips.

While I ate I thought about things. Most civilizations on earth had been geographically and culturally isolated, they peaked and went into decline, taking a lot down with them. If we were going to have a global civilization we better get it right. Various efforts to create sustainability seem ever-and over-focused on economic sustainability as the key, whereas ecological economics looked at the economy as one leg of the sustainability triangle.

Resources are pretty critical, too: imagine the economy as eating, resources as a fish, and air as society. As long as you have a fish and place to eat it, you have potential, though what's the fun if you don't use it?

I had no fork, no place to sit, so I started to pick pieces off the hot fish and pop them into my mouth. People walked by, I was an oil-soaked rain-soaked mess, but they didn't care and for sure they'd seen it before. I got through the fish and down to the fishy-flavored chips all cooked in the same deep fryer.

Economists who say that eating fish is what it's all about—we have to be able to keep eating fish, regardless of how many are in the sea—ignore the fact that when the sea is empty the show's over. Having faith that there will always be another fish is religious. *Techno-optimism is a religion—nothing wrong with that,* I thought, *unless it turned the state into its church.*

I had faith that nature would turn us back into dirt if we were not careful.

I finished off the fishy chips, jammed the dark shreds of paper into a corner of the doorway and looked for something besides my pants or the handlebars of my bicycle to wipe my slick hands on. I walked back up the street to the chippy and grabbed a handful of napkins. "What kind of fish was that?" I asked. "Cod," the woman said to me, and I sensed in the flat tone of her response that it was her only response; no matter what type of white fish she fried: cod, haddock, or hake, should anyone ask: cod.

At the ferry terminal I met another cyclist coming off the boat from the Outer Hebrides, a string of islands forty miles off the northwest coast of Scotland. As we talked, he mentioned that he turned sixty while cycling the islands. "And I had sixty miles an hour of wind to go with it," he said. "You're wise to be starting in the west. What have you got for gear?" I told him and he shook his head. "You'll need a good fleece jacket and some waterproof socks, go now and buy them, you have time. There's nothing once you get out there."

I took part of his advice, and rode back into town to a bike shop where they sold me a cheap polar fleece pullover, I looked at waterproof socks, but at twenty-five pounds a pair I passed, figuring plastic bags would work just as well. I stopped at a Tesco supermarket, stocked up on food and made the four o'clock ferry.

At ten that night and still raining, the boat docked in Castlebay Harbor on the island of Barra, the southwest tip of the Outer Hebrides. I made my way to the hostel with three other cyclists: an Englishman named John, and two women doctors, Claire and Phillipa, from Australia. John the Englishman pushed the door open and we entered a narrow hallway: one side opened into a common room where an older man sat playing solitaire at a table and a young couple, harpists I learned later, chatted in the glow of the fireplace. On the opposite side we saw the kitchen, and at the end of the hall, a stairway. We stood there looking around and dripping on the hardwood floor. On the wall, instructions told us how to check ourselves in.

After putting my bike under a tarp around back I came in and made a cup of tea. The older man still sat in the common room, and we started to chat. He came from the Shetland Islands, just off the north of Scotland, and yes, they had salmon farms aplenty up there, he told me.

"We have a little song we made up about them," he said, and

began singing to the tune of *Oh Christmas Tree*: "Oh salmon farm, oh salmon farm, environmentally you do harm, you bring the jobs that earn the bobs, but most of that goes to the nobs. Oh salmon farm . . . " he repeated the verse, and looked at me when he finished to see if I understood the slang. But the story sounded so familiar that I figured it out by context: bobs are money and the nobs are the wealthy owners. "Exactly," he said.

The morning broke clear and sunny, a breeze blew gently out of the northeast. I lay in bed awhile as the place emptied out. In the bathroom I found a tub and managed to figure out the hot water heater so that I could have a bath, the last I would take for the next ten days. The women doctors had pedaled off by the time I got downstairs. John, a big man dressed in a black polar-fleece jacket and spandex cycling pants, stood out front, smoking a cigarette next to his bike.

"That's quite a lot of gear," I said, sitting down on the front steps with a mug of tea.

"I'm loaded down like a bloody yak," he said, looking at the bags hung from every available place on his bike: front panniers, handlebar bag, rear panniers, rack bag ,and small pack on his back. "But I'm in no hurry."

"No, me neither." I had a map that showed one main road looping around the island, Castlebay Harbor sat in the south-west of Barra, the ferry to South Uist, the next island up, left from the northeast. "What's the best way around?" I asked.

John looked to the west. "If you go that way it'll be longer, but prettier." Then he nodded to the east. "That way is a bit shorter, but the country is not as nice."

"Which way are you going?"

began singing to the tune of *Oh Christmas Tree*: "Oh salmon farm, oh salmon farm, environmentally you do harm, you bring the jobs that earn the bobs, but most of that goes to the nobs. Oh salmon farm . . . " he repeated the verse, and looked at me when he finished to see if I understood the slang. But the story sounded so familiar that I figured it out by context: bobs are money and the nobs are the wealthy owners. "Exactly," he said.

The morning broke clear and sunny, a breeze blew gently out of the northeast. I lay in bed awhile as the place emptied out. In the bathroom I found a tub and managed to figure out the hot water heater so that I could have a bath, the last I would take for the next ten days. The women doctors had pedaled off by the time I got downstairs. John, a big man dressed in a black polar-fleece jacket and spandex cycling pants, stood out front, smoking a cigarette next to his bike.

"That's quite a lot of gear," I said, sitting down on the front steps with a mug of tea.

"I'm loaded down like a bloody yak," he said, looking at the bags hung from every available place on his bike: front panniers, handlebar bag, rear panniers, rack bag ,and small pack on his back. "But I'm in no hurry."

"No, me neither." I had a map that showed one main road looping around the island, Castlebay Harbor sat in the south-west of Barra, the ferry to South Uist, the next island up, left from the northeast. "What's the best way around?" I asked.

John looked to the west. "If you go that way it'll be longer, but prettier." Then he nodded to the east. "That way is a bit shorter, but the country is not as nice."

"Which way are you going?"

12

ECOLOGICAL ECONOMICS: WELCOME TO THE REAL WORLD

The Subasinghes and I parted company on a London street; Ruwan had already disappeared into a record store when Rohana and I said our final good-byes. The next afternoon, I carried a bundle of disintegrating newspaper through the rain in Oban, Scotland—the paper soaked not from water falling out of the sky, but from grease dripping from the fish and chips inside. I passed a gray stone doorway and stepped inside. Peeling away shreds of paper, I found two piping hot fillets on top of a great pile of French fries—chips.

While I ate I thought about things. Most civilizations on earth had been geographically and culturally isolated, they peaked and went into decline, taking a lot down with them. If we were going to have a global civilization we better get it right. Various efforts to create sustainability seem ever-and over-focused on economic sustainability as the key, whereas ecological economics looked at the economy as one leg of the sustainability triangle.

Resources are pretty critical, too: imagine the economy as eating, resources as a fish, and air as society. As long as you have a fish and place to eat it, you have potential, though what's the fun if you don't use it?

I had no fork, no place to sit, so I started to pick pieces off the hot fish and pop them into my mouth. People walked by, I was an oil-soaked rain-soaked mess, but they didn't care and for sure they'd seen it before. I got through the fish and down to the fishy-flavored chips all cooked in the same deep fryer.

Economists who say that eating fish is what it's all about—we have to be able to keep eating fish, regardless of how many are in the sea—ignore the fact that when the sea is empty the show's over. Having faith that there will always be another fish is religious. *Techno-optimism is a religion—nothing wrong with that,* I thought, *unless it turned the state into its church.*

I had faith that nature would turn us back into dirt if we were not careful.

I finished off the fishy chips, jammed the dark shreds of paper into a corner of the doorway and looked for something besides my pants or the handlebars of my bicycle to wipe my slick hands on. I walked back up the street to the chippy and grabbed a handful of napkins. "What kind of fish was that?" I asked. "Cod," the woman said to me, and I sensed in the flat tone of her response that it was her only response; no matter what type of white fish she fried: cod, haddock, or hake, should anyone ask: cod.

At the ferry terminal I met another cyclist coming off the boat from the Outer Hebrides, a string of islands forty miles off the northwest coast of Scotland. As we talked, he mentioned

that he turned sixty while cycling the islands. "And I had sixty miles an hour of wind to go with it," he said. "You're wise to be starting in the west. What have you got for gear?" I told him and he shook his head. "You'll need a good fleece jacket and some waterproof socks, go now and buy them, you have time. There's nothing once you get out there."

I took part of his advice, and rode back into town to a bike shop where they sold me a cheap polar fleece pullover, I looked at waterproof socks, but at twenty-five pounds a pair I passed, figuring plastic bags would work just as well. I stopped at a Tesco supermarket, stocked up on food and made the four o'clock ferry.

At ten that night and still raining, the boat docked in Castlebay Harbor on the island of Barra, the southwest tip of the Outer Hebrides. I made my way to the hostel with three other cyclists: an Englishman named John, and two women doctors, Claire and Phillipa, from Australia. John the Englishman pushed the door open and we entered a narrow hallway: one side opened into a common room where an older man sat playing solitaire at a table and a young couple, harpists I learned later, chatted in the glow of the fireplace. On the opposite side we saw the kitchen, and at the end of the hall, a stairway. We stood there looking around and dripping on the hardwood floor. On the wall, instructions told us how to check ourselves in.

After putting my bike under a tarp around back I came in and made a cup of tea. The older man still sat in the common room, and we started to chat. He came from the Shetland Islands, just off the north of Scotland, and yes, they had salmon farms aplenty up there, he told me.

"We have a little song we made up about them," he said, and

"I haven't made up my mind," he said, the cigarette dangling from his lower lip.

I left him there and went in to pack. When I came out to load up, he was gone. I never saw him again.

Riding dead into the wind of uncertainty on a crisp spring day, I passed newborn lambs everywhere. One that had lost its mother ran alongside me for a quarter mile, *baah*ing insistently as its little hooves battered the asphalt.

The road ran like a long black ribbon through the bright green fields, the steely blue sea to the west. I looked around: white combers rolled in and thundered against the white sand beaches not far from the empty road. In spite of the east wind it was the kind of day that could make you fall in love with a place. Gulls wheeled and glided along the surf. I rode.

Claire and Phillipa stood at the ferry terminal, their bikes leaning against a small building that sat alone in a parking lot. A concrete ramp with pilings along one edge slanted into the bay. It was quiet but for the steady breeze singing a duet of desolation with the sparse landscape, whispering in the dune grass, across the treeless hills, and out to sea. All under a cloudless sky. "We missed the one o'clock ferry; the next comes at four," said Phillipa.

South Uist lay only five miles or so to the north, but we could do nothing except wait. The doctors took a ride up the beach. I unpacked my sleeping bag and stretched out on a bench in the waiting room.

Next thing Phillipa was shaking me awake. "Come on, there's a special boat." It was 2:30 and the ferry, which had made an unscheduled run, had already cast its lines for the return trip.

Quickly, I bundled up my stuff and ran my bike down the ramp. The boat had already pulled away but they backed astern to collect me. "Wow," I said as I lashed my bike down for the trip. "I just made it." But as I sorted out my gear I noticed my raincoat missing. Looking back I saw it, a bright yellow spot lying at the top of the ramp, above the tide line.

I would have to go back. The captain told me not to worry, likely as not nobody would bother it. "And it's out of reach of the tide, so you've had good luck then," he said. As we headed across he and I chatted about fishing and fish farms. His name was Donald John and as the other crewmen came in he introduced me. "A fisherman from America," he told them. Donald John used to work on the pair trawlers catching herring and mackerel. "We learned it from the Irish," he said. "They're the best."

We landed at a remote corner of South Uist and I said goodbye to the doctors. The boat had to wait a half an hour so Donald John invited me down to the galley for a mug up with the rest of the crew.

I asked him about inshore fishing.

"People used to do inshore," he said. "But now the Irish, the Scots, and the Norwegians have followed the fish back to where they gather, out to Rockall and so they never get a chance to come in." Distant Rockall, an isolated uninhabited seamount only one hundred feet wide where it poked its granite point out of the North Atlantic, lay 225 miles to the west, a long way from anywhere.

To make up for the lack of inshore fish, the government gave grants to many small fishermen interested in starting salmon farms, Donald John told me. "But the bigger companies,

McConnell's [owned by Stolt Sea Farms] had the feed and the well boat, so when times got hard it was easy for them to buy out the little guys."

As we talked, the engineer, who also acted as cook, made toast and put out cups of hot water for instant coffee. Sitting in a small booth in the galley we buttered the toast and put jelly on it. The deckhand spooned coffee.

"It doesn't put anything into the local economy except for a few workers," said Donald John. "There's a plant in Lochbois-dale, they have a boat in there that does everything." The auto-mated boats used by the salmon farmers could handle almost all the chores once performed by people, such as offloading feed, pulling up nets for cleaning, and harvesting the fish.

Donald John's crew was a patchwork group from within the interisland ferry company, and they teased each other relent-lessly. Donald John and the mate always worked together, but the deckhand was filling in for someone else.

They were all fishermen once, and still fished a bit, poaching wild salmon from the local rivers. "Just for the pot," as they said, not to make money.

"South Uist is all a corporation; it's all owned by Englishmen, including the fishing rights," said Donald John, who grew up on the island.

"So you see we have to do it," the first mate said of the poaching.

"It's our duty," said the deckhand.

But they had noticed changes in the fish in recent years. "We still get plenty of salmon in the rivers," said Donald John. "But they're a very different color and texture, not like when I was a boy."

The galley suddenly emptied, time for the return run to Barra. The engines picked up their tempo, and the deckhand cast off. We'd exhausted our conversation. I sat by the rail for the run back. At the ramp my jacket sat where I last saw it, and I ran to get it before a waiting car drove over it.

It was four thirty when the boat got back to South Uist. I had twnety-five miles to ride into the wind. I had hoped that the prevailing westerlies would make my ride easier, and the old cyclist in Oban agreed they would. But between his ride and mine, the wind shifted to the northeast, and I ate it all day, every day, as I made my way up the chain of islands. In my favor was the oddity that it did not rain. I had seen this weather pattern before, on the coast of Maine, usually in early May, lots of easterly wind but none of the rain that usually went with it. Here it was late April.

One afternoon I put my bike on a bus in Harris. Not long afterward, the driver pulled over. "Just going to stop here a minute," he said. "In case anybody wants to get some fresh air." I sat in the chair, having had a steady diet of fresh air force-fed to me for the last three days. But I finally got out; I could not resist. The island was the scenic jewel of the Outer Hebrides, granite mountains sloped steeply into the sea; the gray cliffs interspersed with white beaches. Surfers came from all over the world to ride the waves that mounted and broke in sweeping curls along the shore.

Further on we passed a massive construction site. I looked out the window as we went by. Mounds of gravel sat by the side of the road. It meant nothing to me at the time, but Harris gravel would later play a part in my understanding of ecological economics.

At Callanish on the Isle of Lewis I found a pub and went in for some pub grub, sausage and chips. A man sat at the bar, and he watched me get my food. "Ah he's havin' his comfort food, isn't he?"

I laughed, and looked up at him. He had long blond hair and a sea bag at his feet. His name was John, "an itinerant fisherman," he said. He was looking for a job on a prawn boat, but added that things were not too good in any kind of fishing. "Not with the Danes out there suckin' up all the sand eels with great big Hoovers. All to make fish food."

I asked him about salmon farms and he cocked his head back. "Anybody I know with a bit of intelligence hates those damn salmon farms," he said. I nodded.

MATINICUS OCTOBER 2003

Rain beat against the windowpanes and the wind rattled the sashes as I sat in a friend's cottage on Matinicus Island, twenty miles off the coast of Maine. I watched warm and dry as twenty-foot waves broke over the seawall guarding the harbor and a few intrepid lobstermen ran their boats out through the gut, cresting the swells—headed to haul their traps on the lee side of the island. I wondered how far technology and competition would take us in the game of survival, and what would happen to the dispossessed in the race to achieve economic efficiency in all industries, not just fisheries and aquaculture.

In October of 2003, Hurricane Juan drove thirty-foot-high waves into the sea wall guarding Halifax, Nova Scotia, and eighty-mile-an-hour winds toppled giant old oaks across the city's flooded streets. As the storm raged, Peter Tyedmers, an ecological economist at Halifax's Dalhousie University, explained the theory of dissipating structures to me, via a tenuous telephone connection.

"Dissipating structures means as you increase order in a subsystem, it comes at a higher cost to the overarching system. You see more rapid entropy," said Tyedmers, an expert on energy efficiencies in fisheries and aquaculture. "Higher levels of order are possible, but for shorter duration." He was talking about how carbon moved through the economy—when we ate fish, for example. Increasing the order of the subsystem was often about transforming carbon in a way that generated the highest net profit, rather than the smallest ecological footprint.

Economies-of-scale fisheries and aquaculture transformed carbon, in the form of seafood, in a way that created and concentrated money. But according to the theory of dissipating structures, these frenetic forms of economic activity rapidly degenerated the natural and social capital that supported them.

I had long experience with the cascade of dissipating structures. It started in 1976 and followed one fishery's meltdown after another. But as a teenager prowling the docks of various East Coast ports, infectious optimism masked all concerns about sustainability. Congress was pouring millions of dollars into modernizing the fleet. Efficiency, according to the policy makers, amounted to catching more fish faster. In the late 1970s, recently launched steel stern trawlers, all more than eighty feet long, headed to sea equipped with the latest electronic technology, particularly sonars for finding fish and Loran-assisted track plotters that enabled the boats to tow their nets through the schools repeatedly with lethal accuracy. New diesels with increased horsepower enabled the boats to tow larger nets, and like many others, I gravitated toward the new technology without questioning its efficiency—until the bill arrived.

All the new toys had to be paid for with increased landings of fish, which then flooded the market. Prices dropped, requiring fishermen to further increase landings in order to make the same amount of money. Competition drove the most progressive fishermen to invest in more-sophisticated technology: global positioning systems connected to computerized track plotters replaced the old Lorans, and digital sonar displays showed fish more clearly. Every advance led to increased landings, and as soon as everyone in the fleet adopted the technology, prices dropped and landings increased.

I experienced an awakening of sorts one bright summer day in 1984, aboard the ninety-foot-long trawler *Atlantic Harvester*, out of Rockland, Maine. On a ten-day trip in the Gulf of Maine, out near the Canadian boundary, we caught thousands of pounds of hake, much of it too small for our market. Tow after tow we sorted out the bigger fish and shoveled the small ones over the side, dead. Looking up from my work I saw the bodies of juvenile hake—their bellies to the sun, bladders distended from their mouths—floating all around the boat and out toward the horizon for quite a distance. An airplane, bright red against the blue sky and sea, flew past low enough that when I looked up I saw the insignia of the Canadian Coast Guard. A helmeted crewman leaned out an opening in the fuselage and looked down at the scene. Years later I met a former pilot of one of those planes and he told me about seeing fishing boats surrounded by dead bycatch.

"Maybe you saw us," I said.

"Who knows, there were so many," he replied.

Working on deck of the *Atlantic Mariner* in 1984 I started to do the math: the hired captain had to produce something to pay for the trip. Loading the boat with small hake at fifteen cents a pound, we spent at least the first seven or eight days of our ten days at sea, working to cover expenses. In the meantime, we killed and discarded as many fish as we caught. We believed we had no choice but to pay for the trip and make a profit any way we could. We had to maintain our economic sustainability. The sea dotted with dead fish represented an expense, an externality that we would internalize a few years later, in the form of empty nets.

I made only one trip on the *Atlantic Mariner*; working more than a week just to pay the fuel bill of a monster fishing boat may have made sense to some fisheries economists, but it seemed a waste of my time. I went back to the boat I'd worked on the summer before, the *Irene Alton*. Her owner, Bernard Raynes, had built the fifty-seven-foot wooden boat in his backyard. She carried the minimum in technology: an old paper recorder depth sounder, a Loran and a VHF radio. Raynes carried in his head all that he needed to catch fish. He had inherited the accumulated wisdom of eleven generations of his ancestors, all fishing folks in the Gulf of Maine. An image of the sea bottom, formed over the years through the combined observations of those preceding generations, became part of Raynes's own mental landscape. Working with his father and grandfather from the time he could hold an oar, Raynes had learned, as much as anyone can, the ways of fish and how they moved in the sea and seasons. "You have to learn to think like a fish," he once told me.

Raynes's boat required basic maintenance, most of which he accomplished with the help of his crew. The work cost him time, not money, and acted as a bonding exercise for all of us. We laughed a lot on the summer days we spent scraping and painting, and paid close attention as Raynes taught us how to splice new shrouds and stays, and build nets. When the ground-fish landings crashed in the late 1980s and the 1990s, his self-sufficiency paid off.

He continued to fish long after the big fish draggers had all disappeared from the Rockland waterfront one way or another. The owner of the *Atlantic Mariner*, Lee Riley, a man I never met, rerigged her as a purse seiner for herring fishing. (She was later rigged over as a pair trawler, and renamed the *Starbound*. She sank in 2000 after being rammed by a Russian freighter.) The O'Hara fleet, half a dozen ninety-foot steel boats—all built with government subsidies—left for Alaska, where stocks remained healthy enough to support their wasteful mode of fishing.

The *Irene Alton*, with her low fixed and operating costs, survived, and as of 2006 the thirty-year-old boat continued to fish. Unfortunately, the infrastructure that enabled her to take on ice and offload fish vanished. She survived due to her efficiency, only to become functionally obsolete due to the breakdown of the overarching system.

I left Bernard in the late 1980s and moved to an isolated stretch of the coast of Maine, where I began an experiment in efficiency.

Like Raynes, I built my own boat, but lacking his history and confidence in what the existing resources could support, I built a five-meter dory, a lovely little craft that I rowed along the open shore, searching in the intertidal zone for periwinkles, "wrinkles," and later, sea urchins.

From 1988 to 1991, I had the wrinkles all to myself. On spring tides I could earn $120 in six hours. The rest of the time I worked in my garden, cut wood, and read. Wendell Berry's book of essays, *The Unsettling of America*, and Masunobu Fukuoka's *One Straw Revolution* awakened me to definitions of efficiency that made more sense to me than what I had seen in industrial fisheries. Both writers advocated more human effort and less purchased inputs in food production. I learned that a human working by hand in a garden got about ten calories back for every one invested. Petroleum-driven machines reverse the ratio: for every ten calories invested with a tractor or rototiller, the garden returned one. I assumed that by rowing I would get the same sort of calorie-for-calorie return ratio in my fishing as I did in my garden. Following Raynes's example, I kept my fishing expenses low by relying more on my senses and accumulated knowledge than on technology.

One afternoon, as I rowed past a new fiberglass lobster boat anchored in the harbor, the captain hollered over, "Why don't you put a motor on that thing?" I dug my oars in and stopped, then pulled quietly into an eddy next to his boat.

"I want my money in my pocket," I told him. "A motor costs a thousand dollars for something decent; then I have to register my boat; there's another twenty bucks every year; plus gas and all that. Adds up to a lot of goddamn wrinkles, and what's it going to save me? A two-mile row with the tide in my favor."

More than a decade later, I read *The Origins of Ecological Economics* by an eco-economist named Kozo Mayumi, in which he explained what I instinctively knew: that there were two types of efficiency. One measured work accomplished in relation to energy used, the other looked at production in terms of speed. As an example, Mayumi noted that cars have an ideal economical speed in terms of gas consumption and distance covered, but most people used more gas than necessary in order to get to their destinations faster. "Such drivers prefer efficiency in terms of speed of the car to efficiency in terms of gas consumption," wrote Mayumi.

Indeed, as declining fisheries forced more fishermen to turn to wrinkle picking, they arrived with outboard motors, which needed to be paid for with wrinkles. The new entrants to wrinkle picking thought less about efficiency or sustainability than I did. They took the small with the big; they took every wrinkle they could find, and before long the wrinkles had all been picked, the bulk of the money gone to the Honda outboard dealer and the local gas station. But bigger engines would not replace the periwinkles.

As the U.S. economy boomed in the 1990s, wealthy newcomers bought up the shore where I worked, cluttering the view of the coast with their architectural nightmares. I complained, "The value of the land is what it can produce year after year and land around here does not produce much. But these folks decide it's worth a million dollars an acre, and raise my taxes so I have to take more wrinkles, but there are none left."

To increase my earnings I entered the lucrative sea urchin fishery, which lasted only a few years. Nonetheless, many of the most vocal fishermen still seemed enchanted with the myth of infinite abundance.

By 2000, I worked full-time as a freelance journalist, and having run out of fisheries, I became a chronicler of the industry. The stories repeated themselves with depressing regularity, and the same pattern of desperate competition seemed destined to destroy the aquaculture industry. "I feel like I can take any fishery or fish farming story and plug it into the same template for an article," I told Bill Crowe, the editor of *The Fishermen's Voice*.

I sat at his kitchen table piled high with papers and notes from a yellow legal pad. "I don't know how you find room for your ashtray and bourbon," I said.

"Look, I'm right out straight heah, and suckin' wind for ahticles," he said in his thick Massachusetts accent, leaving vacant spaces where the *r*'s should have been. "Did you go to the u'chin meeting?" he asked, as he shuffled through his files.

"Same old story," I told him. "Once again they want natural resources to pay for boats they never should've bought. This guy stood up and said, 'I have two hundred thousand dollars invested in my boat; you gotta let me fish.' Like who asked a finite resource to subsidize your overoptimistic business decision. Eat your two hundred thousand dollar boat."

"That's not front-page," said Crowe. "What else you got?"

"Periwinkles?"

Like the fishermen, Maine salmon farmers complained that regulations did not fit their business plans. Economic sustainability had to come first. At the trial of two companies charged with numerous environmental violations, the growers warned Judge Carter that strict limits he imposed on how many salmon they could stock and how often, would put them out of business.

Carter's harsh terms were a rarity; elected officials and regulators rarely prioritized energy efficiency as a path to sustainable fisheries and aquaculture. Most solutions embraced the efficiency of speed, which required more fish and other resources. While the movers and shakers in government and industry saw through the myth of infinite seafood for what it was, they continued to create systems that relied on infinite resources.

THE LAWS OF NATURE

Unlike the theories of neoclassical economics, which seemed to hold up only in an environmental vacuum, eco-economics focused heavily on the laws of thermodynamics: the first of which states that energy/matter cannot be created, only transformed. The second law adds that energy will always be lost to the surrounding environment in the course of any transformation process—the unstoppable energy leakage known as entropy.

Eco-economists argued that there is no free lunch, no perpetual motion machine, and no infinite economic growth, unless the earth grew, too. The universe tended to disorder; it was dying a slow death, they pointed out; the best society could do was try to diminish its losses through making systems more efficient in terms of energy exchange.

Tyedmers, Mayumi, and other ecological economists put together a strong argument. As a journalist I had written continuously about the breakdown of fisheries, ecosystems, and cultures, while at the same time listening to economists like Hauke Kite-Powell and his neoclassical models that put net profit ahead of all else, including net jobs and net food production, the two things that small-scale fisheries once provided and aquaculture had promised to provide.

The eco-economists examined the patterns of destruction inherent in the neoclassical economic system, due to its inability to register human and environmental well being in terms other than money. Herman Daly in his book *Beyond Growth* pointed out the disconnect between money and well-being. He argued that the world had entered a period of uneconomic growth, where the unmeasured costs of development to human welfare exceeded the financial benefits. Daly, a disaffected World Bank economist like Nobel Prize–winner Joe Stiglitz, ran afoul of the dominant ideology when he began questioning why the economy was being analyzed as separate from the environment, and suggesting there may be limits to growth.

Daly wrote, "The bio-physical limits of growth arise from three interrelated conditions: finitude, entropy, and ecological interdependence." He called on the World Bank to view the economy as a subsystem of the environment. They responded by not responding, marginalizing Daly as much as they could by leaving him out of the discussion.

Mainstream economists did not see the macroeconomy as a subsystem of anything. The natural capital that Thomas Kocherry warned us not to destroy did not register in the neoclassical economic accounting, which measured wealth according to gross national product (GNP). The key point was this: in neoclassical economics there was no depreciation of natural or social capital.

Every log harvested from the forest, every fish landed from the sea was counted as income in the GNP. If the absence of that fish or tree, or if the production of a farmed fish, and its use of clean water and impact on wild stocks, reduced the productive capacity of the ecosystem the depreciation never showed up on anyone's books.

Fish farmers depreciated their pens, but not the valuable and vulnerable water that flowed through them and made the entire enterprise practical. They prepared for maintaining their man-made production capital, but counted water's production contribution as profit. When it came time to maintain water quality through letting cage sites lie fallow, growers complained it would put them out of business.

Within the context of an international agreement to essentially cook the books of global economics, policy makers ignored the impacts of resource extraction and waste disposal on ecosystems and communities. If the accounts were rectified, and most eco-economists believed they would be—one way or another—they would show the world economy deeply in the red. Within ecological economics' hardball definition of sustainability, the *economic growth* championed by certain economists would be a sand castle standing against the tidal wave of reality.

That tidal wave appeared, among other forms, as the breakdown of ecological function, and a domino effect as breakdowns in subsystems disrupted ecological function in all others: dissipating structures. For example, thirteen years after shutting down the Newfoundland cod fishery, regulators and fishermen saw few signs of recovery. Scientists offered wondered if the smaller artic cod, of little commercial value, had taken over the cod's niche in the ecosystem, or global warming was limiting success of reproduction, perhaps disease. Whatever the cause, one fact became apparent: the ecosystem had played a critical role in production, no longer worked, and the resources could not be marshaled to repair it.

All the technology in the world could not compensate for a damaged ecosystem. We saw it in the urchin fishery as well. When areas became completely fished out, the seaweeds that urchins kept in check grew and became habitat for micropredators. When the young urchins settled on bottom, small crabs feasted until they had eaten every one. Overharvesting had destroyed ecosystem function and the process would be expensive to reverse. Once a certain point is passed, as it was with cod and sea urchins, there's no predicting the future.

❧

Daly and many others began developing models to reflect real-world experience. Daly began with an Index of Sustainable Economic Welfare that attempted to measure changes in people's general welfare, their quality of life, as the economy grew. While Daly and his colleagues saw welfare increase with the GNP for several decades after 1947, beginning around 1980, his model saw a steepening decline in welfare, measured in lost leisure time, the stress of congestion, environmental pollution, and poor health. The GNP continued to rise, driven upward by such things as sales of drugs like Paxil, used to treat a condition called Social Anxiety Disorder, which some doctors claimed affected ten million Americans. The economy grew, but so did rates of cancer, depression, divorce, and other signals of trouble.

≈

While Daly strove to frame the big picture, other economists applied the theories in practical ways, such as looking at what directions development decisions might take if planners included inputs such as community values.

When Maine's sea urchin council considered endorsing and funding sea urchin aquaculture development, some council members, including chairman Kristen Porter, participated in a sustainable development experiment. Stewart Smith of the University of Maine met with Porter, sea urchin diver Ian Emory, and several residents of Cutler, Maine, a strong fishing community being used as a hypothetical location for a sea urchin farm. I attended their meeting as a council member.

They met at Porter's house and gathered round his kitchen table. Smith explained the Sustainable Development Evaluative Technique and how it measured an industry's ability to meet a wide range of community values. "What I want everyone to do is fill out these questionnaires," he said, holding up a document consisting of five pages stapled together at the corner. Like the others, I took one from a stack Smith sent around the table. One of the questions asked us to rate in order of importance what we valued more: employment, clean environment, local control of resources, and a couple of other considerations. "You can see the questions are completely subjective," said Smith. "What I want you all to do is rate as best you can what you think is most important for you and your community. Some people may value jobs more highly than a clean environment, others might prefer local control of businesses operating their communities."

Like many college professors, the white-haired, heavy browed Smith explained the process thoroughly; when he finished, the group dove into the task. Smith gathered the papers up half an hour later.

"I'll take these back and some of my grad students will run them through the model," he said. "Your answers will be weighted and assigned points." Smith explained that the total score of the combined questionnaires would be used to create a Mobius triangle, which would show how well the industry met the community's professed values.

Smith presented the information to the council a couple of months later, by a narrow margin urchin aquaculture failed to meet the expressed values of a small cross-section of residents of Cutler, Maine. The one consistent value that cost the industry points was the community's insistence on local control of industry. "The degree of consolidation we've seen in aquaculture leads us to suspect that the proposed project would not meet the community's needs," said Smith, though he added that the model was far from precise.

The economic axis of the industry weighted heavily in terms of economic sustainability, met the community's triangle of values, but the other two corners, social and environmental concerns, were far apart, showing that the benefits of the enterprise flowed disproportionately to the entrepreneurs.

Urchin aquaculture had a small environmental impact, which did not conflict significantly with the way respondents valued their ecosystem. Smith had done a similar experiment with a community considering its first salmon aquaculture site. "That one showed more clearly that salmon aquaculture did not serve the community's values," said Smith.

Ecological economists sought to put the triangles in balance, and had actually taken a formidable step in doing so on the Isle of Harris, the most beautiful of the Outer Hebrides. In 2000, Lafarge Redland Aggregates, one of the largest construction companies in the world, announced plans to open a gravel superquarry on Harris and essentially tear down a mountain to supply Europe's gravel needs.

Alastair McIntosh led the fight against the quarry using ecological economics fundamentals, including intergenerational equity and the rate of natural capital depreciation. McIntosh pointed out that the mountain depreciated at a very slow rate, and delivered a steady flow of services, including views that brought tourism, peat from the lower slopes, fresh streams for salmon, and grazing for sheep. McIntosh said the mountain was already 1.8 billion years old and in some ways, as with peat moss accumulation, had actually appreciated in its ability to deliver services to humans. "Who are we to presume that this mountain will not therefore have some sort of value 'for as long as Earth endures'?" he asked.

"Set against this low-level trickle of utility," wrote McIntosh, "if the mountain is taken away it will provide Harris with thirty-three direct jobs, ten indirect jobs and seventy direct jobs filled by people from other islands and the mainland. Total annual income from these jobs, at full production, which would be for only fifty years of the sixty-year project life, would be £1.3 million . . . .

"The bottom-line consideration, however, is that the mountain that would otherwise yield utility over a very long period of time would be turned into roadstone, which would depreciate over a very short period of time."

The principles made sense to some people. Lafarge Redland backed out of the project and asked McIntosh to help advise the company on how to proceed sustainably.

Like all development in the evolving globalized economy, aquaculture approached a fork in the road that would entail opportunity costs. Salmon and shrimp farming represented the flagships of the past, a commitment to faith in human ingenuity to replace natural capital. Ecological economists sought a commitment to genuine sustainability of the sort McIntosh described, and a realistic accounting of natural capital depreciation.

PART IV

THE END OF THE WILD

13

THE FISH MARKET:
GETTING LESS FOR MORE

The sun crests the Sierra Madre, part of the long range that runs down the western side of North America, from Alaska to Mexico and on through Central and South America as well. A well-worn silver sedan rolls down the road to the fishing port of Yaváros, a place where fishermen and buyers still move top-quality product to consumers they meet face-to-face.

Driver Joel Leal used to be an agronomic engineer, he says. He worked on the ejidos, or communally owned properties, settling land disputes, common enough in the big families many of the ejidatarios had.

But in 1992, when then-president Carlos Salinas de Gortari changed Article 27, Joel's job no longer existed. The ejidatarios received title to their land and, for the first time in history, could sell or lease it to entities outside the ejido; the market would determine the disposition of the land, as it had before the Revolution.

"[The change in] Article 27 was no good for me," Joel says in Spanish. "But Salinas was the best president in my lifetime. He brought a lot of money to Mexico. He was like Porfirio Díaz, who also did a lot of good for Mexico, but they were both corrupt. Corruption seems to go with it.

"That's why the roads are so bad in Mexico, corruption. Look at this," he says, pointing at the bumpy new tar already laced with cracks. "They did this last year and it's already breaking up. It's because the guy who was supposed to buy the tar put the money in his pocket instead and bought this cheap junk."

We pass through the municipal center, Huatabampo, and back into the campo. Signs reading PIONEER mark vast fields of genetically engineered corn.

Joel says after his job vanished he bounced around at a few different jobs and finally got into the fish business three years ago. He likes it, he's his own man, but he needs more working capital. At the moment, he borrows for every buying trip down to the busy port.

We drive across the sparse flood plain, pocketed with dried puddles of salt. He veers left at a fork in the road and continues down the peninsula, passing the forlorn cemetery on the right: the tombstones residing among the cactus and naked soil.

The water of the surrounding bay hems in closer on both sides and we see pangas, twenty-three-foot-long outboard skiffs, lining the shore. In some boats, piles of netting rise above the rails. Others sit idle, at anchor offshore, where roosting pelicans paint them with a thick coat of guano.

Joel drives along the edge of a lagoon, and everywhere people carry buckets of fish and clams. Signs beckon ALMEJAS

CHOCOLATAS, the chocolate clams, hardshell clams dug from the mud of the bay.

Joel turns off the main road and threads among the wide puddles on a dirt road leading down along a saltpan. In the distance, mounds of salt dot the dry areas. We pull into the yard of an unplastered brick house. A fellow comes out smiling at Joel, but he frowns when Joel asks for *jaiba*, crab. No, he doesn't have any, but if Joel will give him some money he can get some. Joel passes him a five-hundred-peso note, worth fifty U.S. dollars, and drives off with his coolers still empty. He heads back down the main drag, past yards fenced with old seines and cluttered with fishing gear, nets and traps of various sorts. Signs advertise items for sale: shrimp, scallops, various types of fish, but the chocolate clams appear to be most plentiful.

Joel pulls into one of the yards where an old man in flip-flops sits in a plastic chair. He gets up when he sees Joel, but shakes his head when Joel asks about product.

Joel gets back in the car. "Lots of competition today and not much shrimp," he says. "My friend gave me ten thousand pesos (one thousand dollars) and told me to buy lots. Tomorrow is Ash Wednesday, the start of Lent, and lots of people want fish." He drives up the street to another yard and walks out back. *"Buenos días, hermano."* Juan, a dark-skinned man with very Mayan features and his shirt buttoned up to the neck, shakes Joel's hand and beckons over to a set of scales. He piles two kilos of blue shrimp onto then and then dumps the shrimp into a plastic bag. He hands Joel the bag and Joel hands him two hundred pesos. We have driven sixty miles and been in town over an hour and this is the first product to go in the coolers: two kilos of shrimp. But Juan says he will try to get more later.

As we get back in the car Joel mentions that Juan is of a different religion, "Hermanos de Cristo," Brothers of Christ. "Many of the indigenous people, mostly Mayan, in Yaváros have converted to this evangelical church," says Joel. "You can tell them by their dress, and they love music. They're always walking around with guitars."

He drives around the back side of town, past fishermen on the beach who wave to Joel and hold up bags of clams. Joel stops to talk to them but does not buy. He deals only with the small-scale wholesalers in town. "If I tried to buy direct from fishermen," he says, "I wouldn't last long."

Further along, we pull into the yard of a house that sits back off the road and looks out onto the bay. We get out of the car again. Near a table out front sits a bucket, and Joel picks a handful of glistening clams out of it, holding them dripping as he examines them. A small, handsome man comes out of the house and walks across the yard, his shirt buttoned to the neck. "*Buenos días hermano*," says Joel. They exchange pleasantries, smiling, but the small man gets serious when they start to haggle. There is much shaking of heads at first as the numbers fly back and forth. But eventually they start to nod to each other. Joel counts out twenty-five hundred pesos and passes them to the small man, who counts them again. He pockets the money and invites us in for coffee.

His wife pours us coffee and then sits down on a sofa against the wall. Our host makes no introduction. The woman wears a long skirt, and a broad scarf covers her head and most of her back, though not completely, and her thick black hair escapes from its lower edge to fall a few inches below her waist. Her eyes are bright; her cheekbones, high.

A white rabbit hops in and comes over to the table; it stands up on its hind legs and sniffs my hand. I scratch it. The woman smiles. The dogs that run everywhere around Mexican villages don't kill it "because they know it belongs here," she says.

At the table we talk; I ask the man his name: "Bernardino," he says. His wife is Sylvia.

For Joel this is all irrelevant, and after the thread thins, he changes the subject back to fish. Bernardino, he tells me, is a fisherman as well as a fish buyer, and suddenly I notice the dive gear and spearguns here and there around the room. Bernardino shows us his gear; wet suits, compressor, flippers. He takes his spearguns down from where they hang on the wall. "*Harpoona*," he says.

Joel has more business to attend to, and he waves for us to leave.

≈

Round and round he goes, back to the main drag, where he stops at a cinderblock wall painted sky blue: "Cosme's," says Joel. He walks through a door in the wall and enters a yard bustling with activity. Cosme greets Joel with open arms, but he looks like the antithesis of Bernardino. Cosme's eyes are sunken in deep, dark circles, his shirt is unbuttoned to the waist and his bald belly hangs over his belt. If Bernardino is a brother of Christ, Cosme may be a brother of the anti-Christ.

Out back, three men stand around a stainless-steel table in a screened-in room. One cuts fillets from the wings of a small manta ray and the others skin them. In the yard sit boxes holding various types of fish waiting to be filleted. Joel opens the door of a big walk-in cooler and looks around nodding. Several large containers are full to the brim with blue shrimp; others hold the less-valuable brown shrimp.

Joel buys some and puts them in his car. It's one thirty and Joel drives over to his favorite eatery, Nancy's *restaurante*, but a woman standing at the door shakes her head, telling him Nancy has left for the day. Joel drives back to Bernardino's. In the yard, Sylvia has brought a plastic chair out and put it against the wall, where she sits smoking a cigarette with regal grace. Her profile against the white wall and the dignity with which she smokes inspires me to take her photo, but before I can reload my camera she finishes the cigarette and gets up.

Joel asks if we can buy a lunch, she waves him to be quiet. She'll feed us for free. Bernardino runs to the store for a few extras, some soda and tortillas. *"Maíz?"* he asks. Do we want corn tortillas, or wheat. We tell him corn.

He comes back and while Sylvia works in the kitchen he invites us outside for an appetizer: *almejas chocolatas,* a Yaváros specialty. Bernardino pushes his knife into the seam of the closed shells and with a twist opens each clam and sets them up on the table. He scoops out the meat and dices it up before scooping it back into the shells and dousing each with lime juice. He offers them to us with salt and chile and we down them one at a time.

Back inside, we eat hotdogs mixed with vegetables, beans, and *panela*, a homemade cheese. Bernardino tells how he searches for clams underwater, poking the mud with a stainless steel spike about eight inches long. He gets four to six hundred clams in a two-hour dive, and figures he makes about five hundred pesos (fifty dollars) after gas and other expenses. Good money in southern Sonora.

For dessert we have *cayo de hacho*—scallops, which he prepares raw, *crudo*, much the way he prepared the clams. Joel smokes a cigarette with Bernardino and Sylvia afterward, and then heads back to Cosme's for more buying.

While I photograph some guys cutting up stingrays, Joel looks over a box of *guachinango*, a type of red snapper, but it is too pricey. Joel has me take pictures of him with various species so he can show his customers. He buys about twenty kilos of brown shrimp, and ten of blue, as much *linguada*, and a few frozen lobsters. Cosme and I sit on boxes against a wall and talk about the gear. Most of the fish are caught on hooks, he says, the shrimp and manta rays in gillnets. Local fishermen also drift at night with an Asian-style net called a *cachuga*. It hangs in the water suspended from poles that project off the bow and stern of the panga. A lantern hung above the mouth of the net attracts the shrimp and they find themselves drifting deeper into the net as the boat drifts downwind. On windless nights the fishermen set sails in the water to catch the tide.

I ask him about aquaculture. It's no good, says Cosme, lowers the price for shrimp, but it's not his biggest concern. The catches are way off, he says. The fishermen are lucky to get eight kilos a night, twelve is exceptional. And the price is down because of the glut on the world market. "Too many farmed shrimp, which are soft and tasteless," he says.

Joel pays Cosme and gets back in the car. Today's the day when you don't haggle, he says. You take what they offer and pay what they ask.

Back to Bernardino's to settle the account. Joel adds a few clams, and another type of scallop called *pata de mula*. He has bought 786 pesos worth of product, but he leaves the change with Bernardino to keep buying. He'll be back Friday, he says.

You can trust the brothers and they give you a better price, he says. Cosme, he's a different story. When the season ends, the brothers respect the law, but Cosme and his crew keep right on fishing. At Cosme's, one of the fishermen explicitly told me not to take his picture. "He's wanted by the law," Joel told me later, putting his wrists together to symbolize handcuffs.

☙

Two days later, I see Joel on his corner, the trunk of his car open. I talk a couple of American tourists into buying the last kilo of shrimp, and I take the last seven clams. Joel laments that if he had had two hundred pounds of *linguada* and *pechuga de angel* he could have sold it all before noon on Wednesday. But it wasn't there.

☙

Joel's experience spoke of a transformation. A trend of dwindling catches for the *pangeros*—the small-boat fishermen. The trend stretches beyond Yaváros to the rest of Mexico and to small-boat coastal fishermen around the world. The small-scale artisanal fishermen operating within a few miles of the coast feel the decline in global fisheries' landings more than any other sector. Though they are in the best position to maintain a sustainable fishery, and they often are the group with the longest historical reliance on the resources, in difficult times they often are the first to be sacrificed.

The wild shrimp harvest held steady only due to increased landings from the *barcos de alta mar*—the high-seas fleet—and in 2004, for the first time ever, aquaculture production exceeded the wild catch. In spite of chronic disease problems, the farm harvest continued to stream northward to the border, where the Mexican Shrimp Council worked to increase its market appeal amid the flood of farmed shrimp on the U.S. market. High-quality fish caught close to shore had its place among savvy consumers in a domestic market. But in the global economy, fishing has been about more than just having the best fish: it's been about moving them in commodity markets.

At Cozy Harbor Seafood in Portland, Maine, John Norton looked at what he had to offer clients who ranged from retail shoppers at his Commercial Street fish market to the Hannaford Brothers supermarket chain. Haddock, cod, flounder, and other wild species he bought at the Portland Fish Auction once dominated his line of products—along with Maine lobsters. But more and more, he featured an assortment of farmed products: shrimp and salmon dominate, but other species include tilapia, catfish, mussels, and clams.

"Figure you're a buyer," said Norton. "I come to you with my wild product. Sometimes I can supply you, sometimes I can't.

Maybe the price'll be high, maybe low, and the quality is all over the map. Then I offer you an aquaculture product, consistent supply, consistent quality, and consistent price. Which are you gonna buy?"

Norton believes wild products are better for his business and his community, but he bends to market forces. "I just put together a suite of products I'm offering," he said, "and less and less of it comes from the wild."

For chain restaurants such as Red Lobster, which buys 5 percent of the world's shrimp, consistency in price and quality are key. These two attributes alone allow the chain seafood restaurants to set up cost-effective nationwide promotions and specials. No need to tailor marketing to specific regions and local products, although that is done to a degree. Aquaculture products purchased in large quantities enable endless shrimp and salmon specials to become the backbone of seafood menus across the United States.

Chain restaurants served the beef industry well in building consumer confidence. With seafood, consumers maintained a much higher level of uncertainty, chain restaurants offered diners an opportunity to eat fish with a sense of safety. Diners who shied away from seafood in the past due to concerns about the type and quality of the fish they were served could now buy with confidence.

The shift in production and marketing changed America's taste in seafood. According to the National Fisheries Institute, a trade group, wild fish dominated America's top-ten favorite seafoods in 1987. By 2003, wild species slid down and off the list; cod dropped from third place to sixth, flounder disappeared.

Shrimp and salmon, much of it farmed, took over first and third places. In 2005 farmed tilapia, which few Americans ever heard of in 1987, was ranked sixth, ahead of cod at eight.

◆

Frank Rier returned from the Boston seafood show in 1989 having sampled farmed salmon from Norway and elsewhere. "I remember thinking how it all tasted really different from ours," he said. "Then my cousin Charlie and I had a salmon cook-out and I was just amazed at the fuller flavor that our fish had compared with what I'd just had at the show in Boston. I think it has to do with our faster currents and the amount of natural feed in the water."

Rier had hoped to capitalize on the unique flavor of Maine farmed salmon, but that ambition got lost with the fish in the commodity market. "We could have had a niche market," he said. "We could have produced a quality product that sold for above the market price. But the State made the regulations to suit the big companies, and we lost an opportunity."

For the thousands of people who had never eaten wild salmon or shrimp, the farmed varieties pouring out of Chile and Norway tasted great. Consumers could count on seafood being consistent, no surprises. The same situation evolved within the shrimp industry, quality took a back seat to consistency and ease of marketing. Vertically integrated companies that understood economies of scale production, global retailing, and control of inputs eventually dominated shrimp and salmon farming, rapidly consolidating both.

In 2002 five companies produced 40 percent of the world's salmon. Several of the big companies had started as feed suppliers who bought farms that owed them money after salmon prices sank in the late 1990s. In 2005 a series of major takeovers put one company, Panfish, owned largely by Norwegian billionaire John Fredriksen, in control of an estimated 30 percent of the 1.25 million tones of global farmed salmon production. Panfish also owned significant stock in other top producing salmon companies, making it the undisputed king of the farmed salmon industry.

❦

Charoen Pokphand (CP) offered one of the best examples of the kind of vertical integration that dominated industrial aquaculture at the beginning of the twenty-first century. The Chia brothers, Chinamen living in Bangkok, started the business 1921, exporting chickens and pigs back to China. They opened their first feed mill in 1954, and in 1986, under the direction of Dhanin Chearavanont, a son of one of the founders, CP diversified into shrimp farming. At that point CP controlled all the aspects of shrimp production, and in 1988 they moved into marketing, opening the restaurant chain, Chester's Grill, and Makro supermarkets followed in 1994 by its Lotus Supercenter chain of superstores. Through vertical integration and continued expansion CP controlled 60 percent of Thailand's domestic shrimp market, by 2005. That year the company exported two billion dollars worth of shrimp from Thailand alone, and became the world's largest exporter of frozen shrimp, with feed mills and farms all over south Asia.

According to its 2005 mission statement CP sought "to become a global agrifoods company, 'Kitchen of the World.'" The company also promised to utilize the best technology, protect animal welfare, and finally, to focus on producing "safe and healthy food."

The shrimp business was a bit more diversified in Mexico, but as the wild stocks struggled against overfishing, habitat destruction, and ecological breakdown, and farmed product flooded the market, more people resign themselves to eating it.

Ocean Garden Products handled 60 percent of the exported shrimp; as a government owned company OGP had "an obligation to the social sector," in the words of operations manager John Filose. The company loaned money to producers of every description: from the pangeros in Agiabampo to the powerful Bours family, whose members owned trawlers and shrimp farms, primarily in Sonora.

At the 2005 International Seafood Show, John Filose sat at his company's booth chatting with *New York Times* food writer Jane Brody. Behind them a chef prepared Ocean Garden shrimp. Shrimp, glistening after a light sauté in white wine, or garlic sat on small plastic dishes. The chef skewered one with a toothpick and pushed it toward me. The shrimp OGP served came from Mexican farms, but it tasted delicious; other farmed shrimp at the show did not compare.

"It's all in the post harvest handling," Filose said. "Ocean Garden figured that out a long time ago." But how did they prevent farmed shrimp from being sold as wild for a higher price? I wondered. According to Filose, OGP developed a tracking process to distinguish between farmed product and the wild shrimp that still made up 30 percent of the company's production, and historically had always been its premier item. "Besides, you can tell wild shrimp," said Filose, describing the different features that distinguished the two products. "Wild shrimp are a mix of sizes and with farmed shrimp you find a lot of times that they have black tails."

In 2006 the Mexican foreign trade bank Bancomext sold OGP to a Sonora based consortium of feed producers, and boat and farm owners, including the some of the Bours family, for 12 million dollars. The Bourses also own Bachoco, a major food retailer in Mexico. Diversification up and down the production and marketing chain within the consortium provided the level of vertical integration they would need to remain players in the highly competitive shrimp industry, where fishermen and growers from around the world competed for the big dollar markets of the Europe, Japan, and the United States.

In 2004 Americans ate 3.5 billion pounds of shrimp, 80 percent of it farmed, over four pounds per person, along with an estimated 500 million pounds of salmon, primarily farmed.

Without differentiating between wild and farmed raised products, marketers touted the benefits of eating fish. Who could tell looking at lovely red salmon fillets in the seafood case, which ones had developed that color through a natural diet and which had been dyed. No labels were required to identify farmed fish, or the chemicals used in their production. In Britain, when the government proposed labeling farmed fish, the five supermarket chains that controlled 80 percent of the country's retail food sales, fought the legislation.

≈

Wild fisheries fought to maintain their place in the market. Roger Flemming, of the Conservation Law Foundation, questioned the entire rationale behind growing salmon in Maine primarily to supply the fresh fish market in the northeast U.S. He believed rebuilding wild fisheries could fill that niche. "The biological maximum sustainable yields of wild fisheries in New England are three to four times current landings," said Flemming. "When those fisheries are rebuilt that's going to satisfy a lot of deman... Groups such as the Marine Stewardship Council (MSC), a certific... n agency established by Unilever LTD in 1996 promoted sust... ble wild fisheries through eco-labeling. In 1998 the Stewardship... ncil certified Alaska salmon as sustainably caught. But the re... filiate Thor Larsen, was that only two percent of consumers responded to eco-labeling if there was a significant difference in price, and beyond a doubt aquaculture put shrimp and salmon on the market cheaper than capture fisheries.

Consumers for the most part made a statement through their buying habits that they put economics ahead of social or environmental considerations. Cheap fish were more important than sustainably produced fish.

U.S. wild shrimp fishermen fought at another level for their product's place in the market. Together with shrimp processors, and with support from Mexican shrimp producers, they petitioned for anti-dumping tariffs against India, China, Vietnam, Thailand, Brazil and Ecuador.

In 2004 the U.S. federal trade commission found in favor of the fishermen and imposed duties on the targeted countries. The tariffs led to a 43 percent drop in Thailand's shrimp exports to the United States in the first quarter of 2005. While the shrimp industries in countries charged with dumping are controlled by large multinationals such as Thailand's Charoen Pokphand, and Mitsubishi of Japan; small farmers too, felt the impacts of anti-dumping actions as their shrimp backed up at the border and prices dropped. Small importers suffered because the U.S. required them to post a bond, equal to the previous year's imports multiplied by the tariff, an amount that sometimes reached into the millions of dollars.

"I spoke at the hearings," said Brian Marks, a native of Houma, Louisiana and an advocate for shrimp fishermen. "At the time the duties seemed like a good idea but in the end they may have done more harm than good. They could end up driving a lot of processing jobs out of the country," said Marks, noting that the anti-dumping duties did not cover breaded shrimp, and that shrimp breading facilities were proliferating in shrimp exporting countries.

"We realize these people need to work," said Marks, who does not consider the duties he helped impose to be the ultimate solution. "What we really need are quotas and floor prices like they have with textiles," he said. "That would raise prices for everyone, and we could share the market without hurting each other so badly."

Margaret Curole, wife of a shrimp fisherman, and the U.S.

representative to the World Forum of Fish Harvesters and Fish-workers (WFF), claimed the anti-dumping duties have done little to help fishermen. "Things are so good right now," she said in a voice full of sarcasm, "that my husband is out driving a tug boat." Like many fishing communities in the United States, her home of Galliano, Louisiana, had undergone a transformation as more fishermen, unable to support their families at a U.S. average standard of living, have sought other work. "We come from 5 generations of fishing families," said Curole. She is descended from the Acadian French refugees expelled from Canada in 1756, and her Cajun accent reveals her heritage. "I never left home till I got involved with the WFF, now I've traveled all over the world."

On a recent visit to China, Curole met a shrimp trade specialist. "He asked me what I thought about duties, and I told him they weren't helping us." Tariffs have raised prices paid to fishermen less than 10 percent on average, not enough to compensate for 50 percent drop between 2000 and 2002 alone.

"We talked about getting people together to explore the option of a quota system and price controls," said Curole. But when she presented the quota idea to the Southern Shrimp Association, the most powerful organization in the Ad Hoc committee that petitioned for anti-dumping duties: "They foo-fooed me out of hand," she said. "They didn't want to talk about it because they figured they were going to get money from the Byrd Amendment," she added, referring to United States legislation that would distribute revenues from anti-dumping duties to the injured parties—mostly processors.

As Curole and others sought creative solutions to the

worldwide shrimp glut and other fisheries issues. Maintaining artisanal fisheries did not appear high on the global policy agenda. The Food and Agriculture Organization, for example, refused to examine how proposed Non-agriculture Market Access (NAMA) rules within the World Trade Organization would affect wild fisheries, though Japan warned that by opening up more markets, NAMA would lead to increased fishing pressure on some species, risking further resource declines.

Marks expressed a similar concern that if NAMA went through it would facilitate the movement of more fish from the developing world to wealthier countries, and continuing negative impacts on quality and sustainability. "It will close off options to long term solutions," he said. "It will also lead to a greater internationalization of fisheries, where species such as New Zealand's orange roughy, and the Patagonian toothfish find international gourmet markets and then that leads to over-fishing."

In spite of the risks to their futures small fishing communities have had little to say about global trade. "The problem we have," said Curole. "Is that most fishermen wouldn't have a clue what you were talking about if you said WTO or NAMA. By the time they feel the impacts, it'll be too late." Efforts by Curole, Marks and many others to remove the institutionalized blinders from fishing communities worldwide, aim ultimately to enable small-scale seafood producers to reap the benefits of trade without destroying cultures and ecosystems.

But the focus of many activists, NGOs, and quasi-private organizations such as the Marine Stewardship Council, remained global. These groups and individuals operated within a paradigm defined by corporate objectives. Mexican fish-monger, Joel Leal, driving around with 200 pounds of fish and shrimp in the back of a beat up Subaru, did not show up on their radar. But if a chance for sustainable seafood production existed, odds are it would be rooted in small-scale local activities such as his.

At the opening of the twenty-first century a critical point had arrived in seafood production—a choice between three fundamental worldviews. First came those, somewhat abandoned by scientists, governments, and investors, who sought to create sustainable seafood production that included sustainable societies: the cultures and communities with long histories in fisheries and aquaculture. Then came those who wanted to rebuild wild stocks and develop harvest and marketing systems that would enable commercial fisheries to compete within a market defined by farmed products. Another path, promoted by the many in governments around the world, would move full bore toward an aquaculture dominated seafood market, and the end of the wild.

14

VOICES FROM HOME

EDINBURGH, SCOTLAND

Alan Berry, a former oyster farmer from west of Glasgow, Scotland, believed that salmon farms wiped his out his small shellfish operation. In 1996, a year after a salmon farm was established in the same sea loch where Berry had his farm, all his oysters died.

"They died from the tributyl used to treat the salmon nets. It's deadly to oysters," said Berry, who began investigating the environmental impacts of salmon farming, and soon became an avid foe of the industry. He arrived in Maine in the fall of 1999, after Atlantic Salmon of Maine applied for a lease in the middle of Blue Hill Bay, within sight of the upscale community of Blue Hill. Wealthy landowners along the shore, concerned about the loss of their pristine view and consequent lowering of property values, formed the "Friends of Blue Hill Bay" and sought to intervene in the lease application process. Maine regulations did not recognize aesthetics as a legitimate issue in siting salmon farms, so the group flew Berry in to educate them on how to oppose salmon farming.

Dorothy Hayes invited me to meet Berry at a party she was throwing at her summer home: a house and outbuildings that stood on a promontory overlooking the bay. The proposed farm would be in view of some of the most expensive real estate in Maine.

"I have a friend who owns salmon farms in Chile," quipped Hayes as we waited for Berry. "He asked what I was doing and I had to tell him, fighting salmon farms. He said whose? And I said Atlantic Salmon of Maine, and he said, 'Go for it, Dorothy, they're rotten.'"

Berry, a balding man in his early sixties, arrived and gave a lengthy presentation on the biochemistry of salmon farms. Somewhat reserved, he answered questions afterward and it seemed he had confidence that the assembled crowd understood him perfectly. "Salmon farming on an industrial scale is organized environmental crime," he said.

But after the members of Save Blue Hill Bay stopped the lease in their bay, most ignored the issue. I e-mailed Berry several times afterward, and in 2005 we spoke again in Scotland. Berry fumed at what he considered the collusion of industry, science, academia, and mainstream NGOs.

"The marine-science establishment failed to properly assess the damage," said Berry. "In the United States they stopped applying the law, the Clean Water Act."

One of the key points that Berry made again and again was that the nutrients from salmon farms change the ecology of the waters over a wide area.

"They've suckered the environmentalists into believing the problem is the wee patch under the cage. But you have an incredible level of nutrients going into the water, especially in summer, and it forms a plume that stretches far beyond the cages." According to Berry, the increased nitrate levels lead to the formation of ammonia and the growth of toxic bacteria that leads to amnesiac shellfish poisoning (ASP). The closure of ten thousand square miles of scallop beds off western Scotland due to ASP added weight to his contention.

In the United States, government agencies sent mixed messages on the subject. NOAA called bacteria and oxygen-depleting substances—such as those generated by wastes from salmon and shrimp farms—the biggest threats to estuarine systems. At the same time, Dr. Sherwood Hall, a phytoplankton expert with the Food and Drug Administration dismissed aquaculture's contribution to pollution as minimal. On a large scale, Hall may have been correct, overall aquaculture generated pollutants hardly comparable with those from other sources such as sewer runoff, but Berry looked at impacts on a local scale.

"We never had a toxic algae bloom in all my life, until the salmon farming started," said Berry, who tried to present three papers at a 2004 meeting of the International Committee for Environmental Science (ICES). "I wanted to talk about toxins, ASP, and nitrates. They refused the papers because they said I was using other people's data. It was government data!"

According to Berry, the industry used intimidation to quiet dissent. "They frighten any academic who shows his head. Sherwood Hall, the biggest protector of the world's biggest polluters, called me a communist. We're being discredited as eco-terrorists."

Berry also raised the alarm about sea lice proliferating among farmed salmon and attacking wild fish. In 1999, the Scottish Executive, Scotland's ruling body, put a limit of two lice per fish in an effort to control the problem, but did not admit that salmon farms had any negative effect on wild salmon stocks.

Berry was dismayed. "It's not beyond the wit of man to solve problems within limits," he said. "But this is a misadventure. The scale is so big that even if you allow two lice per fish, that's millions of egg strands going into the water. Smolts going out to sea swim through clouds of this and get loaded up with lice, they weaken and become easy prey for other species."

Feeling the pressure of the forces he opposed, Berry, too, began to waver in his commitment to his cause of over ten years. "I've gone broke fighting salmon farms," he said. "I'm sixty-eight years old, somebody else will have to take over."

Among others, Bruce Sandison, chairman of the Salmon Farm Protest Group, took over, and he was adamant. "Parasitic sea lice breed in billions in farm salmon cages. They attack and kill wild salmon and sea trout as they pass by on their way to and from natal rivers. Many west highland and island rivers and lochs that once supported large populations of wild salmonids are now devoid of these species," Sandison wrote in 2005. He kept the pressure and focus on the sea lice issue, and in March of 2006, the Scottish Executive admitted that sea lice were having a negative impact on wild salmon. Amid strong objections from salmon farmers, the government imposed stricter limits on where salmon cages could be placed and in what densities. "Too much regulation," according to the salmon farmers; "not enough," said people like Sandison.

BANGOR, MAINE

In Maine, too, a few agitators continued to raise issues about the impacts of salmon farms, and regulators sought to come to grips with the industry's problems. The salmon farmers fought for their commercial existence.

> Bangor Daily News, *Augusta, Maine (February 8, 2002) Salmon-farm workers and their families packed into a legislative hearing room Thursday and ripped into a proposed law that they said would destroy a vital industry in their Down East communities.*
>
> *Also in the crowd were environmentalists and coastal residents who supported the bill. They argued with equal passion that strict new rules are needed to keep the fish farms from destroying the health and character of the Maine coast.*
>
> *More than 200 people attended* [bussed to the hearing by their employers] *packing the State House hearing room, spilling into the hallway and filling a second room set up with speakers to broadcast the arguments. The contentious public hearing lasted more than five hours, but provided few hints about what lawmakers will do with the proposal.*

In 2000, Maine had the largest Atlantic salmon aquaculture industry in the United States. Output that year reached thirty-six million pounds; eight million more pounds than the state's groundfish landings, but by 2002 the aquaculture boom seemed to be winding down. The salmon industry managed to marshal its rank and file to make a showing at the hearing, where they made a point to blame well-funded environmental groups from out of state for destroying their industry. But contrary to the industry's claims, the most formidable opposition to its expansion often came from local people. Resistance from people who lost money by fighting salmon farms carried more weight than attacks by hired dogs.

"We need to stop and think about how we're going about this," Marsden Brewer, a lobsterman out of Stonington, Maine, said of salmon aquaculture. "With fisheries' management all we hear about is effort reductions, with aquaculture it's all about expansion," he said.

"It's time for a moratorium," Brewer told the state legislature's Committee on Marine Resources in February. The committee debated the merits of a two-year moratorium on salmon aquaculture leases, but in its final aquaculture reform bill, dropped that provision and instead gave municipalities power to govern aquaculture within two thousand five hundred feet of their shorelines.

While the legislature compromised salmon aquaculture on one front, more legal action hit on another. Federal judge Margaret Kravchuk recommended that three salmon aquaculture companies operating in Maine, be found in violation of the Clean Water Act.

According to the Maine Aquaculture Association's Sebastian Belle, it was a bum rap. Yes, the farms had been operating since their inception without wastewater discharge permits, but they had applied for the permits. "The Environmental Protection Agency told them they did not have the criteria for granting permits and turned it over to the state." Belle expressed frustration, noting that the technical issues of aquaculture are too varied and complex for citizen legislatures and overburdened bureaucrats. "It's a lot to ask of fisheries managers to reeducate themselves around a whole new industry," he said. "It's very frustrating when we have to debate simple things that have already been settled elsewhere. People need to read the literature."

But the literature Belle referred to generally promoted the tedious stakeholder approach, where all interested parties had a voice. Belle supported that process, with qualifications. "The demographics of many coastal municipalities have changed," he claimed, "so that they no longer reflect the interests of those who make their living from the sea." Belle contended that such gentrified coastal towns "should not have veto power over aquaculture and fisheries development."

GRAND MANAN, NEW BRUNSWICK

On the island of Grand Manan, New Brunswick, fishermen's representative Klaus Sonnenberg, executive director of the Grand Manan Fishermen's Association, pointed out that the three companies running the salmon industry in Maine and New Brunswick were all European. "These farms are not locally owned," said Sonnenberg. "The people here will end up as servants to corporations with their headquarters in another country."

Lobstering and herring fishing had always been the mainstays of the island, and those industries had proven themselves over the test of time, argues Sonnenberg. "It would be a shame to see these fisheries pushed out of the bay to make room for what is essentially a young and unproven industry," he says.

Fishermen on the island pointed out many other problems with salmon aquaculture. Cypermethrin, a common pesticide used to treat salmon, broke down the chitin of sea louse shells, but chitin also formed lobster shells. In a famous case at a lobster pound in Back Bay, New Brunswick, lobster buyer George Guptil claimed a shift in the tide at the time the farm was treating its salmon with cypermethrin carried the pesticide into his pound and killed ten thousand pounds of lobster. Guptil had no backing from any national or international environmental group, and in 2006 he was still seeking compensation from Cooke Aquaculture.

BAR HARBOR, MAINE

In 1992, Inka Milewski, an environmental consultant for the Conservation Council of New Brunswick, began examining the impacts of salmon farming on the coastal waters of Maine and neighboring New Brunswick. She noted that in 1992 salmon farms put 290 metric tons of nitrogen into New Brunswick's L'Etang Inlet, compared to 130 tons from all other sources, including human sewage.

"It's just another human-generated stress," said the intense and energetic Milewski, speaking at a conference on the impacts of climate change, held at the College of the Atlantic, in Bar Harbor, Maine. In a book, coauthored with Heike Lotze of Dalhousie University in Halifax, Milewski documented an increase in dinoflagellates in the waters of Passamaquoddy Bay and the outer Bay of Fundy, the most heavily farmed salmon aquaculture region in North America.

"The elevation of ammonium levels on a local scale," said Milewski, "has led to a shift in the phytoplankton favoring dinoflagellates."

Milewski suggested that the controlled nature of aquaculture would enable fish farmers to apply technological solutions to problems caused by climate change, while enjoying the benefits of enhanced growth rates for northern aquaculture species predicted in the Intergovernmental Panel on Climate Change (IPCC) report.

I tried to talk to Milewski after the conference. She couldn't stay, she said, she had a lot of work to do and it was a four hour drive back to her home in Fredericton. I walked her to her car, a Toyota Corolla, and waved good-bye. Before she left, she handed me a free copy of her book, *Two Hundred Years of Ecosystem and Food Web Changes in the Quoddy Region, Outer Bay of Fundy*. "Read this," she said. "It should answer a lot of your questions."

Indeed, the book tracked the utilization of the bay from extrapolations of indigenous food-gathering to the present. It revealed the rapidly intensifying exploitation of the bay, as a source for raw materials, a sink for waste disposal, and a means of transportation after the arrival of Europeans in North America. By the year 2000, the bay served less as a source of food—the millennia-old scallop, pollack, and herring fisheries were virtually extinct—and more as a sink for effluents from paper mills and towns throughout the watershed, and salmon farm waste.

Milewski's book classed the term "farming the sea as a misnomer." From her perspective, the business of growing salmon in net pens in open water looked more like "fouling the sea."

"That's why the New Brunswick Conservation Council decided not to go at aquaculture from a consumer perspective," Milewski said in a later interview. "Other groups are working on consumer concerns, but we're most concerned with ecological issues: sustainability and impacts on communities and ecosystems."

Unlike many observers of the aquaculture industry, Milewski did not let shellfish farmers off the hook. "Jamming the bays and estuaries with suspension culture of oysters and mussels has impacts, too," she said. "Tracadie Bay is 35 percent full of mussel lines. These are filter feeders and when you grow them in huge systems they strip the water of nutrients that other organisms need."

According to Milewski, aquaculture did not offer an innovative solution to the problem of feeding the world, it acted instead as a BandAid for a terminally ill ecosystem. "Why are we turning to aquaculture?" she asked. "Our regulators have given up on managing wild resources. It's become out of fashion to be a fisherman. It's more efficient to concentrate aquaculture production and rationalize all the ill effects."

She blamed human ingenuity for what she saw as the ongoing destruction of Passamaquoddy Bay and the global ecosystem. "Every creature has something," she said. "Tuna, for example, evolved incredible speed, but they can't stop swimming. We evolved these incredible brains: they're the very best and the very worst. They create so many unecological systems, and they don't stop."

The conservation industry, as Milewski saw it, would not stop the spread of aquaculture. "Salmon aquaculture is a cash cow for environmental groups," she said. According to Milewski, in the 1960s, when DDT was being sprayed throughout the watershed critical to wild Atlantic salmon, the Atlantic Salmon Federation (SFA) was working to protect salmon by paying a bounty for shooting mergansers—ducks that ate salmon smolts. "The SFA got fourteen million dollars for salmon restoration, but they've never gone after the CEOs of big polluters," she said, referring to the organization's relationship with industry. "I worry that most big NGOs are going down that same road."

Milewski worked for over twenty years to bring sustainable use to in the unique ecosystem of Passamaquoddy Bay and continued to do so as of this writing. "I do it for my children, my grandchildren," said the fifty-year-old activist. "Let's face it, my life is ending. One out of two women gets cancer in this province. I'll be happy if I see another ten years."

Broughton Archipelago, British Columbia

While Milewski took on salmon farming in New Brunswick, another Canadian woman, Alexandra Morton, fought the industry on the Pacific Coast. Salmon farming pilot projects began in British Columbia in 1970s, and by 2005 the province produced 61,800 metric tons of fish. The salmon farming industry claimed to provide 1,800 direct jobs to coastal communities, but as far as Morton was concerned the industry took far more than it gave. "In terms of jobs, environmental health, and community pride we've seen a loss," said Morton.

In her efforts to compel the salmon farming industry to take more responsibility for what she saw as its environmental and social impacts, Morton became something of an amateur expert in salmon diseases, parasites and the biology of wild fish.

"This is not what I came to British Columbia to do," said Morton. "I came with my husband to study orcas." Morton's husband drowned while studying killer whales, leaving her with a two-year-old baby and not much else. She stayed in the small community and over the years repaid their support by doing her utmost to protect the wild fish and the way of life they sustain.

Morton worked to document the spread of disease from farmed to wild salmon, escapees, the spread of sea lice to wild fish, and even a situation where farmed fish in the cages feed on wild smelt coming out of the rivers, competing directly for food with wild populations while never leaving the cages. "A guy told me, when the oolichan are running we cut our feed by half."

Speaking at meetings and public hearings, Morton hammered at the DFO, demanding action and accountability. "They don't want to do the research because they don't want to know the answers," she said.

Berry, Milewski, Morton, and others all sought to fill a void left by science—a void noticed on many fronts. Economic writers from Phillip Murowski (*The Effortless Economy of Science*) to Michael Polyani (*The Republic of Science*) looked deeply into the shifting philosophy of science as a tool of government and business. Ecological economist Gilberto Gallopin and several colleagues published a paper in 2002 entitled "Science for the Twenty-First Century: From Social Contract to the Scientific Core," in which they contended that since World War II science had become the domain "where 'solutions can be found.'" At the same time, they noted "a strong ideological privileging of the intended purpose, a desired outcome, over the unintended side effects." Or to paraphrase Morton: science was intended to find solutions, not more problems.

"Any uncontrolled change effects [disease outbreaks, for example] are interpreted as symptoms of the imperfection in the current knowledge and/or its application," wrote Gallopin, "with the presumption that more knowledge will reduce uncertainties, increase capacity for control, and permit the remedying of past mistakes."

Essentially, Gallopin described the view of the techno-optimists, which included, in fact, required, certain blind spots. According to Gallopin, the problems of development were of as much interest as the solutions, and bore examination rather than disregard. Gallopin noted that science for the future would have to include "drastic broadening to account for the inter-linkages between the object of study and other parts of reality." Other parts of the social and environmental dimensions of applied reality included industrial seafood farming and biotechnology.

The scientific work conducted by people like Berry, Milewski and Morton sought to shed light on those linkages. But their work flew in the face of the dominant system, and they often became marginal characters at the conferences, such as ICES, where global scientific ideas were formed. In the fishing communities under siege on a variety of fronts, other individuals fought to maintain their cultures in the face of rapid change. Many felt that capture fisheries still offered the surest way to provide sustainable seafood for the most people, but development funds, science and political force had aligned behind aquaculture.

15

Go Wild

There are some limiting factors that may begin to slow the rate of growth of aquaculture: tightening of fish-based meal prices; growing commercial and residential demand for coastal real estate; and a belated public concern for environmental and social costs. But there is no doubt that the beast will grow rapidly in the near term. I wish the same energy and money could be devoted to better management and resolute rebuilding schedules for the capture fisheries.
— James Crutchfield, former member of the Stratton Commission

GLOUCESTER, MASSACHUSETTS

For over ten years, Niaz Dorry worked to preserve the small boat fleet of United States fishermen. She began as a Greenpeace Ocean's Campaigner in 1996 and by 1998 *Time* magazine named her one of its "Heroes of the Planet." Dorry left Greenpeace in 2000 and has since worked on her own, establishing the NGO Clean Catch in 2004.

While maintaining her focus on small-boat fisheries, Dorry expressed strong views on fish farming and aquaculture in general. "I don't see the need for any of it in the ocean," she said as she stood in the hall during the Maine Fishermen's Forum, at the Samoset Resort in Rockport, Maine. "It all lowers prices and that sends the wrong signal to the consumers: the price of seafood is low, there must be plenty."

Dorry wanted a future where healthy fishing communities harvested sustainable resources in ways that did not destroy the environment. Not too much to ask. To that end, she attended countless meetings of the New England Fishery Management Council, conducted field research and wrote the lengthy articles for the *Fishermen's Voice*.

Paradoxically, she and her perceived opponents expressed the same desires. "I had this strange conversation with Jeff Kaelin," said Dorry, referring to a lobbyist for the high tech sector of the herring industry. "He said 'all I want is sustainable fisheries.' I said, well that's all I want, why are we on opposite sides of the table?"

The answer to her question seemed fairly apparent. Everyone from John Filose to Thomas Kocherry sought sustainability, each in their own way. They simply prioritized different legs of the sustainability triangle. The Subasinghes, for example, agreed on the ends—solidarity and fair trade—but differed on the means. Rohana held up economic sustainability while his son put more importance on social and environmental issues. Kaelin, a lobbyist for the herring industry, sided with Rohana and the crowd that saw net profit as the measure of sustainability. As long as the resource could provide a continuous monetary return on the harvester's investment it could be considered sustained. Any problems, Kaelin believed, could be solved through the wise use of existing technology, or the development of better technology.

"The other side thinks ahead. They cast us as reactionary and they're the future," said activist Dorry. "We need to change that."

Dorry sees the situation holistically. Her view of the future goes beyond Kaelin's, to include healthy cultures, resources, and ecosystems that increased in their ability to produce real wealth: fish.

"Turn-of-the-century industrialization became irreversible," said Dorry. "The trawler allowed fishing nonstop, twelve months a year. Post-war technology took that a step further—took us past sustainability, demanding more from the ocean than it could ever give, and destroying its ability to generate fish at the same time. The old fashioned notion that the sea can support infinite exploitation has to go."

CORDOVA, ALASKA

For a number of years, Ann Mossness's e-mail address has been: eatwildfish@aol.com. Mossness was a fisher-turned-activist. She started gillnetting salmon as a teenager, working with her Norwegian-born father in Bristol Bay, Alaska, in 1972. She was shaking sleek silver salmon out of the meshes long before the word *aquaculture* became part of her vocabulary. Once fish farming took off, however, she saw prices for sockeye salmon, one of her mainstays, drop from $2.48 a pound in 1988 to $ 0.40 cents a pound in 1991.

In 2001 Mossness started the Go Wild campaign to promote wild fish and worked under the umbrella of the Institute for Agriculture and Trade Policy (IATP) Marine and Fish Conservation Program. Five years later, she accepted a grant from the National

Environmental Trust to help direct a consumer awareness campaign highlighting the benefits of eating wild fish.

☙

"I'm concerned about environmental funders completely willing to end commercial fishing," said Mossness. "But I feel like I've been able to educate a lot of environmentalists that all fishing is not the same. Comparing our gillnet fishery in Bristol Bay to the high seas drift net fishery is ridiculous," she said, referring to the misconceptions she often faced when she tells people she uses a gillnet. "They have these images of sharks and dolphins wrapped up the nets. I'll bet last year we didn't have one thing in our nets that wasn't a salmon."

In 2006, Mossness bought twenty thousand dollars worth of salmon fillets that she sold through mail order and around her off-season home in Bellingham, Washington. "I'm trying to convince the big buyers that there's a strong domestic demand for sustainably harvested wild fish," she said.

Mossness saw aquaculture as a major threat to Alaska's wild fisheries and fishing culture, and she worked to focus people's attention on the effects salmon farming has on fish stocks and fishing communities in British Columbia. Mossness contended that escapees would spread disease and colonize Alaskan streams, and the Alaska Department of Fish and Game supported her assertions. The state banned salmon farming in 1990, and maintained its prohibition in the face of ever-increasing pressure, including the proximity of Canadian salmon farms on the southern border.

"The annual release of tens of thousand of Atlantic salmon into the already-challenged Pacific Coast ecosystem amounts to biological pollution," said a 1999 Alaska Department of Fish and Game (ADF&G) white paper on Atlantic salmon.

The report pointed out that the cultured salmon were inoculated against disease, and raised concerns that the "use of antibiotics may result in diseases mutated into more virulent or antibiotic-resistant forms." Although the risk of disease transfer is deemed low, "documentation of the passage of diseases from farmed salmon to wild stocks is difficult given the lack of baseline information on the prevalence of disease organisms in wild fish populations."

The biggest threat that surfaced in the report highlighted competition from Atlantic salmon escapees that had already spawned successfully in British Columbia's Tsitika River, and had showed up in spawning condition in southeast Alaska streams. Equally real was the problem of farm raised coho and Chinook salmon escaping and breeding with wild fish. "The potential for genetic damage is high," said the report.

Alaska recommended a number of measures to contain the problems in British Columbia, including "the eventual closing down of the industry" if problems persist.

"We don't want to see the industry expand north," said Glenn Oliver, of the ADF&G. But in 2002 British Columbia lifted its moratorium and the farms moved closer to the Alaska border.

By the end of 2005, the Offshore Aquaculture Act, which threatened to bring fish farms to federal waters only three miles from shore anywhere off the coast of Alaska, became Mossness's biggest target.

Mossness pointed out that nine out of sixteen people on the president's Ocean Commission, which spent three years formulating an oceans policy for the twenty-first century, had ties to extractive industries. "They're all looking at the EEZ for the next get-rich-quick scheme," she said, noting that the OAA threatened to undermine Alaska's aquaculture ban by putting fish pens just outside state waters. Mossness referred to an Alaskan economist, Gunnar Knapp, who advocated ending the ban on salmon aquaculture and making fisheries and aquaculture more economically efficient. "Our inefficiency is intentional," said Mossness. "That's what makes small-scale fishing operations sustainable." Unlike Dorry, Mossness did not haunt the hall at fisheries meetings. "Corporations and bureaucrats would like to wear us out with meetings, so we go directly to the public," she said.

STONINGTON, MAINE

Maine lobsterman Ted Ames achieved instant notoriety in 2005, when the MacArthur Foundation awarded him a five-hundred-thousand-dollar fellowship to help create sustainable fisheries in the Gulf of Maine. Ames had long been a familiar figure in the Maine fishing community. I first heard him on the VHF radio in 1983, talking to Bernard Raynes as the *Irene Alton* passed Ames's boat, the *Dorothy M*. When I met him in person three years later in Eastport, Maine, Ames had run the hundred miles from his home in Stonington to the Canadian border to catch the fall run of cod and winter flounder in Passamaquoddy Bay. "Quite a lot of tide down here," he said as he repaired his net at the Eastport breakwater. He managed to tear it up on every tow but the fish filling his hold more than paid for the damage. Ames made it downeast for the last big year. After 1986 the cod never came back in numbers to justify the effort.

I did not see him again until I arrived in Stonington ten years later, chasing sea urchins. Ames had sold the *Dorothy M*. "She was an old boat when I got her," he said, "and getting a bit tender for going offshore."

Ames earned his money lobstering and spent his spare time accumulating historical data about cod spawning grounds. He interviewed old fishermen, reviewed their logbooks and charts, and chased down information anywhere he could find it. By the late 1990s, copies of his paper on the cod spawning grounds of inshore Maine had circulated throughout the regulatory and scientific arenas of New England fisheries. His work was used to justify the closure of all Maine waters to groundfish gear during the spawning season, May to November.

A thin, wiry man with a narrow face, high forehead, and sharp eyes, Ames usually spoke in a cultivated tone. With his ever-present pipe in his mouth, he often seemed more like a professor than a fisherman. He had grown up in a fishing family on Vinalhaven, an island in Penobscot Bay, but he showed some smarts and they sent him off to Bowdoin College. He went on to earn a PhD and taught school for a while, but in the end he could not get fishing out of his blood. His community was proud when he went off and proved himself in academia, prouder still when he returned to become known as "the educated fisherman." When I saw him in 1983, he had been back on the water for a year. When we last spoke, in 2006, he was sixty years old, still fishing, and wondering how to proceed with his fellowship.

He wanted to expand on his work, trying to rebuild the inshore cod stocks and protect their spawning grounds. I asked him where aquaculture fit in.

"I think it could be great for the inshore fisheries if we used it right," said Ames. "There are a lot of these nursery areas that we haven't lost yet and we could use aquaculture to raise fish that we could put in to hold these areas from being lost." Ames pointed out that when species get fished down, their effect on the ecology disappears. The ecosystem shifts in unpredictable ways; even as stocks rebuild in some areas it can take decades to recolonize former habitat, if it can ever be recolonized at all.

"If we could raise cod to, say, fingerling size and then let them go in these areas, that might make all the difference."

For Ames, the promise of finfish aquaculture rested in its ability to help restore wild fisheries. He felt that anything else, such as raising fish to market size, worked against that. "If somebody can make a few bucks that's fine, but what about its impact? These juvenile fish we're trying to protect smell all that feed, they get attracted to it and swim into the pen where they become feed themselves."

Ames had not heard about ecological economics or the sustainable development evaluation technique, but he knew that communities with a vested interest in maintaining an ecosystem that produced the wealth they lived on offered the best hope for management with a long-term view. Investment capital inevitably discounted the future, leading to management decisions that favored the short term view.

According to Ames, 80 percent of the fish landed in Maine are caught by 5 percent of the boats. "The balance is dangerously shifting," he said, warning that consolidation would leave most small fishermen working for a few large companies. Ames joined several others in founding the "Downeast Initiative," a program to create viable community-based management. "The bottom line is that we need to develop a strategy that allows stocks to recover. And we need to find a logical way to remove pressure from habitats, improve what we have left and not cut anyone out. Fishermen need to take an active role in conservation of stocks and gain more control over their livelihoods." He admitted, however, that the goal seemed a long way off. "Perhaps if some of these aquaculture people would work with us, we could do something for the habitats," he said.

KERALA, INDIA

The efforts of Ames and Mossness offered examples of a global movement toward sustainability on the premise of community control and an economy that valued more than money. The World Forum of Fishworkers and Fish Harvesters launched in India in the 1990s spread its message throughout the world. Among other things, it demanded the recognition of women's contributions to fisheries. In places such as Kerala, India, fisheries cooperatives took a new and enlightened approach to shepherding their resources, and maintaining their resource base, including aquaculture geared to the artisanal sector.

Nalini Nayak, of the International Collective in Support of Fish Workers (ICSF), wrote that the last decades of the twentieth century brought on the organization of artisanal fishworkers in southern India. Groups organized by ICSF and the National Forum of Fishworkers marched to protest the expansion of industrial shrimp farms, trawlers, and the destruction of their resource base. At the same time, activists such as Nayak worked within fishing communities to address the problem of fishermen participating in their own downfall. "Ironically, while artisanal fishworkers fought against trawlers, they themselves contributed to the bust by going increasingly for outboard motors and destructive gear," Nayak wrote in 2006. Citing ecological economist John Kurien, Nayak framed the dilemma that entrapped fishing people all over the world. "[Kurien] shows that high energy use from a certain level makes equity impossible, and shows how beating entropy and inequality by higher energy use (high tech gears, boats, motors) is a self-destructive reflex which fritters away the gains of political struggle to assert rights of the artisanal fishworkers over coastal waters."

People working to create a future for large communities of small producers fought against an old system where capital and technology appropriated resources. Proponents of that system also seek sustainability, but they see it in terms of a reorganization of fisheries and aquaculture according to free market principles. The future appears a continuation of late twentieth century methods of harnessing fossil fuel energy and human ingenuity to further exploit the productivity of the sea.

16

FISHERIES SURVIVORS

On a brisk bright morning, Halloween day 2001, the crews of several scallop boats crowded the wharves of Lunenburg, Nova Scotia. Dressed in an assortment of plaid hunting jackets and hooded sweatshirts, they stood in clusters, smoking and talking. Some held bundles of new gloves. The 110-foot scalloper *Ernest E. Pierce*, one of seven such boats operated by Clearwater Fine Foods, lay ready: fueled, iced, and grubbed up for a ten-day trip with a crew of nineteen. The reflection of her deep blue hull and white cabin shimmered in the calm harbor water.

Captain Gary McLeod, a neat, trim man wearing a leather jacket and fisherman's cap, hugged his wife good-bye and stepped aboard the big vessel. At fifty years old, he had thirty-seven years' experience aboard offshore scallop boats. "I quit school when I was thirteen, to help my mother with the family," he said. "But I never quit learning."

In the wheelhouse overlooking the deck, he blew several long blasts on the ship's horn. The noise resonated off the buildings of the old town: the brightly painted warehouses, homes, and stores that rose up in a rainbow of color on the hill above the harbor and culminated in the steeple of the 248-year-old Anglican church.

At the sound of the blast, the eighteen men under McLeod's command all came aboard, donned life jackets, and took their stations for the monthly emergency drill. Once they were aboard, McLeod sounded the horn again—four prolonged blasts: there would be no late sleepers in Lunenburg. The men went to work. One climbed aloft to change the wire on the tackle, something the Clearwater boats did every trip.

While the boat prepared to leave, a computer programmer for Deep Sea Trawlers—the company that runs Clearwater Fine Food's scallop fleet—came aboard with a floppy disc for McLeod. It contained computer-generated charts compiled from extensive surveys using multibeam and side scan sonar, along with underwater video, and extensive ground truthing by fishermen and biologists: all part of Canada's Seamap Program. Clearwater and four other fishing companies cooperated with the Canadian government to create these charts, which many believed would revolutionize fisheries, fisheries management, and other marine issues.

As McLeod booted up his computer and looked over what he called the 3D chart, Roy Rose, captain of another Clearwater boat, the *Ocean Lady*, just in from Brown's Bank, stepped into the wheelhouse. Rose's last tows had been overlaid on the chart and he pointed to the colored lines on McLeod's screen. "We were getting fifteen bushel a side of sixteen count here when we left," he said.

"Ooo, that's my kind of tow," McLeod said, imagining the mountains of big scallops covering his deck. Close to 9:00 A.M., sailing time, McLeod seemed anxious to cast the lines, but one of the crew appeared at the door. McLeod looked at him.

"We still need a port light in the starboard shucking house," said the older crewman. "Somebody pulled the gasket off and the glass must've gone overboard."

McLeod sent word to the maintenance crew ashore. Another Clearwater boat, the *Penny Luck*, left the dock on schedule. An hour and a half later, the *Ernest E. Pierce* followed, with a new port light in the starboard shucking house. Her 1200 Caterpillar pushed her along at eleven knots, and by late afternoon she overtook and passed the *Penny Luck*.

Just before the mate's watch turned out at midnight, McLeod prepared to make his first tow. He blew a short blast on the horn, and men came forward on either side of the boat. They hooked the tackles to the fifteen-foot-wide steel dredges, called rakes by the Nova Scotia fishermen, and lifted them onto the rails ready to set.

McLeod turned to his computer. The Seamap charts had been integrated into a computer program called Ocean Vision. He hit a button and a color-coded picture of the bottom appeared, its topography clearly visible, as if the water had been drained away. An icon for his vessel, connected to a GPS, flashed on the screen. "This Ocean Vision with the 3D overlay lets me see what the bottom really looks like, and where I am. Look at the difference," said McLeod, clicking a standard chart up on the computer. "This is what I used to go by," he said, pointing to a general contour line that bears as much resemblance to the real shape of the bottom as a smiley face does to a portrait photo. McLeod clicked back to the graphic 3D image. "This gives me resolution down to one meter," he said.

It was apparent that he could tell almost exactly where he would tow his rakes. "Before this, we would have been dragging all over, wasting time and effort and doing more harm than good."

He rang a bell. The boat rolled to port; deckhand John Conrad slammed his hammer down on the knock-out block, and the two-ton dredge slid off the rail and splashed into the sea. As the boat rolled to starboard, deckhand Todd Publicover, a survivor of the 1993 sinking of the offshore scalloper *Cape Aspy*, knocked out the starboard dredge.

The gear dug in and McLeod revved up the RPMs until the boat towed the gear at five knots. He watched a plot line grow along the top of a clearly defined ridge. The chart did not show a real-time image, but a graphic illustration of the bottom as it existed at the time of the multibeam survey.

"I checked it against my old tows," said McLeod, pointing at the shadows of two underwater cliffs. "You see these hook-ups? I knew they were there, but I didn't know I could tow between them." McLeod had found other hangs that coincided exactly with his old charts and numbers. He had grown to trust the multibeam data sets as dead-on accurate.

But the high-tech revolution still could not identify scallops on bottom. The color-coded overlays of bottom type, created by backscatter interpretation, only showed preferred bottom for scallops. "The scientist came out here with us and did some correlation studies to see if that's actually where we caught the scallops," said McLeod. "It came out pretty good."

Not this time. "A lot of it is still hit or miss," said McLeod, as the drags came aboard with only a few bushels of scallops.

After another fruitless experimental tow, he turned the wheel over to mate Wayne Knickle with instructions to head north and pick up Roy Rose's tow. At dawn, McLeod took command again and set his gear on Rose's tow. "We'll shoot away here and see if we can't get a rakeful," he said, and rang the bell. The hammers slammed down and the dredges—rakes, as McLeod called them—slid into forty-three fathoms. After twenty minutes, he hauled back a few bushels of large scallops. He kept the rakes aboard and steamed across what looked like rough sledding below.

"Years ago we would have plowed right through this," he said, nodding toward the plot line traversing the rubble pile. "I'll bet there must be twenty or thirty rakes in there. I know one of them's mine." He shot away again and after six minutes loaded the deck with good-size scallops. They came out twenty-seven to the pound.

"We'll load up here for the double watch and then go exploring." From his perch McLeod watched as the crew picked through the mountains of shell on either side of the deck. With much of the quota still in the water he ran double watches. The men worked a continuous rotation, seven hours on deck, five off; nonstop, night and day. The clatter of shells slamming into the wall of the shucking house seldom ceased.

❧

At the big galley table that seated ten men, the crew ate three big meals a day in two shifts. Cook Donald Smith, a Newfoundlander, had been aboard the *Ernest* since she rolled down the ways at Pictou, Nova Scotia in 1981. "Cheeks and tongues," he said as he passed a large bowl of deep fried cod cheeks and tongues to waiting hands at the table. The fishermen shoveled their plates full and dug in. Joey Mullock, a thirty-five-year veteran of the Lunenburg scallop fleet, muttered and made a sandwich. "I ain't eating that shit."

While the crew ground through its demanding routine, hoping for small graces such as clean tows, fair weather, and easy shucking, McLeod studied his chart and plotted out his strategy for putting a trip together. In the past he would have stayed and pounded the twenty-seven-count scallops.

"That was rape," he said. "Now we can utilize that bed. I can jump in there to keep the boxes full, and then look around, because I have an efficient tool to do that with." By the end of the first full day, his looking around had paid off, and McLeod and Knickle traded off working a bed of older scallops in sixty-three fathoms. The meats were small and the shells worm-ridden, but they made a thousand pounds a watch, and stayed on the tow for the next two days.

"These are old," McLeod said of the scallops. "They need to be wiped out. If we don't take them now, we'll come back next year and find a bunch of clappers [empty shells]." The tow looped between to outcroppings of hard bottom. "That's habitat for creatures," said McLeod. "And we don't have to plow through it anymore. We don't want to go there anyway."

Like many of the best fishermen, McLeod used to visualize a picture of the bottom. He had a 3D chart in his mind. He still had to exercise his ability to envision complex abstractions, like when the dredges came up tangled together beneath the boat. Working blind, McLeod untangled them with a slow turning of the boat and raising and dropping of the wires.

But he depended more on the new charts. He admitted he was losing the art of being able to imagine the bottom. "The numbers are leaving me," he said. "I hope that computer never crashes, 'cause it's going to take a part of my brain with it."

McLeod described the epiphany he experienced when he first used the multibeam charts. "It was like we were stumbling around a room, with a pen flashlight and somebody comes in and turns the lights on. Suddenly we can see where the furniture is and we don't have to bump into it any more."

Some observers worried that multibeam generated charts would be used to wipe out the resource, and McLeod admitted that without regulation the technology could be devastating. "It's like a loaded gun," he said. "It comes with a responsibility." McLeod claimed, however, that with quota management and rotational closures, the resource could be fished efficiently and sustainably.

He believed that the charts gave fishermen and environmentalists what they had been looking for: access to resources and protection of habitat. "I think eventually this will be the only way you're allowed to fish. I think the environmentalists will force it. Why hurt bottom when you don't have to."

McLeod continued to average over one thousand pounds of twenty-seven-count scallops a watch. At eight o'clock, on the morning of the fifth day—about half way through his trip—he set a dory over the side, and the relieving mate and I rowed across fifty yards of open sea to the *A.F. Pierce*, sister ship to the *Ernest*. I climbed up the Jacob's ladder of the homeward bound boat, and twelve hours later we steamed into Lunenburg harbor. But the town's skyline looked different. While we were gone, vandals had burned down the old church. The surprised crew vanished as soon as the lines were tied, and the town was quiet.

➤

The technology aboard the *E. E. Pierce* took scallopers a long way toward meeting the needs of the market in the age of aquaculture, but when I met McLeod a year later, I found him standing in the wheelhouse of a boat light-years ahead of anything the industry had seen. Mike Pittman, manager of the Clearwater subsidiary Deep Sea Trawlers, was giving me a tour of the company's new automated scalloper, the *Atlantic Leader*, and McLeod had earned the spot as her captain.

According to Pittman, who managed the 130-foot-long, 964-ton vessel, the *Atlantic Leader* was more than a new boat; it was a new concept. Aside from the dredges, winches, and shucking knives, there was little about the innovative vessel that resembled scallop boats of the past. "We're not 'fishin' any-more," said Pittman, as the 3.5 ton crane amidships loaded equipment aboard in preparation for the boat's first trip. "We're harvesting."

Since the early 1990s, wild-caught seafood had lost significant market share to aquaculture products. Seafood farmers could reduce uncertainty by offering consistent quality, steady price, and predictable delivery. According to Pittman, the *Atlantic Leader* and her sister ship, then under construction, would allow Clearwater to mimic the market advantages of aquaculture and deliver a higher-quality wild-caught product. "We're not stuck going into the American fresh market anymore," he said.

Pittman expected the boat to make up to eleven 30-day trips a year, an unheard of 330 sea days a year. "We have two alternating crews," he said. "No more stuck five days at the dock." The twenty-five-man crew would process frozen product for roughly the first twenty days and fresh for the last ten.

The mapping technology Clearwater had helped develop allowed the company to identify many existing scallop beds and their condition. "With the captain's database he knows what's out there and where it is," said Pittman.

At the time, processors processed what the boats brought them. "The system is production-based," said Pittman. The *Atlantic Leader,* he pointed out, could harvest and process what the market wanted, creating a demand-based system. The vessel's satellite communications systems allowed Pittman to transmit and alter production schedules while the vessel was at sea. "If the market wants twenty count or ten count, we can call the captain and he knows where to get it," he said. "We can now sign five year contracts and deliver the product the buyers want, when they want it."

Although the system relied on natural production, it eliminated much of the hunter-gatherer aspect of fishing. "We're like the farmer who knows what he's growing and for what market," said Pittman. Unlike the fish farmer, however, Clearwater did not have to pay the cost of hatching animals and tending them every day, although the company still made a big investment.

"Clearwater had to buy its quota," said Pittman. "And the company pays over one million a year in access fees."

Pittman expected the production and marketing advantages of the twelve-million-dollar *Atlantic Leader* to reward investors with a quota increase over the long run. "If we get say, an eighteen-hundred-ton quota on Georges, and turn around and take fewer animals to get that poundage, that's going to leave more animals on bottom to spawn. We could end up with a quota increase the next year."

On the downside, they busted the fishermen's union over the new boats. Fishermen who had worked on a share system signed on for wages, and once Clearwater had its new boats fully operational they planned significant job cuts. Before that came to pass, however, Clearwater sold their scallop business and pulled out of Lunenburg completely.

Almost Aquaculture

The lobster industry survived the late twentieth century bust in fishing because on the continuum of fisheries and aquaculture, it looked a lot like aquaculture. The product spent a good portion of its life in a trap, safe from predators and well fed. When harvesters hauled their traps they simply took out the market-size individuals and tossed the rest back unharmed. The lobster industry thrived, unthreatened by farm-raised competition.

June 1993, Trescott, Maine

A midnight in mid-June, Bill Anderson drives his tractor from his house down the dirt track to his wharf. Located at the head of Moose Cove on Maine's "Bold Coast," a stretch of cliffs that run along the last ten miles of the state's coast before hitting the New Brunswick border, the wharf is only usable for about six hours out of every twelve.

Anderson arrives and turns on a spotlight to illuminate his work. With the tractor, he lifts a pallet of boxes full of small net bags, each stuffed with rotting herring, and sets it down at the end of the wharf. Just above is the deck of his thirty-six-foot boat, the *Eleanor Kathryn*, named for his mother. Luna moths, rare giant green moths that live briefly on the June nights, have been attracted to the lights. Their long, graceful forked tails and lime-green backs stand out in stark contrast to the bait bags they land on.

Anderson nonchalantly ignores the moths and uses a hoist to lower twelve boxes, each holding over a hundred pounds of bait, onto the deck of his boat. He stacks them aft of the small wheelhouse, and grabbing his lunch pail he climbs down. In addition to the boxes of bait already on the boat, he has almost 2,000 pounds of salted herring aboard. (Maine lobstermen put an estimated 73,000 tons of herring in the water every year to catch 20,000 tons of lobster, which yield about 4,000 tons of lobster meat.)

❧

The tide has dropped perilously low and he will have to race it out of the cove. He has lost that race on occasion and run aground on the sand, where he has waited seven hours for the tide to return. He guns the engine and snakes down the thin channel that he knows intimately.

Behind him the propeller churns up the sand but he makes it over the bar and into the outer cove, where he motors over to a mooring ball and ties on. He climbs down into the small cuddy cabin in the bow and stretches out in his bunk. At dawn he awakens, starts the engine again, unties from the mooring and heads offshore.

Anderson is one of the most systematic and hardworking lobstermen on the coast. He has gone through numerous crewmen, including me. No one can keep up with him, so he works alone.

In the first light he searches the waters along the Canadian boundary, an imaginary line through the outer Bay of Fundy. He looks at the Loran, two rows of numbers that give him his position. The buoy he seeks should be visible, but the fast-running tide has dragged it under water. He'll come back to it. He pushes the throttle forward to search for another. He finds it, the water surging past a large polyurethane ball with his boat's name painted on it.

Anderson reaches down with a long gaff hook, snags the rope and pulls it up as he runs the boat back against the tide, creating slack. He slips the rope through a block above him and down between the sheaves of a hydraulic hauler that lifts the heavy string of traps off the bottom. The first trap is the worst. Anderson has weighted it with close to two hundred pounds of cement and steel so that it will hold the string in the tide. It comes up alongside. He lets it down, guiding it on to the rail.

Since sailing singlehanded he has built a crane that he uses to shift the trap to the far side of the boat, but first he opens it. He pulls out three lobsters: two are too short, and one has a V-notch tail. All go back into the water, along with a small crab and a half dozen starfish. Anderson pulls out the old bait and dumps what is left over the side. He pulls a full bag from the box nearby and hooks it inside the trap. He closes the trap, latches it, and uses his crane to swing the trap out of the way.

Back at the helm, he steers the boat into the tide as he raises the next trap on the string. He pulls two legal sized lobsters from the second trap. With special pliers, he puts thick rubber bands on their claws and drops them into a holding tank. He throws back the bycatch of two small lobsters and a crab, all healthy and alive, baits the trap with another three pounds of herring and continues on until eleven traps line the far rail, ready to be set back over. Anderson holds the heavy end trap ready. When he gets to the numbers he's looking for, he tosses the buoy over and dumps the end trap. It in turn drags the other traps, one by one, back into the water. When the final trap goes, Anderson tosses the other buoy and moves on to the next string.

On a day like today, when the lobsters are not too plentiful, he can handle up to forty trawls. At the end of the day, as the tide drifts up into the cove, he waits on his mooring, banding the last lobsters and sorting them in crates. Most are hard shell, but he encounters some early shedders, lobsters that have recently shed their old shells as part of their growth process. The shedders have far less meat than the hard shells and fetch a lower price. After almost thirty years lobstering, Anderson knows a shedder from a hard shell as soon as he picks it up. Once all the lobsters are sorted and ready he hoses down the boat and covers the remaining bait.

Just after supper, with plenty of light left in the day, he manages to thread his way up the channel to the wharf. He lifts five crates of lobsters onto the dock, a little under four hundred pounds.

He has exchanged two thousand pounds of herring, worth five hundred dollars at most, for four hundred pounds of lobster worth over eighteen hundred dollars.

Anderson has a heavy investment, however. Each trawl costs close to a thousand dollars to put in the water. And he must maintain his wharf, boat and the holding tanks he has built to keep his lobsters alive until he negotiates a price that he can live with.

FEEDING THE FISH

In the age of aquaculture, the lobster and scallop industries stand out as closely mimicking the market advantages that give farmed products an edge. Another booming industry is the one that provides the feed that both the aquaculture and lobster industries use in massive amounts. Bait and feed are the highest production costs in both industries.

❧

According to Peter Tyedmers' data, the main wild-caught fish ingredients of salmon feed are South Pacific sardines and anchovies, menhaden from the Gulf of Mexico, and herring from the North Atlantic, as well as blue whiting, sand lance, and fish waste. All around the world, stock assessments for forage fish had jumped and fleets of low-and high-tech vessels had developed the capacity to harvest twenty-seven million tons annually.

While older boats such as the *Propomex 3* harvested fish along the coast of Mexico, an upgraded fleet of midwater trawlers had taken over the herring fishery of the North Atlantic.

In the mid 1980s, the research division of Canada's Department of Fisheries and Oceans experimented with midwater trawling for herring on the Georges Bank, the rich fishing grounds between Nova Scotia and New England. "We found it was too hard on groundfish," said Rob Stephenson, of the DFO's St. Andrew's Biological Research Station in New Brunswick, Canada. "Too much bycatch."

The East Germans used midwater trawlers in the 1960s and early '70s to wipe out the Georges Bank herring. Nonetheless, those stocks had since bounced back, though to what degree remained a point of contention between U.S. and Canadian scientists, as did the United States fleet's switch adoption of the effective midwater gear as a way to catch deep water herring.

From 1994 to 2005, the number of midwater boats participating in the northeast herring and mackerel fisheries went from zero to twenty-five, and the ports of Gloucester and New Bedford Massachusetts invested heavily in their infrastructure to support the new fleets. Existing boats cost two million dollars to retrofit, and millions more dollars went into turning urban coastal property into fish processing space.

Norpel, a West Coast–based company, built a forty-thousand-square-foot processing and storage facility in the port of New Bedford, and Whole Foods Market built a herring processing plant in Gloucester, alongside Dave Ellenton's World Traders, which also processed herring. These investments demanded a high return, and NOAA's Northeast Fisheries Science Center in Woods Hole assured the trawler and processing plant owners that the region's herring stock had reached the record level of 1.8 million tons, and they said mackerel stocks were equally robust. The United States shared the Georges Bank herring stock with Canada, however, and having lost their cod, the Canadians refused to endorse the U.S. stock assessment.

The 1.8 million ton herring stock that U.S. scientists expected fishermen to find proved elusive. After a forty-thousand-ton harvest in 2002, landings from Georges Bank dropped, adding fuel to the debate about the accuracy of the NMFS stock assessment. The Canadian assessment of the same herring stock indicated a biomass of six hundred thousand tons, two-thirds smaller than United States estimates, a significant difference.

"I think what fishermen are seeing supports the lower estimate," said the DFO's Rob Stephenson. But herring represented a lifeline to the future for Massachusetts fishing ports, and the boats kept working and opening new markets. Norpel shipped food-grade herring and mackerel to Africa in frozen blocks, and advertised its capacity to produce twenty-thousand tons of mackerel annually as feed for tuna ranches. In a mix of fishing and farming, tuna caught on the high seas were held in net pens in the open water and fed large quantities of whole fish. Tuna consumed roughly twenty pounds of fish for every pound of weight gain. Tuna feed shipped to Australia was blamed for an outbreak of septacimia that wiped out wild sardine stocks in the south coast in the 1990s.

❧

When the New England boats came under fire for landing thousands of pounds of juvenile haddock as bycatch in 2004, the New England Fishery Management Council (NEFMC) amended regulations to allow the boats to land as much as a thousand pounds a trip. "I thought we were trying to protect fish, not midwater trawlers," said a disgruntled council member who voted against the amendment.

All around the world, forage fisheries boomed. In order to protect the stocks and the business interests of the investors who were building up the industry, many regulators advocated a shift to rights based management schemes such as individual transferable quotas (ITQs). Beginning in the 1990s, New England fishermen fought ITQs, the management tool, which privatized fisheries and led to consolidation of ownership. But in the global economy, policy makers argued that consolidation was what the industry needed. While New England groundfishermen stood strong against ITQs, supporting a ban that lasted from 1994 to 2002, chinks in the wall appeared around the fisheries that were doing well.

"I think the scallopers and the herring boats would be happy to go to ITQs," said Dana Rice, a member of the NEFMC. Indeed, council members with interests in midwater trawlers had broken ranks as early as 1998, calling for inclusion of ITQs in management options while it was illegal to do so. In 2005, Maine lobstermen began discussing the idea.

❧

Within the context of these market solutions, policy makers and regulators continued to measure efficiency primarily in terms of speed, ignoring impacts on communities and the inefficient energy use of many technically advanced sectors. Small-boat fishermen of New England survived where they had strong foundations and lucrative niche markets.

In Mexico, the inshore fleet hung on thanks to a commitment within the government that reserved inshore waters for the panga fleet. But as the country embraced trade liberalization and turned more toward market solutions, the pangeros became more vulnerable. For the most part, fisheries survivors either supported the aquaculture industry, mimicked its market advantages, or found niches.

17

AGIABAMPO TO LUBEC

In 2002, the World Bank sponsored a review of the prospects of shrimp farming in Mexico, and engaged anthropologist Billie DeWalt of the University of Pittsburgh as the lead author. DeWalt had tracked shrimp farming in Mexico for almost as long as Maria Cruz-Torres, but he worked on a broader scale, looking at nationwide trends within the global context. The lens through which he looked at shrimp farming did not resolve issues down to a personal level, and to DeWalt the situation in Mexico, while far from perfect, looked encouraging.

In the report, DeWalt and his coauthors identified numerous problems including the laundering of drug money, as well as social and environmental impacts. But in his conclusions DeWalt expressed optimism for Mexico's shrimp farms. Like many aqua-culture industry proponents he believed that humanity had to make the leap from hunter-gatherer to farmer of the sea, and in that regard shrimp farming looked like the future.

"Many of the major global environmental organizations have a presence in Mexico, and local environmental organizations exist in several regions," wrote DeWalt, inferring that even under the heavy scrutiny of environmental groups, Mexican shrimp farming looked sustainable. "Although a number of these organizations met in Juchitán, Oaxaca, and in San Blas, Nayarít, and produced declarations on aquaculture . . . there has been relatively little systematic opposition to shrimp farming in the country. For the major NGOs, other industries and issues have a higher priority than does shrimp aquaculture. This probably reflects the relatively benign effects of aquaculture on coastal Mexico to this point."

Such was the official report. Sonoran governor Eduardo Bours rode it as far as he could. Bours unveiled a plan in 2006 to make Sonora, already the fastest growing economy in Mexico, a global player. Shrimp farming played a key role in that plan. For those in the expanding universe such as Bours inhabited, the boom was just beginning, elsewhere, less well-positioned players wondered where they fit into the big picture.

❧

On a late February afternoon in 2005, Kenny Dessain guided me through the labyrinth of dirt tracks along the coast from Navopatia to Agiabampo. We came to a bluff looking south over the main body of the bay, the mountains of Sinaloa forming a ragged gray wall in the background. Below us long rafts of oysters peeked above the water's surface at low tide. We passed through the oyster camp and Kenny noted that the family's young daughter had come outside and watched our passing car, but I was too busy staying out of the ruts to notice. We headed inland across a perilous salt flat where muddy gashes told stories of cars that had broken through the thin crust of soil.

"We could be on a beautiful road along the coast," said Kenny. "But they cut it open to make a canal for another shrimp farm. Then the biologists told them the water here was too salty so they abandoned the project. Luckily they didn't desmonte [clear] the whole area like Clej did. At least it's still up," he said as we left the saltpan and climbed back into the ancient pitahaya forest.

We came to an arroyo, a deep narrow ditch filled with rutted sand and the signs of past struggles to get vehicles through it. We got out and looked it over, walking across to scout out the best route. I looked back at my wife's minivan with its eight inches of clearance.

We got in, started it up, put it in low gear and cascaded down the steep bank through the sand and up the other side. Scraping bottom as we crested the other bank and regained the road. Down the narrow track we drove. "What happens if we meet another car?" I asked.

"Oh, you sort of wiggle around each other and get by."

We found our way into Agiabampo ejido and to the house of the new president, Alfredo Gastelum. I had met him the year before, when in the midst of massive shrimp farm failure, he had met with a group of entrepreneurs looking at eco-tourism and the sale of desert products as possible cash sources for the ejido.

Some wanted to establish a reserve, but Gastelum was reticent to commit.

As we entered Gastelum's yard, a young man in white boots greeted us. "Are you a fisherman?" I asked.

"Yes," he said, as he picked up a small pair of what looked

like the doors used to keep the mouth of a shrimp trawl open, and put them into a truck that had pulled into the yard.

Gastelum received us in the backyard as the sun sank. He sat leaning back in his chair, reticent again, answering questions but offering little. The shrimp farms had paid nothing to the ejido, he said. Parada had gone bankrupt only three years into a 30-year lease, and the bank that had foreclosed on him was also in liquidation. The other farm, on the Bolsa, had also gone bust, as had the ejido project. The two private farms had been hit with disease. "*Mancha Blanca*," said Gastelum. White spot syndrome virus. The ejido sponsored project? "*Falta dinero*." It had run out of money. Banks had become leery of ejido projects.

"The only shrimp farm that was making it was Orrantia, on the far northern end of the bay. Its sister company, the eighty-acre Baceran, had also managed to survive the white spot epizootic of last May, and being on ejido land, was paying some rent, said Gastelum.

"In the past ejido fishermen have caught fifty thousand dollars' worth of shrimp in a season," said Gastelum. He said he thought shrimp production had dropped at least 50 percent in the bay and the shrimp they were getting were much smaller than in the past. "We used to get eighty pesos a kilo," he said. "Now we're lucky to get forty-five. You have to catch a lot of shrimp at that price to make fifty thousand dollars."

In order to make ends meet the ejido has leased more farm-land, three thousand acres, said Gastelum. But land is tight. A week earlier members of a neighboring ejido who had been involved in a lengthy land war with Agiabampo shot an ejidatario dead off his tractor.

Fishermen were also looking into growing tilapia, an African fish that could be grown in smaller ponds with far less inputs, Gastelum said.

As we sat in the growing darkness, almost unable to see each other's faces, the director of the ejido, Jesus Lopez, arrived and proved more talkative than Gastelum. Lopez complained of low prices for shrimp and increasing contamination in the bay. "Shrimp farming could have been good for us," he said. "But it wasn't. The land Clej built on was too high, and the soil too sandy."

Would they welcome new offers for leases?

"No," said both Lopez and Gastelum simultaneously, although they expressed an interest in small floating nets being developed for small-scale shrimp farming.

I asked about the crab processing plant on the ejido. Lopez's brother had established it. Lopez shrugged, not knowing what to say. What often happened on government-sponsored deals such as the crab plant was that the controlling interests milked the company for grandiose salaries and then went broke. "The price dropped and they couldn't make a go of it," he finally said.

In terms of managing the fisheries, Lopez said that the ejido itself had no plan, and he complained that the problem came from too many fishermen from Sinaloa crowding the fishing grounds, and a lot of poaching going on.

Gastelum returned and took over the conversation on management. "We have the seasons and mesh sizes for the *chinchurros* and *churuperros*—drift nets. The nets are restricted to two-inch mesh at the beginning of the season and 3 inches later on.

Do fishermen obey the rules?

"Yes," said Gastelum. Kenny Dessain and I left Agiabampo Ejido after our obscure meeting with the members of the board of directors, and drove four miles to the neighboring ejido, El Tinente, where we reconnected with Lalo Mendivil. We arrived at the big compound occupied by Lalo's extended family. His father greeted us, and invited us into the main house. The old man sent one daughter to fetch Lalo while another served us coffee. Cups of hot water arrived, and a jar of Nescafé. I sat in the living room, in a folding chair, looking around at the unplastered brick walls. His family had once owned four big houses in Chihuahua, Lalo's father said. He spread his hands wide to show the thickness of the adobes, over two feet, and raised one hand, pointing to the height of the ceilings, fifteen feet at least. That was before the revolution. Between 1910 and 1920, Pancho Villa's army turned the state of Chihuahua upside down. The Mendivils lost their ranch, carved up among Villa's peasant army.

Lalo came in and invited us back to his house. We sat in his kitchen bundled against the cool desert night. He had changed jobs again, and was working as a bricklayer, building the tract homes Sergio Larraguibel and I passed outside of Navojoa.

"When I saw what was happening with fisheries I learned about agriculture," he said. "Now the rich are taking over agriculture, I am learning construction." Mendivil tried to plan for the future, but he managed to stay only a step ahead in the fast-changing game. "But my heart is always in the sea," he said. On weekends, he rowed out into the bay and caught what he could with his ataraya. "Everything is dying out there," he said and ran down the litany of species, including cultivated oysters, and manta rays, which had declined in number and size. "The red snapper from the sea hardly come into the bay anymore," he said. "What few show up are small and not worth much.

"It is because the bay has become so contaminated from the farms and shrimp tanks. This bay does not flush well, so the contamination builds up. Even the mangroves are suffering; they are getting weak.

"As far as managing, we need someone who can educate the fishermen about how to care for the resources. They poach the shrimp with their *chango* nets, and destroy the bottom."

I told him that most fishermen were starving and appear unable to look beyond the moment.

Lalo's wife came into the kitchen at nine thirty and put her arms around him. We took the hint and stood up to leave. Lalo recommended we take the highway back to Navopatia. But that would add twelve miles to the journey and Dessain voted instead for the coast road, a challenge I declined. "Then we'll go up the trunk road," said Kenny. "It's better than the coast road and only about three miles out of our way."

So we headed back through Agiabampo and turned north on the trunk road. The lights of the town vanished behind us and we rattled along the washboard road under a night sky thick with stars. The headlights illuminated the narrow track through the matoral—the pitahayas towered thirty feet high on either side of the road and jackrabbits skittered across our path.

"What the hell is a *chango* net?" I asked Kenny.

"They drag it along the bottom and it has these boards that spread the net and funnel the shrimp into it."

"It sounds like a regular shrimp trawl."

"Yeah, it's a panga-size towel."

"Well that's what I think that kid had at Gastelum's: a pair of small trawl doors that he was putting in the back of the truck."

Kenny shook his head. "Obeying the regulations. Those changos are illegal everywhere."

We came to a fork.

"Which way?"

Kenny leaned forward and looked at the tire tracks. "Always follow the most tracks," he said. We bore to the right, and continued on through the desert. The flat alluvial plain covered with the monotonous columns of cactus offered few landmarks and we sniffed our way along for an hour, talking in a mix of Spanish and English about the breakdown of ecological function, and how wild shrimp no longer exist because they are interbred with farm escapes. Industry, we realized, had replaced ecology. "From what I've seen, by the time you have to choose between eco-tourism and aquaculture you're screwed," I said.

The key point was that when the ecosystem broke down on any critical level, the life cycles of so many interdependent organisms were thrown out of kilter and the system went haywire. Things usually stabilized at a point where the environment could not produce the level of seafood it used to.

Kenny understood Spanish much better than I and he looked at me. "That's exactly what Lalo was saying," he said.

"I was getting something like that."

"No he was saying exactly what you are, that the ecosystem is not working any more."

"So if you're already a refugee on the coast, your only option is to use the available technology to bypass the difficult life stages of say shrimp, and grow them from post-larvae to market size in what's left of the ecosystem. But this downgrades the connected ecosystems further—according to the law of dissipating structures—if you want to wrap your mind around that."

"Dissipating structures makes sense."

"It is sort of like using your credit card to pay off your mortgage. Borrowing from the future at higher interest rates. And if enough of these shrimp farms go environmentally bankrupt, as they have gone financially bankrupt, it will break the ecological bank in the same way that failed shrimp farms have taken several banks down around here." We changed the subject.

❧

Before we left for Agiabampo, our friend Reuben had told us a story. Kenny filled me in on the details I had not understood. Two weeks earlier, a dozen narcos—mafia drug lords—came into Navopatia with two wounded from a big shootout in Obregón. Reuben poked his own body with a pointed finger to show where the wounds were: one in the chest, another in the side, and one in the leg. He said a mafia helicopter came in and took the wounded out. Then came back for some of the others, the rest commandeered some pangas and hid in the mangroves, then made their way south and got on buses in Sinaloa.

"Joaquin was right there," said Kenny, referring to another friend who had shared his version of the story. "He said the guy got out of the helicopter with the biggest gun he ever saw. He said the entire village was on edge." As Kenny, who had been away when it all happened, understood it, the army had cordoned off the area but did not come in for another round of gunplay. "They sat there for two days while these guys got their wounded out by helicopter. Those soldiers shot it out with them in Obregon, and again in Navajo, but they wouldn't come in here. Makes you wonder what's going on, doesn't it?."

"Well, why would they want to come in and get shot up for a drug war they are never going to win?"

Joaquin told Kenny that before leaving Navopatia the narcos gave everyone in town a thousand pesos (one hundred dollars) for their trouble. So everyone was happy.

"Taking care of *narco* wounded could be the next big thing," joked Kenny. "Compare that with tomorrow. We have a group of New Age women coming in from the States to channel dolphins, and do *inner work*," he said.

"Boy, it would have been interesting if that had overlapped with the mafia thing."

Such is life in Sonora's fog desert. The road improved, and after a while we saw haloes of light on the horizon, marking the ejidos to the north. "Turn here," said Kenny, "it's a shortcut home." We drove across a dry reservoir and made our way into Kenny's camp around midnight and made a cup of tea. From the beach we watched the lights of the shrimp boats, drifting with their butterfly nets for their three or four kilos a night. The illegal chango fishermen worked in darkness.

Early next morning, Kenny and I launched his leaky canoe to go see what remained of Carlos Parada's shrimp farm. We paddled north past the dolphin channellers lighting candles near the shore. We struck a bar in the middle of the bay and got out of the canoe. We walked for a quarter mile across the shallows dragging the canoe behind us. We must have looked interesting from shore, walking ankle-deep in the middle of the broad estuary. By the time we found deep water, Kenny expressed some concern about the depth of water in the canoe. I cut the bottom out of the plastic bottle and tossed the homemade bailer back to Kenny, who sat in the stern with water up over his ankles. He bailed while I paddled on toward the entrance of Clej.

We paddled up toward what was left of the massive pumps, which sat disassembled and rusting. Half way up the canal, Kenny found himself drowning again and we beached the canoe on a narrow shelf of sand in the manmade canyon. Kenny found some rags and tarpaper to plug the biggest hole in the canoe and started jamming it in.

"I know some caulking tricks," I said.

"Well, what am I doing it for, then," he said and invited me to apply what skill I had. I folded the rag into the hole bit by bit as I had seen the master caulkers do, and when we launched again the canoe stayed fairly dry. We beached again at the base of the pumps, and looked at the colossal dike already collapsing.

"They knew it was too high here and that the soil was too soft, but they built it anyway," said Kenny as he looked at a wall of torn sandbags, the failed efforts to stop erosion around the pumps. "I wonder if they even came to look at this place, or just picked it out on a map."

We climbed up to look over the two-hundred-acre array of shrimp ponds that I had walked two years earlier with Parada's foreman. Part of one of the massive pumps, its two-inch-diameter twenty-foot long stainless steel drive shaft still intact, lay abandoned in the sand. A hundred yards away on the edge of the matoral, the tall arms of the pitahaya spiked above the mass of thorn scrub in silent witness.

"Thank god they stopped before they took down the whole thousand acres," said Kenny. We took pictures of the wasted site and headed home—back across the bar, past the women on the beach, to the camp.

Some fishermen felt the bay was coming back since the farms quit operation. But the fishermen's bodega stood empty. "They've all gone to Melchior Ocampo to get their dole," said Kenny.

By 2006, Clej had new owners and they were working on bringing the farm back online.

GOLD FROM SEA WATER!

Lubec, Maine had a moment in history that its longtime residents often joke about but can not live down. In 1897, a former minister named Prescott Ford Jernegan arrived from Middletown, Connecticut with a machine he claimed would extract gold from seawater. After selling five hundred thousand dollars' worth of stock in his Electrolytic Marine Salts Company, Jernegan set up two of his "gold accumulators in North Lubec. Each accumulator held a small battery, mercury, and other chemicals. Saltwater flowed over the mercury and apparently left behind traces of gold: about two dollars' worth in a twenty-four-hour period.

But in July 1898, a New York bank raised questions about the inconsistent quality of the gold, and Jernegan disappeared. Charles Fisher, a professional diver who worked for Jernegan, presumably stoking the accumulators with gold, left town hot on the heels of his boss. The machines quit working as soon as he vanished.

Word spread through town that Jernegan had gone to Europe with two hundred thousand dollars of the investors' money, and the truth sank in: what had seemed too good to be true, was in fact not true, Lubeckers realized they had been swindled, their own desperation and wishful thinking led them to believe the unbelievable.

≈

When the blue revolution arrived in Lubec it promised a new kind of gold from seawater, and the community bought in again. This time the scheme worked, salmon actually did, after a fashion, create gold from seawater. To the chagrin of the town though, most of that gold still ended up in Europe, or Canada, in the coffers of consolidated salmon aquaculture companies. As the industry positioned itself for what the Maine Aquaculture Alliance promised was a comeback, one Canadian company owned every lease in Washington County. The comeback might keep Cooke Aquaculture in the black, but towns like Lubec, and Bucks Harbor, the former home of Atlantic Salmon on Maine, sought new opportunities, in a seascape of diminishing options.

≈

In 2005 a relatively new Lubec business, the Bold Coast Smoke House, processed five thousand pounds of salmon a year for the local retail trade. The company's owner, Capt. Vinnie Gartmayer, arrived in town from New York in the late '90s and began smoking the farmed salmon. He built a vending stand on a trailer and used it to peddle salmon at various events. At the Lubec Fourth of July parade, the town's biggest annual event, Gartmayer did a brisk trade in smoked salmon sticks, thin slivers of salmon impaled on eight-inch long sticks, and doused with teriyaki sauce. His noble efforts kept alive the dream that salmon farming would contribute to the Lubec economy, but he felt no great love for the big companies taking over the business. "They've totally destroyed the bay," he said.

Most of the former salmon farm workers had abandoned the dream. "It gave us a few jobs for a little while but now it offers us nothing, or worse than nothing," said Gene Blake, a former salmon processing plant worker. "They promised us the jobs," he said. "Then they sent them over to Canada where they're subsidized."

Gartmayer did construction work in between salmon gigs, people like Gene Blake took jobs thirty miles or more away. A chocolate candy factory run by Peruvian immigrants took over part of Peacock's Sardine Cannery, but folded after a few years. Without an economic base the town slipped quickly into decline. One vital business after another folded: the laundromat, the pharmacy, the combination gas station, hotel, restaurant, marine supply store, and dive shop, which also filled scuba tanks for urchin divers.

I ran into a guy from the defunct dive shop stocking shelves in the Machias grocery store. "You lost?" I asked.

"Gotta have a job, cap," he said.

I knew that the store only paid $7.50 or so an hour. In eight hours this guy made sixty bucks before taxes, at thirty cents a mile his daily round trip cost him eighteen dollars, in the end he took less than forty dollars a day back to Lubec. He could not live on that.

～

An old movie shown one evening at the local high school offered sharp contrast to the town's funk. A film company had come to Lubec in the summer of 1936 and made a short movie called *The Movie Queen*. In 1989, it seemed Lubec's entire population turned out to see it and gave a raucous round of applause when the star of the film, Evangeline Morrison, who still lived in town, took a front row seat.

What startled the audience, many commented later, was the bustling life on Water Street. In the black-and-white film, people moved in quick jerky motions produced by the old cameras along crowded sidewalks, passing storefronts advertising everything anyone might need, from shoes to corsets. There were ship chandleries and a butcher shop. In 1989, most folks drove a hundred miles round trip to buy a pair of shoes, and window shopping on Water Street amounted to a survey of the plywood covering the store windows.

In a somewhat bizarre development that year, the Food and Drug Administration closed John McCurdy's smokehouse, the last herring smokehouse in the United States, because the fish used were not eviscerated beforehand. The uneviscerated smoked herring could be imported from across the bridge in Canada, but not produced in Lubec. No one had ever died, or even gotten sick, from eating McCurdy's bloaters, as they were called, but that did not matter. Rules designed to police industrial-scale facilities could not be bent for a small reputable producer.

To make up for the loss, the town received a grant to turn the smokehouse into a museum. Money intended to restore the buildings evaporated. A storm washed one of the smokehouses into the narrows in 1994. But the committee in charge of the project did manage to dress up an adjacent storefront to look as it did in *The Movie Queen*. Freshly painted old-fashioned lettering on a dusty window advertised "dry goods," but there was nothing inside but a lifeless room with a few bits of furniture stored in it.

The town invested what was left of its scarce resources in a floating marina intended to attract yachts. Most of the selectmen owned companies that would help build the marina. Against the advice of many local fishermen, the selectmen placed the marina in an exposed location. After a few years the floating marina started to sink; it could no longer stand the pounding it received every winter, and the town sold the pieces to Eastport. In one hard-luck story after another, Lubec repeatedly ventured its capital on desperate gambles, and lost.

In 1999, a real estate broker named Al Rummel arrived in town from Key West, Florida. Rummel bought or brokered properties all over the U.S. "You look for the three *D*'s when buying real estate," he said to me one day. "Death, Divorce, and Distress." No surprise that his philosophy brought him to Lubec.

Young folks generally left Lubec, and it had become a town

of old people, many of whom died or went to the old age home—
one of the few growing businesses in town. Divorce was on the
rise everywhere. But when it came to distress, few American
towns could rival Lubec. Distress seeped into every conversation: two people shaking their heads saying, "I don't know," was
a normal exchange, at the post office, the bank, or the remaining
gas station; one might have thought distress was taught in the
school, and in some ways it was. Since not long after the making
of *The Movie Queen*, and the demise of its herring industry,
Lubec had been steeped in distress, and ripe for exploitation.

Lubec presented as easy a mark for the fish farming industry
as it did for Al Rummel. Aquaculture developers tended to follow
similar patterns, the industry searched for areas where capture
fisheries had declined and local populations had run out of
options.

Lubec fit the bill, the town had seen one fishery decline
after another. Long before the salmon farms arrived, the real
wild salmon vanished, sustained after 1900 only through
intense hatchery programs. Haddock once filled Cobscook Bay
in such numbers, "you could walk across on their backs," the
older fishermen said.

As late as 1986, the small-boat fishermen of Eastport and
Lubec, Maine, and Campobello Island, New Brunswick, fished
together for cod and pollock in the border waters of the bay. The
fishermen worked both sides of the international boundary, but
authorities on both sides looked the other way. A few hours
before high water, a dozen twenty-foot-long open boats driven
by twenty-five horsepower outboard motors would buzz out of
the harbor, and locals called them "the mosquito fleet." The

fishermen would head for the hot spots, mostly on the Canadian side: Cherry Island, Head Harbor. Fishermen would look for the edges where the tide eddied and drop their jigs, three hooks, each covered with two or three inches of fluorescent red tubing, and weighted with as much as five pounds of lead to get them to bottom in the swift-running tide. Some like Reedy Wilson filled their boats every day, and became famous around the bay.

Reedy was still fishing when I arrived downeast in 1986. He would stand in his boat, drop his jigs over the side, and rock back and forth, bouncing them on bottom. Sometimes he would load up, which meant manhandling as much as 150 pounds of cod or pollock up off the bottom, sliding the fish into his boat one at a time. Then he would toss his line back. Often the fish hit as the line sank, and he would haul it back.

The cod ran big, all large; what the market called whales. I bought them from the fleet when I could and shipped them south to buyers in southern New England. I sent a load to a fishmonger named Carter Star in Rhode Island and he called me the next day deeply concerned. "What's wrong with these fish?" he asked. "I've never seen anything like them."

"They're too fresh. They weren't even twenty-four hours out of the water when you got 'em. Give 'em a week and they'll start to look familiar," I reassured him.

Up until the mideighties, people around the bay pursued a variety of fisheries with a variety of gear types. A guy I knew named Ronnie Small trapped eels in the estuaries, dug clams, and gathered mussels. Sometimes he worked for a lobsterman. A few fellows from Lubec took long-lines offshore in the spring and set them for halibut. If they managed to catch a few they could get over three dollars a pound for them. Gene Greenlaw from Peacock's was among those who set up weirs to trap herring. Every spring he rebuilt his weir in Boot Cove, where herring had been trapped for thousands of years. Many fishermen had small boats rigged with dredges that they used for scalloping in winter. The nearby Passamaquoddy tribe had traditional fisheries for porpoise and seal. Plenty of folks hunted ducks in the fall and Jim Robinson's fishing camp stayed busy with anglers coming to catch Atlantic salmon, and hunt deer.

But by the time the salmon farms arrived in the region in the mid-1980s, almost every fishery was in decline. The high seas fishery off Greenland had ravaged what remained of the hatchery-reared salmon, and due to contamination in the rivers, the eels contained so much mercury they could not be eaten.

The state had developed emergency plans to restock the clam flats. Big boats caught most of the herring offshore, so that processors had to buy fish and truck them to their plants rather than process locally caught product, and the only thing that made scalloping worth it was desperation: the fifty dollars a day a deckhand earned shucking scallops in subzero weather was better than nothing. People's distress was so great that they latched onto salmon farming the way a drowning person latches onto a life preserver.

Other solutions existed, but they would have entailed sacrifice. The general public would have had to learn how to eliminate small sources of pollution: indiscriminant use of home lawn chemicals, chemicals flushed down drains and toilets, cars that leaked oil. The rivers could have been cleaned, but that would have required a change in Maine's logging, agricultural, and paper processing practices. The commercial changes in the region's natural resource industries would have come at a cost of efficiency—the ability to harvest more, faster—which would have made the resources from Maine's forests and oceans less competitive in the global market.

While people began to realize that resources did not always last forever, they discounted the future value of those resources to the point that it didn't matter. Resources might be exhaustible, they figured, but not human ingenuity. "We'll find new technology," they said, and some of the best minds in economics agreed with them. The cultural mindset of eastern Maine could not accept the idea of conservation. Most people had lived poor all their lives and did not want their incomes limited by affluent urban environmentalists. They believed the economy would outgrow the resource base.

Salmon farming offered a painless way to cash in on what remained of the bay's productivity. So the Brahmins among local fishing families—the Harrises, the Prenniars, and the Riers— leased sites and set up fish pens. They hired their friends and family members, they bought feed in Eastport, put nets together in their backyards. At the lease hearings no one fought their neighbors. It took about two hours to go through the formalities.

When the price of salmon dropped in the early 1990s, the small holders sold out to the big companies, many of whom had financed the initial ventures. By the mid-1990s, all that remained of the locally owned industry were the processing plants that cleaned and packed the salmon. A decade later, they too had vanished.

By 2005, the scallops had not rebounded, and some had been found to contain Slice, a sea lice pesticide used on salmon farms. A few boats managed to survive by dragging small sea urchins out of deep water. ISA continued to infect salmon, and the fish farming industry offered so little to Lubec that people hardly paid it any mind. "That's all done," shrugged a clam digger who once worked on the farms. Ralph DeWitt moved to Connecticut to find work.

In 2003, Sebastian Belle told me that salmon farming still provided close to twelve hundred jobs in Maine. According to the labor department, however, Maine's entire aquaculture industry, including mussel and oyster farms, employed a little over two hundred people.

At Uncle Kippy's restaurant in Lubec, owner George Olsen smiled behind his handlebar mustache. "Things are going to be booming here soon," he said. "As soon as they get this LNG terminal in you'll see things change." Olsen believed that the latest economic engine destined for the area, a liquefied natural gas terminal, would bring lasting economic growth. He didn't see LNG as the next attempt to wring gold from seawater.

18

THE LAST WILD EGGS

By standard measures of poverty, few populations could match the poverty of wild fish and shrimp. Lubec and Agiabampo can hardly compare. Wild fish and shrimp are 100 percent illiterate, have astounding infant mortality rates, and no title to any property. Fish have no political voice except in the form of environmental groups that campaign for high-profile species such as whales and tuna, and seldom advocate "saving the phytoplankton."

Marine creatures have no legal rights; they also live in some of the most polluted environments in the world, which often leads to birth defects in their offspring. Unlike poor people, fish will never be compensated, their cases never heard. They live an existence below poverty, below the lowest caste; for the most part they are invisible except in restaurants and fish markets.

Nobody checks their food for contaminants; nobody makes sure they have enough. They eat what they can. Aquaculture at least increased people's understanding of how hard wild fish had to work to survive, and how vulnerable they were.

But the life of farmed salmon is brutal. Salmon packed into cages with two to three fish per square meter live high-stress lives on a good day, unable to escape temperature fluctuations, rough seas, parasites, and pathogens. They endure on a monotonous diet of chemical-laden processed food.

"I never realized how fragile these fish were until I started to raise them," said John Malloch, one of the last small-scale Canadian fish farmers. "It makes me realize how much damage we did chasing them around with nets."

In late February 2006, Josh Wilkenfeld, a shrimp biologist with over thirty years' experience, worked twelve hours a day to set up the largest shrimp hatchery in Mexico. At the site near a deserted beach north of San Carlos, Sonora, Wilkenfeld and his crew batted ideas around as to why 60 percent of the larvae they produced morphed into deformed creatures and died. It took them a while to zero in on the water quality problems that were killing their babies. "It turned out to be too much iodine, I think," said Wilkenfeld. "We tried a number of different things, but that seems to be what shifted it."

Offshore, the wild vannamei mingled with escapees from the farms. After a few years of such crossbreeding, the gene pool had become irreversibly altered. Fewer and fewer shrimp living in the open ocean could be irrefutably called wild.

"That may not be a bad thing," one scientist told me. "These shrimp are bred to be disease resistant, and that may be an advantage to the wild stocks."

In July the shrimp post-larvae rode the tide inshore, rising in the water column as the pull of the moon signaled the beginning of the flood. They traveled about five kilometers a tide before sinking to the bottom again at high water.

During the height of the rainy season, July and August, as the influx of fresh water lowered salinity, the shrimp moved far into the estuary where the runoff from a new mango orchard accumulated after the downpours. Pesticide residue in the water attacked the chitin of the shrimps' shells, and within minutes thousands died.

The local shrimp farm shut down its intake pumps until the scourge flushed out of the area. Negotiations began to protect the farms from agricultural runoff. The shrimp in the wild were on their own.

≈

In late winter off the coast of Greenland, fishermen consider the drift of nearby icebergs before setting their gillnets. On the surface, lines of corks mark the positions of the nets. Below, walls of fine monofilament net hang in the waters where huge schools of Atlantic salmon, many of which have traveled over a thousand miles, swim in search of prey. The fishes' silver flanks flash in the increasing winter sun as the fishermen haul the nets out of the water. These salmon live in the wild but many, like the shrimp, have lost their genetic integrity. Thousands were born in hatcheries in Maine and Canada, others escaped from salmon farms and joined their wild cousins, and others were the products of crossbreeding between wild Atlantic salmon and escapees.

In small groups, the survivors from the fishing grounds move back toward the coasts. By midsummer, a dozen fish swim through the seal-infested waters of Cobscook Bay and up the St. Croix River. From the St. Croix, they enter Passamaquoddy Bay and on up New Brunswick's Magaguadavic River. Swimming past the net pens, they encounter methane, reduced oxygen, and tons of particulate matter. Their gills burn in the acidic water. Strange smells, chemicals from the paper mill upstream, choke them but they continue on. They still recognize something about their home river and their instincts override all other stimulations. They spawn in a redd. The eggs incubate below the gravel, safe from alewives. The larval fish emerge with yolk sacks hanging and hide in the shallows under rocks and fallen logs. Largemouth bass prowl the waters searching for feed, and young salmon fry are choice morsels.

The salmon grow and pass through different development stages. After two years they leave the river as a smolt. After two or three years they return.

Passing the salmon farms, they swim fast past the lice they can smell, and the rot below the cages drives the returning fish toward water with adequate oxygen levels. They move into the mouth of the river. Below the first bridge, they enter a weir: nets guide them into an aluminum cage where they swim in tight circles. An escaped salmon, infected with ISA, enters the weir. The wild fish smell the sickness in the fat, lethargic fish and frantically try to to avoid the disease carrier, but they cannot. The farmers had been told to eradicate their infected fish, but refused. According to an aquaculture spokesperson, without an indemnity program, farmers could not afford to kill fish.

The team that checks the weirs runs into problems and does not get to the weir until the next day. By then it is too late. An RT-PCR test that shows the wild fish have become carriers of ISA. They must be destroyed.

❧

Cod eggs float among the plankton. The cod larva bursts from its egg case into the wide ocean, sensitive only to its need for food. Cod must eat as soon as they emerge and the density of feed at the time they are born determines their survival rate. Global warming and chemical pollution have reduced the levels of plankton. It ingests whatever it can find that is smaller than it: microscopic prey. In turn, the juveniles of its future prey, lobster and herring, seek out the cod larvae and gobble them up.

Increasing nutrient levels in the Bay of Fundy have changed the phytoplankton ecosystem. The diatoms the cod hatchlings need to live are no longer there. A few late hatches find enough to live. The survivors move toward shore. Like the young of many other species, they seek the sanctuary of the coastal fauna, the kelps and rockweed forests that lined the shores.

❧

Juvenile cod often schooled inshore around Nova Scotia. In the kelp and rockweed that grew thick along its shores they found sanctuary from numerous predators, including their own parents. In 2000, Acadian Sea Plants, a Canadian rockweed processing company, received permission to harvest the seaweed. Working from open boats, harvesters cut great rafts of rocks weed. The thick wet skeins streamed with life as they hauled them aboard. The bilges of their boats grew thick with marine invertebrates and small fish.

Rockweed endures the worst the North Atlantic can throw at it, and holds tenaciously to the rocks that bound the island, but it cannot regrow if harvesters take too much. After Acadian Sea Plant's harvesters permanently stripped areas of the Nova Scotia shoreline, New Brunswick's Department of Fisheries Agriculture and Aquaculture set limits on the percentage of seaweed harvesters can take from any given area. But the limits are difficult to enforce, and all actions remain confidential between the company and the province.

❧

A small school of juvenile cod feels the seaweed surrounding them pulled in a violent and awkward motion. Some become trapped in the tightly pulled skeins, others escape into the cloudy water full of debris and bottom mud from the disturbed rocks. Exposed, a small cod darts away toward a dark mass in the deeper water. It slips through the tiny holes in the pen and encounters more of its own. The cod there are slightly larger than the rockweed refugee, but not large enough to pose a threat. The smaller fish joins them as they swim aimlessly in the pen. Periodically, small bits of what smells like fish floats down from the surface and the small cod gobbles them up in the frenzy with the other fish.

After a month, the farmed fish have grown markedly, the wild cod less so. When the net is changed, it can swim in and out of the pen at leisure, feeding where it pleases and dashing to safety from the jaws of the seals that haunt the perimeter. In a fit of fear it dives to the sanctuary of the bottom one night and swims off, out of the cove and into deeper water.

The fish and others move offshore and find their way to the waters off Nova Scotia, where many fish carry a noda virus that poses slight harm to the adults.

The cod from Grand Manan pick up the virus and in the spring the school returns to the island. In the cove they swim beneath pens and become infected with the loma worm, but pass on the noda virus, which wiped out the pen full of farmed cod.

❧

In 2006, Nel Halse announced the first harvest of farmed cod from Cooke Aquaculture's New Brunswick–based cod farms. The fish raised there came from a hatchery in Nova Scotia. No one has any way to know if the few escapees have yet crossed with local wild cod.

EPILOGUE: THE RACE

Many books of this nature end on an upbeat note; they point to all the places that look hopeful—organic aquaculture, recirculating systems, biotechnology—without noticing that similar "promising initiatives" have preceded many fisheries disasters.

Mark Weisbrot's graph of economic growth in Latin America offers a more accurate vision of the future trajectory of fisheries and aquaculture development. Its arching line represents the classic feast of harvesting virgin resources: the peak at maximum yield, followed by famine, the steep decline that leads investors/harvesters to chew into natural capital in their bid for economic survival. Rather than solve fisheries problems, industrial aquaculture continues to consume natural capital.

Jim McVey and I talked again just before this book went to press. We discussed how energetically the Chinese were pursuing aquaculture development. They had experienced a famine in the twentieth century in which 30 million people starved, and

Jim is convinced that technologically complex fish farming systems will be critical to preventing starvation in the future. Like most problem solvers in fisheries and

aquaculture he sees his work as producing food, not as a symptom of global economic famine in which fisheries and aquaculture consume natural capital in desperate quests for profit. The only difference between the global situation and the Maine sea urchin meeting of 1996, in which fishermen insisted on harvesting beyond sustainable limits, is scale. Economic hunger drove the urchin harvesters, and it is driving the push into industrial aquaculture.

It is a race, as McVey says, but not to survival.

❧

Herman Daly calls the current situation "uneconomic growth," and gauges it by the decline in human welfare. But I return to Weisbrot's graph; it's simple and I've seen it many times before. "There's still tremendous capacity for growth," he said, and I recognized those words as an integral part of the presentation, a necessary perpetuation of the myth of abundance.

What he referred to by "growth" however, was simply the capacity for expensive technology to substitute for natural capital. But in the world of dissipating structures the cost of technology in terms of its tendency to accelerate resource decline, soon exceeds its benefits.

❧

Nothing in my thirty years of experience in fisheries and aquaculture indicates that the patterns of exploitation will change. They are old. In the 1913, a Captain William H. Thomas of Gloucester, wrote disparagingly of trawling:

> *It Scrapes and Tears and Scrapes and Tears the Fishing Grounds! It Kills and Kills the Small Fish*—How many, man cannot tell. This mode of fishing is like the selfish man who "Killed the goose that laid the golden egg." Let this method alone, and not many years hence, in my opinion, a dearth of fresh fish will be certain, and the owners . . . will wonder how they were ever induced to engage in such a murderous mode of fishing

While trawling promised to feed the world cheaply, it did irremediable damage to ecosystems—the future of the ocean envisioned by aquaculture pioneers claiming it as their Manifest Destiny will look far worse. Through its negative impacts on wild resources, aquaculture could become the only option, and it won't be cheap.

❧

For readers hoping to be cheered after this somewhat dismal journey, I can offer little comfort. Technology will continue to mask the depreciation of natural capital, and economic models geared for abundance will continue to guide development down the cascade of dissipation, calling it growth.

The only hope springs from a sober realization of how far off course the ship of humanity has strayed, and how absurd the suite of technological solutions we are presented with really is. If the future belongs to everyone, then it requires new models and a different way of thinking.

❧

I met many intelligent people in the course of writing this book. I suspect that creating genuinely sustainable aquaculture practices and fisheries will take all of them working together with a common vision. Though that prospect seems very improbable, I can't give it up.

Unfortunately, while humans believe they have time, the ocean makes no guarantees. It may desert us before cooperation occurs on the necessary scale. It is a race.

BIBLIOGRAPHY
AND
SELECTED REFERENCES

Alaska Department of Fish and Game. "Atlantic Salmon White Paper: Southeast Region." 1999.

Anderson, James L. "Aquaculture and the Future: Why Fisheries Economists Should Care." *Marine Resource Economics*, Volume 17 (2002).

———. *Sustainable Aquaculture: What Does It Mean and How Do We Get There?* University of Rhode Island, 2005.

Aquaculture magazine. *2005 Buyer's Guide*. World Aquaculture Outlook, 2005.

Atlantic States Marine Fisheries Commission. "Report of the Ad Hoc Committee on Aquaculture," 2002.

Bagwell, Kyle, and Robert W. Staiger. *The Economics of the World Trading System*. MIT Press: Cambridge, Massachusetts, 2002.

Bartlett, Ed, and Ray Robinson. *Salmon on the Dennys: Struggle for Survival*. Published by the Authors: Dennysville, Maine, 1988.

Belle, Sebastian. Personal communications 2001–2006.

Benbrook, Dr. Charles M. *Antibiotic Drug Use in U.S. Aquaculture.* The Northwest Science and Environmental Policy Center: Sandpoint, Idaho, 2002.

Bigelow, Henry and William C. Schroeder. *Fishes of the Gulf of Maine*; U.S. Government Printing Office: Washington, D.C., 1953.

Bottomore, T. B. *Karl Marx: Early Writings.* McGraw Hill: New York, 1964.

Brennan, William. "Aquaculture in the Gulf of Maine: A Compendium of Federal, Provincial and State Regulatory Controls, Policies and Issues." The Gulf of Maine Council on the Marine Environment, 1999.

Bricknell, Ian and Rob Raynard. "Viral Disease Risks to and from Emerging Marine Aquaculture Species." FRS Marine Laboratory, Aberdeen, Scotland, 2002.

Brigder, Christopher J. and Timothy Reid, eds. *Open Ocean Aquaculture IV: Symposium and Abstracts.* St. Andrews, NB, Canada; Mississippi-Alabama Sea Grant Consortium, Ocean Springs, MS; June 17–20, 2001.
MASGP-01-006

Brooks, David A. *Modeling Tidal Circulation and Exchange in Cobscook Bay, Maine*; Department of Oceanography, Texas A&M University: College Station, Texas, 2004.

Buck, Eugene H., and Rachel Borgatti. *Open Ocean Aquaculture*; Congressional Research Service, August 18, 2004.

Bureau of Commercial Fisheries, U.S. Department of the Interior. *Fisheries of the United States*, 1960–1970.

Carter, Judge Gene. "Memorandum of Decision and Order." *State of Maine v. U.S. Dept. of the Interior, U.S. Geological Survey, U.S. Fish and Wildlife Service, U.S. Dept. of Commerce, and National Marine Fisheries Service.* U.S. District Court, District of Maine, 2000.

———. "Findings of Fact, Memorandum of Decision and Order on Remedial and Injunctive Relief," Order and Injunction. *Public Interest Research Group v. Atlantic Salmon of Maine LLC,* and *Public Interest Research Group v. Stolt Sea Farm Inc.* U.S. District Court, District of Maine, 2003.

Calderon-Aguilera, L. E., et al. "Influence of Oceanographic Processes on the Early Life Stages of the Blue Shrimp (Litopenaeus stylirostris) in the Upper Gulf of California." *Journal of Marine Systems* 39 (2003).

Cicin-Sain, Biliana. Arguments used by the U.S. Navy against applying the National Environmental Protection Act in U.S. Territorial Waters outside the three-mile limit. Personal communication, 2005.

Clifford, Henry C. and Harry L. Cook. "Poaching: Security Aspects of Shrimp Culture." *Aquaculture Magazine,* January/February 2002.

Coastal Resources Center, University of Rhode Island. *Promoting Good Management Practices for Integrated Mariculture Management in Sinaloa, Mexico*; University of Rhode Island: Narragansett, Rhode Island, 2001.

CONAPESCA. Alianza Contigo 2004: Proyectos Productivos Aprobados en Sonora; Sonora; 2004.

Cortright, Joseph. "New Growth Theory, Technology and Learning: A Practitioners Guide." *Reviews of Economic Development Literature and Practice*, No. 4, (2001).

Crutchfield, James. *The Fisheries: Problems in Resource Management.* University of Washington Press: Seattle, 1965.

Cruz-Torres, Maria L. *Lives of Dust and Water: An Anthropology of Change and Resistance in Northwestern Mexico.* University of Arizona Press: Tucson, Arizona, 2004.

Cushing, D.H. *Marine Ecology and Fisheries.* Cambridge University Press: London, 1975.

Daly, Herman. *Beyond Growth: The Economics of Sustainable Development.* Beacon Press: Boston, 1996.

Daly, Herman and Joshua Farley. *Ecological Economics: Principles and Applications.* Island Press: Washington, D.C, 2004.

Della Penna, Jeff. "Fish Farm Fiasco." *Fishermen's Voice,* Vol. 7, No. 5 (May 2002).

De Orellana, Margarita. *Villa y Zapata: La Revolución Mexicana.* Biblioteca Iberoamericana: Mexico, 1989.

De Soto, Hernando. *The Mystery of Capital: Why Capitalism Triumphs in the West and Fails Everywhere Else.* Basic Books: New York, 2000.

DeWalt, Billie R., Lorena Noriega, Jaime Renán Ramírez Zavala, and Rosa Esthela González. *Shrimp Aquaculture, People and the Environment in Coastal Mexico.* World Bank, World Wildlife Fund, Food and Agriculture Organization, Network of Aquaculture Centres in Asia-Pacific, 2000.

Dewar, Margaret. *Industry in Trouble: The Federal Government and New England Fisheries.* Temple University Press: Philadelphia, 1983.

Doré, Ian. *Shrimp: Supply, Products and Marketing in the Aquaculture Age.* Urner Barry Publications: Tom's River, New Jersey, 1993.

Eagle, Josh, Rosamond Naylor, and Whitney Smith. *Why Farm Salmon Outcompete Fishery Salmon.* Marine Policy, 2003.

FAO. "Fish and the WTO." *Subsidies, Market Access and Anti-Dumping;* Bridges Trade BioRes; Vol. 5 No. 21; 25 November 2005.

FAO/NACA. *Asia Regional Technical Guidelines on Health Management for the Responsible Movement of Live Aquatic Animals and the Beijing Consensus and Implementation Strategy.* FAO Fisheries Technical Paper, No. 402; Rome, 2000.

FAO. "*State of the World Fisheries.*"Rome, 1998–2004.
State of the World Fisheries; 2000.
State of the World Fisheries; 2002.
State of the World Fisheries; 2004.

FAO. "Report of the Technical Sessions." Kyoto, 1976.

Forster, John. "Aquaculture Chickens, Salmon: A Case Study." *World Aquaculture Magazine.* (September 1999).

Finlayson, Alan Christopher, et al. "The Invisible Hand: Neo-Classical Economics and the Ordering of Society." Direct correspondence to Thomas A. Lyson, Cornell University: Ithaca, New York, 2002.

Finlayson, Alan Christopher. *Fishing for Truth: A Sociological Analysis of Northern Cod Stock Assessments from 1977 to 1990.* Institute of Social and Economic Research (ISER): St. John's, Newfoundland., Canada, 1994.

Personal notes on Polyani, Karl. *The Great Transformation.* Beacon Press: Boston, 1957 (1944).

Personal notes on Mirowski, Philip. "Physics and the 'Marginalist Revolution." *Against Mechanism: Protecting Economics from Science*, Rowman & Littlefield: Totown, New Jersey, 1988.

Galindo-Bect, Manuel S. and Edward P. Glenn. *Penaeid Shrimp Landings in the Upper Gulf of California in Relation to Colorado River Freshwater Discharge.* Fish. Bull. 98.222–225; 2000.

Gallopín, Gilberto C. Silvio Funtowicz, Martin O'Connor, and Jerry Ravetz. "Science for the Twenty-First Century: From Social Contract to the Scientific Core." *International Journal of Social Science* 168 (2001).

Garcia, Serge. "Trends in Aquaculture." FAO, Rome, 2002.

Glenn, K. L., et al. Examining Genetic Differences in Farm Raised Pacific White Shrimp. Iowa State University Animal Industry Report, 2004.

Goldburg, Rebecca and Pamela Baker. Letter to the EPA regarding effluent limitations guidelines and new source performance standards for the concentrated aquatic animal production point source category. Docket Number W-02-01 (2003).

Goldburg, Rebecca. Testimony Concerning Marine Aquaculture Before the U.S. Commission on Ocean Policy. Boston, 2002.

Gomes, Luis Antonio. "The Toa of Aquaculture: Cultivating Aquatic Organisms in Concert with Their Microscopic World." *World Aquaculture Magazine.* (December 2000).

Hagler, Mike. *Shrimp the Devastating Delicacy: The Explosion of Shrimp Farming and the Negative Impacts in People and the Environment.* Greenpeace: Washington, D.C., 1997.

Harvey, David. Aquaculture Outlook. Electronic Outlook Report from the Economic Research Service; www.ers.usda.gov; 2002, 2003.

Hoegland, Porter, et al. "A Comparison of Access Systems for Natural Resources: Drawing Lessons for Ocean Aquaculture in the U.S. Exclusive Economic Zone." Marine Policy Center, Woods Hole Oceanographic Institution. Woods Hole, Massachusetts, 2003.

Hoegland, Porter, et al. "The Optimal Allocation of Ocean Space: Aquaculture and Wild-Harvest Fisheries." *Marine Resource Economics* Volume 18 (2003).

Howlett, Michael, and Jeremy Rayner. "Studying Canadian Aquaculture Policy: Issues, Gaps, and Directions." Paper destined for the annual general meeting of the Canadian Political Science Association. Dalhousie University, Halifax, Nova Scotia, 2003.

Kite-Powell, Hauke L. "Down on the Farm . . . Raising Fish: Aquaculture Offers More Reliable Seafood Sources, but Raises its own Set of Problems." *Oceanus Magazine* Volume 43, Number 1, (2004).

Kite-Powell, Hauke L., et al. "Open Ocean Grow-Out of Finfish in New England: A Bioeconomic Model." Marine Policy Center, Woods Hole Oceanographic Institution. Woods Hole, Massachusetts, 2003.

Instituto Nacional de la Pesca. *Memorias, Secundo Foro de Investigacion Camaron de Pacifico.* Dirección General de Investigación y Desarrollo Tecnológico Centro Regional de Investigación Pesquera en Salina Cruz, Oaxaca, 2000.

IUCN (World Conservation Union). *Trade Matters! Why Addressing the International Trade Regime Is Important for Biodiversity.* Gland, Switzerland, 2005.

Josupeit, Helga. *Shrimp Market Access: Tariffs and Regulations*; Food and Agriculture Organization of the United Nations, Rome; 2004.

Lamb, John E., Julian A. Velez, and Robert W. Barclay. "The Challenge of Compliance with SPS and Other Standards Associated with the Export of Shrimp and Selected Fresh Produce Items to the United States Market." The World Bank, Washington, D.C., 2005.

Lightner, Donald V. "The Penaeid Shrimp Viral Pandemics due to IHHNV, WSSV, TSV and YHV: History in the Americas and Current Status." Department of Veterinary Science and Microbiology, University of Arizona. Tucson, AZ, 2004.

Llosa, Alvero Vargas. *Liberty for Latin America: How to Undo 500 years of State Oppression*. Farrar, Straus and Giroux: New York, 2005.

Lotze, Heike, and Inka Milewski. *Two Hundred Years of Ecosystem and Food Web Changes in the Quoddy Region, Outer Bay of Fundy*. Conservation Council of New Brunswick. Fredericton, New Brunswick, 2002.

Mageean, Deidre. "Identifying Childhood Hunger in Maine." Margaret Chase Smith Center for Public Policy, University of Maine, 1993.

Mander, Jerry and Edward Goldsmith. *The Case Against the Global Economy*. Sierra Club Books: San Francisco, 1996.

Mayumi, Kozo, et al. "Georgescu-Roegen/Daly versus Solow/Stiglitz Revisited." *Ecological Economics* 27, (1998).

McClennen, Caleb. "White Spot Syndrome Virus: The Economic Environmental and Technical Implications on the Development of Latin American Shrimp Farming." Master of Arts in Law and Diplomacy thesis, submitted to Tufts University. Boston, 2004.

McFarland, Raymond. *A History of the New England Fisheries with Maps*. Elibron Classics. Replica of 1911 edition by University of Pennsylvania. D. Appleton and Co.: New York.

McPhee, John. *The Founding Fish*. Farrar, Straus and Giroux: New York, 2002.

Mirowski, Philip. *The Effortless Economy of Science?* Duke University Press: Durham, North Carolina, 2004.

Molyneaux, Paul. "Economic Efficiency in Fisheries and Aquaculture." *International Journal of TransDisciplinary Research* Volume 1, Number 1, (2006).

———. "Aquaculture Moves Offshore." *APF Reporter.* Volume 21, Number 2, (2003).

———. "Disease: Shrimp Farming's Biggest Problem." *APF Reporter.* Volume 21, Number 1, (2003).

———. "Down on the Farm." *National Fisherman Magazine.* (September 2001).

———. "Manifest Destiny." *Fishermen's Voice.* Volume 10, Number 7, (July 2005).

———. "Salmon Disease." *APF Reporter.* Yet to be published.

———. *The Doryman's Reflection: A Fisherman's Life.* Thunder's Mouth Press: New York, 2005.

———. "Threats to Wild Populations." *Fishermen's Voice.* Volume 7, Number 5, (May 2002).

NMFS. *Our Living Oceans: Report on the Status of U.S. Living Marine Resources,* 1999. U.S. Dep. of Commer., NOAA Tech. Memo. NMFS-F/SPO-41.

———. *The Rationale for a New Initiative in Marine Aquaculture;* NOAA Publications, Silver Springs, MD; 2002.

———. *A Code of Conduct for the Responsible Development of Aquaculture in the U.S. Exclusive Economic Zone;* 2000.

———. *Estimated Aquaculture Production, 1985–1996,* Fisheries Statistics and Economic Division.

National Research Council of Norway. *Evaluation of the Idea to Use Cod as a Species for Genome Sequencing and Functional Genomic Studies in Norway.* Oslo, 2004.

Naylor, Rosmond and Marshall Burke. *Aquaculture and Ocean Resources: Raising Tigers of the Sea;* Annual Review of Environment and Resources 30; 2005.

Naylor, Rosmond et al. "Effects of Aquaculture on World Fish Supplies." *Issue in Ecology,* (Winter 2001).

Nunan, Linda M., Steve M. Arce, Ronald J. Statha, and Donald V. Lightner. "Prevalence of Infectious Hypodermal and Hematopoietic Necrosis Virus (IHHNV) and White Spot Syndrome Virus (WSSV) in Litopenaeus vannamei in the Pacific Ocean off the Coast of Panama." *Journal of the World Aquaculture Society.* Volume 32, Number 3, (September, 2001).

Ormerod, Paul. *The Death of Economics.* Wiley: Hoboken: New Jersey, 1997.

Páez Osuna, Federico, ed. *Camaronicultura y Medio Ambiente.* Instituto de Ciencias del Mar y Limnología, Programa Universitariode Alimentos. El Colegio de Sinaloa. Mazatlán, Sinaloa, 2001.

Perkins, John. *Confessions of an Economic Hit Man.* Berret-Koehler Publishers: San Francisco, 2004.

Polk, Marie, ed. *Open Ocean Aquaculture: Proceedings from an International Conference*; University of New Hampshire/ University of Maine Sea Grant College Program; 1996.

Power, Melanie D. "Lots of Fish in the Sea: Salmon Aquaculture, Genomics and Ethics." Paper Number DEG 004, University of British Columbia, 2003.

Public Citizen, *Shrimp Stockpile: America's Favorite Imported Seafood*; Washington, D.C.; 2005.

———. *Fishy Currency: How International Finance Institutions Fund Shrimp Farms Introduction*; 2005.

Roberts, J. Timmons and Nikki Demetria Thanos, *Trouble in Paradise: Globalization and Environmental Crisis in Latin America.* Routledge: New York, 2003.

Roque, A., et al. *Evaluation of Oxytetracycline Concentration in Shrimp Post-larval Tissues Offered Through Artemia Nauplii and Medicated Bath*; 30(1B): 219–226, *Ciencias Marinas* (2004).

An Overview of the Shrimp Disease Problem in Mexico with emphasis on Taura and White Spot Syndrome; Centro de Investigación en Alimentación y Desarrollo, A.C.; Mazatlán, 2000.

Rosenberry, Bob. *World Shrimp Farming*. Shrimp News International: San Diego, 1998–2006.

Rulfo, Juan. *The Burning Plain, and Other Stories*. University of Texas Press: Austin, TX, 1971.

Sachs, Jeffery. *The End of Poverty: Economic Possibilities for Our Time*. Penguin Press: New York, 2005.

SAGARPA; Norma Oficial Mexicana de Emergencia: *Que Establece Los Requisitos de Sanidad Acuícola Para la Producción de Crustáceos Aquáticos Vivos, Muertos, Sus Productos y Subproductos, Así Como Para Su Introducción a Los Estados Unidos Mexicanos*; NOM-EM-006-PESC-2004.

Shiffrin, Anya and Amer Bisat, eds. *Covering Globalization: A Handbook For Reporters*. Columbia University Press: New York, 2004.

Shiva, Vandana. *Water Wars: Privatization, Pollution, and Profit*. South End Press: Cambridge, MA, 2002.

Society for Positive Aquaculture Awareness (SPAA). "News Release: Antiaquaculture Activist David Suzuki's Slanderous Remark Suggests He Has Abandoned Science for Hysteria; PAA demands apology." Campbell River, British Columbia; 2004.

———. *The Real Salmon Story*: Farmed & Nutritious; 2001.

State of Maine Department of Environmental Protection. "*Pollutant Discharge Elimination System General Permit for Atlantic Salmon Aquaculture*," 2003.

Steinbeck, John. *Zapata*. Penguin Books: New York, 1991.

Stiglitz, Joseph E. *Globalization and Its Discontents*. Norton: New York, 2002.

Subasinghe, Rohana (senior fisheries officer, FAO). Personal communications, 2003–2006.

Tacconi, Luca. *Biodiversity and Ecological Economics: Participation Values and Resource Management*. Earthscan Publications: London, 2000.

Travis, Steven E. Population Genetic Structure of Pacific White Shrimp from the Gulf of Fonseca, Honduras. U.S. Geological Survey, USGS open file report OFR 03-174, (2002).

Tyedmers, Peter H. *Salmon and Sustainability: The Biophysical Cost of Producing Salmon Through the Commercial Salmon Fishery and the Intensive Salmon Culture Industry*. University of British Columbia. Vancouver, British Columbia, 1992.

United States Congress. *National Aquaculture Act of 1980*; Public Law 96-362, 94 Stat. 1198, 16 U.S.C. 2801, et seq. (1980).

Villaba, Armando and Donald Robidue Jr. "Decentralizing Coastal Management: Just in Time: Conservation and Development Strategy for Santa María Bay, Mexico." *Intercoast*, (Fall 2002).

Villaba, Armando. "Conservation of Critical Coastal Ecosystems in Mexico: Santa Maria Bay." Coastal Resources Center at the University of Rhode Island, 2000.

Wallach, Lori and Michelle Sorza. *The WTO: Five Years of Reasons to Resist Corporate Globalization*. Seven Stories Press: New York, 1999.

Weber, Michael. *From Abundance to Scarcity: A History of U.S. Marine Fisheries Policy*. Island Press: Washington, D.C., 2001.

———. "What Price Farmed Fish?" *SeaWeb Aquaculture Clearinghouse*, Washington, D.C., 2002.

White, Kathryn, Brendan O'Neill, and Zdravka Tzankova. "At a Crossroads: Will Aquaculture Fulfill the Promise of the Blue Revolution?" *SeaWeb Aquaculture Clearinghouse*, Washington, D.C., 2003.

Wilson, Diane. *An Unreasonable Woman; A True Story of Shrimpers, Politicos, Polluters, and the Fight for Seadrift, Texas*, Chelsea Green Publishing Company: White River Junction, Vermont, 2005.

World Trade Organization. *WTO After 10 Years: Global Problems and Multilateral*

Solutions; WTO Public Symposium – programme; Geneva, Switzerland; 2005. List of seminars and workshops organized by the Office International des Epizooties [World Organization for Animal Health] (OIE) in 2002 and planned for 2003.

Zarain-Herzberg, Martha. *Seguimento de Granjas Acuícolas del Estado de Sinaloa Druante Años de 1995 al 2001.* Centro de Ciencias de Sinaloa, Culiacán Rosales, Sinaloa, 2003.

———. Personal communications, 2003–2006.

ACKNOWLEDGMENTS

This book would not have been possible conceptually without the help of the Alicia Patterson Foundation. I owe a great deal to all my sources, particularly Bob Rosenberry, who continues to highlight the bright side of the shrimp farming industry, Sebastian Belle, who over the last five years has offered me an ongoing commentary on salmon farming in Maine, and Rohana Subasinghe of the FAO. I must mention, too, among the many people who contributed to this book, a few who have offered me their time and expertise: Joel Leal, Sergio Larraguibel, Alejo Aquilera, and Kenny Dessain, with whom I pounded the back roads of the Sonoran Coast; Dr. Martha Zarain, Dr. Cristina Chavez, Dr. Leobardo Montoya, and Dr. Federico Páez Osuna in Mexico, who provided valuable information regarding the biology of shrimp farming in Mexico; Bob Peacock, Frank Rier, Ralph Dewitt, Chris Duffy, Joe McGonigle, Jim McVey, Dr. Michael Chambers, Dr. Hauke Kite-Powell, Bob Hukki, and Jimmy Robinson, who shared details on the economics and realities of fish farming and the fate of wild salmon in New England. To Dr. Mike Beattie, Dr. Steve Ellis, Dr. David Scarfe, Kurt Klimpel, Donald V. Lightner, and Henry Clifford for their generous contributions regarding salmon and shrimp diseases. I also owe a great deal to the 2005 Covering Globalization Workshop led by Dr. Joesph Stiglitz at Columbia University in New York. I want to thank the people who reviewed my drafts, Aaron Porter, Bob Rosenberry, Anne Dubuisson Dr. Peter Tyedmers, Dr. Maribel Molyneaux, John Oakes at Thunder's Mouth Press, and my wife, Regina Grabrovac. I would have liked to spend more time polishing much of the text, but there was no time.

To those of you who contributed and are not mentioned here, my apologies, and appreciation.